AMAZING
TALES FROM THE
CHICAGO CUBS
DUGOUT

A COLLECTION OF THE GREATEST
CUBS STORIES EVER TOLD

PETE CAVA
AND BOB LOGAN
WITH STUART SHEA

FOREWORD BY BILLY WILLIAMS

SPORTS
PUBLISHING

Sports Publishing books may be purchased in bulk at special
discounts for sales promotion, corporate gifts, fund-raising,
or educational purposes. Special editions can also be created
to specifications. For details, contact the Special Sales
Department, Sports Publishing, 307 West 36th Street, 11th
Floor, New York, NY 10018 or
sportspubbooks@skyhorsepublishing.com.

Sports Publishing® is a registered trademark of Skyhorse
Publishing, Inc.®, a Delaware corporation.

Visit our website at www.sportspubbooks.com

10 9 8 7 6 5 4 3 2 1

Library of Congress Cataloging-in-Publication Data available
on file.

ISBN: 978-1-61321-022-2

Printed in China

*For my wife, Molly Megahan Cava,
born four days after her beloved Cubs played their
last World Series Game to date.
—Pete Cava*

❧

*To the best fans in baseball—Cubs fans.
—Bob Logan*

CONTENTS

Part II

FOREWORD

By Billy Williams

Author's Note: The No. 26 flag atop Wrigley Field's right field foul pole teaches new generations of Cubs fans that Billy Williams was—and is—part of Chicago sports history. Nobody has worn a Cubs uniform longer than he—16 years as a player, 15 as a coach. And few hitters have provided more pleasure for Cubs fans than No. 26, the Sweet Swinger, piling up 2,510 hits, 392 homers and 1,353 RBIs. Now in his third North Side career as an aide to Cubs president Andy MacPhail, Williams adds the same character and class he displayed on the field.

*   *   *   *

When I came to Chicago in 1959, there were a lot of empty seats in Wrigley Field, because the Cubs weren't winning. All that changed when Leo Durocher took over as our manager (1966), and since then, the excitement among our fans has been growing, year by year. With Dusty Baker coming aboard to manage the Cubs, I have a new role, working with the young outfielders and doing whatever I can to help Andy and Ted [Hendry] get the Cubs to where we all want to go—the World Series.

The one thing that's never changed for all these years in Wrigley Field has been the fans. Cubs fans are unbelievable. They never give up, sticking with us through some tough times and bitter disappointments. My biggest regret in baseball is not bringing the World Series to Chicago in 1969, after the Cubs lit up the whole town all summer. I still believe we had the best team in baseball that year, but we just couldn't get it done.

Another thing I grew to enjoy was the way the veteran Chicago sportswriters did their jobs. I wasn't much of a talker when I first got to the Cubs, but they were fair and honest about the way I played the game. Writers like Ed Prell, Jim Enright,

Jerome Holtzman, and Bob Logan had a lot to do with the fans' support for me. I want a World Series ring for myself, but I want it even more for those fans.

PREFACE

By Bob Logan

The easiest part of writing this book was deciding on the dedication.

When it comes to being dedicated, nobody can outfinish Cub fans. That's all the more amazing, because the Cubs have been outfinished by almost everybody in baseball since I started covering them in 1970. Now into my fourth decade as a Cubwatcher, I've run the gamut of emotions with this flummoxed franchise and many of the lummoxes wandering around Wrigley Field in their uniform.

Through it all, the lone hard core of Cubs consistency has been these indescribable, indomitable fans. I've seen them roasting in the summer sun, shivering under blankets through the raw winds of April and chilling fog that blots out the scoreboard in September, roaring—and pouring—while torrents of rain pour into the bleachers.

Ah, those Wrigley bleachers. Lots more about them in chapter 3 of this book, the fans' own turn at bat. But for all of you, in or out of the bleachers, you've earned my admiration and respect. Cubs fans everywhere, this book's for you.

I am grateful to John McDonough, the Cubs' outstanding marketing and broadcasting chief, for his friendship and assistance over the years. Also, many thanks to Cubs publicists Blake Cullen, Chuck Shriver, Bob Ibach, Ned Colletti, Sharon Pannozzo, Chuck Wasserstrom and Samantha Newby for their able assistance.

ACKNOWLEDGMENTS

By Pete Cava

The author gratefully acknowledges the contributions and cooperation of Hal Bateman, Dr. Peter Bjarkman, Ollan Cassell, Dick Cassin, Andy Cava, Molly Cava, Nancy Cava, Paul Debono, Dick Denny, Reid Duffy, Jim Fisherman, Kurt Freudenthal, Charlie Holdaway, Margaret Mavor, Gen McMicken, Mark Murrow, Dan O'Brien, Anne Phillips, Dale Ratermann, Tom Surber, and the late Harold Rosenthal, as well as the Soceity for American Baseball Research, the sports department of the *Indianapolis Star*, the Indiana State Library, Indianapolis/Marion County Library, Butler Univeristy's Irwin Library, and the Ziffren Sports Resource Center Library of the Amateur Athletic Foundation of Los Angeles.

PART I

GROVER ALEXANDER

Grover Alexander won 373 games between 1911 and 1930 and was elected to the Hall of Fame in 1937. He was with the Phillies from 1911 to 1917, the Cubs from 1918 through 1926 and the Cardinals from 1926 through 1929.

The right-hander's greatest years were with Philadelphia, and his most unforgettable performance took place when he pitched for St. Louis during the 1926 World Series.

Yet Alexander the Great pitched more games for the Cubs than for any other team.

*   *   *   *

When Alexander was a boy, a younger brother had trouble pronouncing his name and called him "Doder". The nickname stuck, and gradually evolved into "Dode". That's what folks called Alexander back in his hometown of St. Paul, Nebraska.

In the big leagues, however, Grover was known as "Alex", "Ol' Pete", or "Alexander the Great".

*   *   *   *

Alexander was named for Grover Cleveland, the President of the United States from 1885 to 1889 and from 1893 to 1897.

In *The Winning Team*, a 1952 film about Alexander's life, a former Cubs radio broadcaster named Dutch Reagan played the role of Ol' Pete. Dutch, better known as Ronald Wilson Reagan, would later become President of the United States in 1981... making Ol' Pete Alexander the only athlete portrayed on-screen by a future U.S. President.

*   *   *   *

Although he'd averaged over 30 wins a season for the Phillies from 1914 through 1917, Philadelphia owner William Baker traded Alexander to the Cubs prior to the 1918 season. The United States was at war with Germany, and Baker was concerned about the possibility of losing Alexander to military service.

Baker traded Alexander and catcher Bill Killefer for Pickles Dillhoefer, another backstop, pitcher Mike Prendergast, and cash. Baker was also concerned about Alexander's age since, by then, Ol' Pete was 30 years old.

*   *   *   *

The trade was one of the biggest steals in Cubs history. Prendergast, 9-17 in two seasons with the Cubs, won 13 of 28 decisions in a couple of years at Philadelphia.

With the Cubs from 1918 through June 1926, Alexander won 128 games against 83 defeats, including a 27-14 log in 1920 with a league-leading 173 strikeouts.

*   *   *   *

Alexander was the Cubs' Opening Day pitcher for 1918, but pitched just twice more before he was drafted into the army. Ol' Pete served in France as a frontline sergeant in the artillery.

He returned home deaf in one ear. Worse, he had developed epilepsy and was drinking heavily.

*   *   *   *

After the war, Alexander's favorite drinking partner in Chicago was "Shufflin' Phil" Douglas, a lanky Southerner. When sober, Douglas could be a topnotch pitcher. By July 1919, he'd won ten games for the Cubs against six losses.

Hoping to keep his star pitcher out of the saloons, club president William Veeck (whose son, Bill Veeck, later owned the White Sox), decided it was time to separate Alexander and Douglas. On July 25, 1919, just two days after the hard-drinking teammates had thrown back-to-back shutouts in a double header with Brooklyn, Veeck traded Douglas to the New York Giants.

The deal didn't help, as Alexander lapsed deeper into the bottle.

Douglas was barred from baseball for life after confiding to a Cardinals player he would leave the Giants in the middle of the 1922 pennant race in return for "an inducement".

*   *   *   *

Teammates remembered Alexander as a big guy with a fine build who liked chewing tobacco. He wore his baseball cap one size too small, and tugged it down rakishly to one side. Unlike most of the other pitchers of his era, Alexander managed to stay in shape without running between starts.

Alexander had short fingers and threw a heavy ball. Hans Lobert, a big league catcher form 1903 to 1917, got hit above the heart by an Alexander fastball. Lobert said it "bore in like a lump of lead… I couldn't get my breath for 10 minutes afterward."

*   *   *   *

Several times a season, Alexander would suffer an epileptic seizure on the bench. As teammates tried to keep the luckless pitcher from swallowing his tongue, Alexander would thrash around and froth at the mouth.

Once the players had Alexander pinned to the ground, one of them would pour a shot of brandy down his throat in the belief the spirits would revive him. Alexander's teammates usually kept a bottle on hand in the event of an emergency.

Amazingly, Alexander never suffered a seizure while he was on the mound. Sometimes he sipped ammonia on the bench, hoping to ward off attacks.

*   *   *   *

Alexander's 300th career win came in a Cubs uniform on September 20, 1924. His opening Day win on April 14, 1925, the first Cubs game ever aired on radio, was his 301st.

Alexander helped his own cause in the 8-2 win over the Pirates, homering his first time up. He also had a double and a single.

*   *   *   *

Alcoholism eventually led to Alexander's departure from Chicago. By 1926 Joe McCarthy was managing the Cubs. Marse Joe believed Ol' Pete was a bad influence on the younger players.

"A fellow once asked me one time if Alex followed the rules," said McCarthy. "'Sure he did,' I said. 'But they were always Alex's rules.' So I had to let him go."

McCarthy also had his hands full with another carouser, outfielder Hack Wilson. While Wilson was only 26 and just coming into his own as a slugger, Alexander was a shopworn 39-year-old.

In mid-June McCarthy unloaded the veteran pitcher to St. Louis for the $4,000 waiver price.

*   *   *   *

Ol' Pete made history that fall in the World Series. After winning two starts against the mighty Yankees, Alexander came on in relief with the bases loaded in the seventh inning of the seventh game. He struck out Tony Lazzeri, a dangerous batter, and went on to preserve a 3-2 Cardinals victory.

Some teammates claimed Alexander had been out on the town the night before the game, and was still feeling the effects when he came in to face Lazzeri.

*   *   *   *

Despite the ravages of combat, drink, and illness, Alexander was one of the greatest pitchers of all time. He could throw a fastball, curve, screwball, sinker, and change-up.

Unfortunately, Ol' Pete was his own worst enemy.

"I had control of everything," he lamented, "but myself."

BOB ANDERSON AND THE TWO-BALLS-IN-PLAY INCIDENT

A strapping, blond right-hander from Hammond, Indiana, Bob Anderson pitched for the Cubs from 1957 through 1962. He was supposed to be the Cubs' starter for the opening day game with the Los Angeles Dodgers in 1959, but a spring blizzard hit Chicago and the contest was postponed.

Before the game was canceled, however, the 6'4", 210-pound Anderson came ambling out of the Cubs' dugout bundled up in his bright blue warm-up jacket and a pair of winter gloves. He sculpted a melon-sized snowball and, to the delight of newspaper wire services photographers, cheerfully tossed it around with batterymate Sammy Taylor.

*   *   *   *

Anderson pitched for the 1956 Los Angeles Angels, one of the best teams in Pacific Coast League history. The Angels went 107-56 that year, with Anderson winning 12 of 16 decisions. The pitching staff also included future Cubbies Dave Hillman (21-7), Gene Fodge (19-7), Dick Drott, and Johnny Briggs (5-5).

After his fine work with the Los Angeles squad, Bob Scheffing took over as Chicago's skipper. Scheffing and pitching coach Fred Fitzsimmons pinned their hopes on the new kids, as well as a young right-hander out of Trinity College in Connecticut named Moe Drabowsky.

With the Cubs, however, Anderson, Hillman, Fodge, Drott, Briggs, and Drabowsky would combine for just 113 wins against 159 losses.

*   *   *   *

Anderson holds a unique niche in baseball lore. Of the hundreds of big league hurlers from Don Aase to George Zuverink, he's the only one ever to be on the mound while more than one baseball was in play.

This bizarre incident took place during a Cubs-Cardinals game on June 30, 1959. With one out in the fourth inning, Stan Musial came to the plate. Stan the Man worked the count to 3-and-1, and Anderson threw him a high, inside fastball.

Musial turned into the pitch, then seemed to hold up. The ball jumped, nicked home plate umpire Vic Delmore's shoulder, and traveled all the way to the backstop. Delmore called ball four and motioned Musial toward first base. Catcher Sammy Taylor spun around to argue, claiming the ball had ticked Musial's bat before it grazed Delmore.

While Taylor stood with his back to the field, Anderson strolled toward home plate as Musial sauntered to first. Cubs manager Bob Scheffing rumbled out of the dugout to add his voice to the protest. No one, however, asked for time.

The ump, seeing Anderson coming toward him with upraised palms, assumed the hurler wanted a new baseball. As Delmore tossed one to Anderson, Cubs' third baseman Alvin Dark alertly scampered toward the backstop for the original ball.

Musial, hoping to take advantage of the confusion, rounded first base and took off for second. At about that time, Dark reached the backstop, where Cubs' on-field announcer Pat Pieper had grabbed the original baseball and had dropped it into a ball bag.

Meanhile, Anderson spotted Musial's dash and whirled and fired toward second base. As Anderson threw, another baseball whizzed over his head toward second. Musial slid as Anderson's toss sailed into center field. Musial scrambled to his feet with an eye on third base. As he stepped off the bag, he was tagged out by Chicago shortstop Ernie Banks.

Dark had retrieved a ball from Pieper, and he and Anderson had simultaneously thrown toward second. While a stunned Musial tried to figure out what was going on, both dugouts emptied. Scheffing and St. Louis manager Solly Hemus engaged in a three-way shouting match with Delmore and fellow umps Al Barlick, Bill Jackowski, and Shag Crawford.

The umpires finally decided that the first baseball—the one thrown by Dark—was indeed the ball in play, and the one thrown by Anderson was a dead ball. Musial, they declared, was out at second. Enraged, the Cardinals announced the game was under protest. They dropped it, however, after posting a 4-1 victory.

*   *   *   *

Anderson finished the '59 season year with a 12-13 record and was 9-11 in 1960. After that, arm trouble diminished his fast ball. He spent most of 1961 and 1962 in the Cubs bullpen, and was traded to Detroit. He bowed out of the major leagues following a 3-1 record with a 3.30 earned run average for the Tigers in '63.

A graduate of Western Michigan University, Anderson retired from Inland Steel in 1993. He still gets frequent requests for details of the two-balls-in-play incident from over four decades ago.

CAP ANSON

The history of the Cubs dates back to 1871, when a franchise called the Chicago White Stockings played in the National Association of Professional Baseball Players, commonly called the National Association.

After sputtering in and out of the professional ranks, the White Stockings joined the fledgling National League and played their first game on April 25, 1876—exactly two months before Custer and the Seventh Cavalry met their fate at Little Big Horn.

One of the original White Stockings was third baseman Adrian "Cap" Anson, baseball's first superstar.

*   *   *   *

Anson was a five-year National Association veteran who had played for Rockford, Illinois, and the Philadelphia Athletics. Al Spalding signed him to a contract with Chicago for 1876, but the Athletics offered Anson $500 more than Chicago was paying to tear up the contract and return to Philadelphia.

Anson's fiancee was a Philadelphian and didn't want to leave her hometown. She begged Anson to accept the offer from the Athletics and renege on the deal with Chicago. Anson asked Spalding to tear up the Chicago contract, but Spalding insisted that Anson stick by the terms of the agreement.

Anson took the unprecedented step of offering to buy out his own contract for $1,000... but Spalding—who was building a championship team—wouldn't budge. Anson finally gave in. So did Anson's fiancee, who reluctantly agreed to leave Philadelphia.

It was a recalcitrant Anson who joined his Chicago teammates in the spring of 1876.

*   *   *   *

On his first day with his new club, Anson showed up in street clothes. He couldn't resist tossing the ball around with his new teammates. When Spalding saw Anson in mufti, playing catch with the other Chicago players, he issued an order.

"Now Anse," Spalding informed his prize recruit, "come tomorrow in uniform."

Anson would stay in a Chicago uniform for the next 22 seasons.

*   *   *   *

Anson helped the White Stockings to the 1876 N.L. title and, after taking over as manager and shifting to first base in 1879, he led the club to pennants in 1880, 1881, 1882, 1885, and 1886.

The White Stockings were also known as Anson's Colts and, after Cap's departure, they were dubbed the Orphans.

The March 27, 1902, edition of the *Chicago Daily News* referred to Chicago's youthful newcomers as "Cubs." Several years later, that became the team's official nickname.

*   *   *   *

The first player to accumulate 3,000 career hits, Anson batted over .300 in all but two of his 22 N.L. seasons. He was the first batter to hit three consecutive home runs in a game. Anson was an innovator who insisted on training rules for his players and a formalized spring training regimen.

His teams were among the first to employ base stealing and hit-and-run plays on a regular basis, and Anson was the first manager to experiment with a pitching rotation. He took part in a baseball tour of England in 1874 and a global junket in 1888-1889. In 1939 Anson—who was once elected city clerk of Chicago—was voted into baseball's Hall of Fame.

*   *   *   *

Anson was still an everyday player when he turned 40 in 1892. Sportswriters had begun calling him "Pop" and "Old Man." Some suggested Anson should hang up his spikes and make room for a younger player. The jibes began to irritate Anson, who felt he was still one of the league's top players.

The Chicago captain decided on a satirical revenge. He trotted out to his position one day sporting a shaggy, gray wig and a long, gray fake beard. Anson played the entire contest wearing the wig and beard. Even the reporters had to chuckle.

Anson, noted a sympathetic scribe, "undertook to revenge himself on his critics in a manner every way worthy of his great intellect… it was daring; it was original and conspicuous and particularly humorous…"

The burly 6', 200-pound Iowa native played before fielder's gloves came into fashion and, for much of his career, the pitcher's mound was 45' or 50' from home plate, instead of the present 60' 6" distance. He was a strict disciplinarian who wouldn't hesitate to back his words with his fists.

Although a college man—he helped form Notre Dame's first baseball team while attending school there in 1869—the light-haired, ruddy-complected Anson was a vicious bench jockey and a well-known umpire-baiter. If Anson didn't like an umpire's decision, he would launch into a profanity-laced tirade.

Anson was generally despised throughout the league, but Chicago fans loved him.

*   *   *   *

Although honest and religious, Anson was also an unapologetic bigot. He frequently told ethnic jokes about the Irish, Jews, and blacks and openly used racial slurs.

In July 1887 the White Stockings scheduled an exhibition game with Newark of the International League. Newark's starting pitcher was to be a black man named George Stovey.

While African American players were rare in the 19th Century, there was no institutionalized color barrier. Two blacks had played for Toledo's major league team in the American Association, and over thirty more had competed at the minor league level.

Anson insisted the White Stockings wouldn't take the field against a team with a black player in the line-up. Backing down to Anson, who was one of the most influential men in baseball, the Newark club benched Stovey.

*   *   *   *

Anson's attitude toward African Americans was never fully explained and completely unjustified.

"His repugnant feeling... toward colored ball players," observed Negro League player and historian Sol White, "... and his opposition, with his great popularity and power in baseball circles, hastened the exclusion of the black man from the white leagues."

Part of Anson's legacy was the segregation of professional baseball, which remained in place until the advent of Jackie Robinson.

ERNIE BANKS

Ernie Banks swung a bat like Babe Ruth, had the soft hands of Marty Marion at shortstop, and the saintly disposition of Mother Teresa.

Even Dick Young, the acerbic New York baseball writer whose truculence once drove Tom Seaver to demand a trade from the Mets, had nothing but praise for Mister Cub.

"Ernie Banks," observed Young, "is a beautiful man."

*   *   *   *

A Dallas native, Banks never played a day in the minor leagues. He joined the Cubs late in 1953 from the Kansas City Monarchs of the Negro American League, and took over as the starting shortstop the following season.

The slender, quick-wristed Banks blossomed into an awesome slugger, compiling 512 career homers. He had a single-season high of 47 in 1958. From 1955 to 1960 Banks out-homered everyone in baseball, including Henry Aaron, Willie Mays, and Mickey Mantle.

He won back-to-back Most Valuable Player Awards in 1958-1959.

*   *   *   *

A fine fielder, leg injuries curtailed Banks' career as the Cubs shortstop and he shifted to first base. Before moving to first, Banks had a brief, unhappy stint as an outfielder.

When the leg ailments moved him off shortstop late in May 1961, acting manager Vedie Himsl announced Banks would shift to left field. The outfield was strange and lonesome territory for Banks, a career infielder.

"Only a duck out of water could have shared my loneliness in left field," he recalled, claiming he would even agree to become a catcher to escape his exile to the outfield.

A few weeks later, in mid-June, the Cubs installed Banks at first base, where he developed into a terrific gloveman.

*   *   *   *

Banks and second baseman Gene Baker, another former Kansas City Monarch, were the Cubs' first black players. Baker came to Chicago from Los Angeles of the Pacific Coast League, and he and Banks formed an excellent middle infield combination.

Banks had replaced Baker at shortstop in Kansas City, but the two men met for the first time as members of the Cubs. On their first day of infield practice, Baker offered some advice. "Just watch me," he told Banks, "and everything will be all right."

Banks and Baker became good friends—"He helped me plenty," Ernie recalled—and they roomed together on the road through May 1957, when Baker was traded to Pittsburgh.

*   *   *   *

On his first day as a Cub, Banks borrowed a bat from slugging outfielder Ralph Kiner, the seven-time N.L. homer king. Stepping up to home plate, Banks sent the first pitch from Cubs coach Roy Johnson into Wrigley Field's left field bleachers.

A crowd had gathered around the batting cage to watch the rookie. After Banks blasted the ball into the bleachers, there was an awed silence that was finally broken by Kiner.

"Hey, Banks," the impressed veteran hollered, "you can use all my bats if you promise to keep on hitting like that!"

*   *   *   *

Ernie had nothing but praise for his white teammates on the Cubs, particularly Kiner and another hard-hitting outfielder, Hank Sauer. Banks recalled only one "color"-related incident during his early days in Chicago.

When Ernie joined the Cubs from the Kansas City Monarchs, equipment manager Yosh Kawano noticed the yellow laces on Banks' well-worn baseball shoes. After staring for a moment with a look of disapproval on his face, Kawano bustled off and reappeared with a pair of black shoelaces.

"At the major league level," noted Ernie, "those bright yellow laces were for hot dogs. Yosh wanted to be sure I wouldn't be classed as one."

*   *   *   *

At the start of his career, Banks used a 33 ½-ounce Babe Ruth-model bat. He eventually switched to a lighter bat, the same model used by Giants outfielder Monte Irvin.

Later in his career, Banks started using a 35", 36-ounce Louisville Slugger, the same type used by Vern "Junior" Stephens, a shortstop with the St. Louis Browns, Red Sox, White Sox, and Orioles from 1941 to 1955.

Ironically, it was Stephens who set the major league record for homers by a shortstop (39, with Boston in 1949) that Banks broke when he hit 44 in 1955.

*   *   *   *

Leo Durocher was never an Ernie Banks fan when he managed Chicago. Durocher, a member of the notorious St. Louis Cardinals' Gashouse Gang during his playing days, leaned

toward more flamboyant players rather than the gentlemanly—
although no less competitive—Banks.

"He's too old to play the game anymore," grumbled Durocher
after taking the Cubs' reins in 1966, when Ernie was 35.

Durocher's criticism spurred Banks. After a career-low
15-homer, .272 season in '66, Banks bounced back, pounding
23, 32, and 23 round-trippers in his final three seasons as a
regular.

*   *   *   *

Banks spent his entire 19-year career with chronically mediocre
Cubs teams. He is one of a handful of Hall of Famers who never
had the chance to play in a World Series.

Asked if he had any regrets about not playing for perennial
winners like the Yankees or Dodgers, Ernie had this response:
"I figure that Ernie Banks is the luckiest person in the world to
be associated with the very best organization in baseball—the
Chicago Cubs."

*   *   *   *

By current standards, the enthusiasm of Ernie Banks seems too
good to be true. But Ernie's love of baseball was as genuine as
his smile.

"What you saw publicly with Ernie," insists Ron Santo, "was
the way he was on the field and in the clubhouse. It wasn't a facade; he truly wanted to play two games every day, three if there
had been enough sunshine…"

ROSS BARNES

Over the years, the Cubs have had their share of power hitters... thumpers like Hack Wilson, Rogers Hornsby, Bill Nicholson, Hank Sauer, Ernie Banks, Billy Williams, Ron Santo, Dave Kingman, Andre Dawson, and Sammy Sosa.

It's only fitting, since the man who hit the first homer in National League history wore a Chicago uniform.

*　　*　　*　　*

When Al Spalding wanted to make Chicago the top team in the newly-formed National League in 1876, he set his sights on Adrian Anson, catcher Deacon White, first sacker Cal McVey, and Ross Barnes.

Spalding and Barnes had known each other for a decade, They'd been teammates on Rockford's Forest Cities clubs, and Henry Chadwick—the true Father of Baseball—described Barnes as "the model second baseman."

*　　*　　*　　*

Barnes was Chicago's second baseman when the White Stockings played their first game. He was the first batter in team history when he stepped up against Jim Devlin in a game at Louisville on April 25, 1876.

In a May 2 game at Cincinnati, Barnes hit an inside-the-park home run off Reds pitcher Cherokee Bill Fisher in a 15-9 Chicago victory.

*   *   *   *

Oddly, the dapper-looking infielder's historic homer was the next-to-last of his four-year major league career. Barnes played in an era where home runs were scarce, and his only other round-tripper came in 1879 when he played for the Reds.

Considered by many peers to be the finest player of the Nineteenth Century, Barnes was also the N.L.'s first batting champion.

GLENN BECKERT

Although the Cubs' Tinker-to-Evers-to-Chance infield is immortalized in verse, the Cubs had another great double play combo from 1965 to 1973 in second baseman Glenn Beckert and shortstop Don Kessinger.

Beckert began his professional career as a shortstop in the Red Sox-organization. When Boston decided Rico Petrocelli was their shortstop of the future, Beckert was left unprotected in the 1962 winter draft.

The Cubs gambled on the Pittsburgh native, and moved him from short to second base in 1964 following the tragic death of Kenny Hubbs.

* * * *

In 1965 Beckert replaced journeyman Joey Amalfitano at second base. That same year, Kessinger took the shortstop post from Roberto Pena.

With Kessinger leading off and Beckert in the number-two spot, the Cubs had excellent table-setters for a line-up that included Ernie Banks, Billy Williams, and Ron Santo. Beckert was an excellent contact hitter who had the fewest strikeouts of any N.L. regular for five straight seasons.

* * * *

When Leo Durocher came to Chicago, he was patient with the Cubs' younger players, including pitcher Ken Holtzman, catcher Randy Hundley, Kessinger, and Beckert. His handling of the younger players helped the Cubs jump from tenth place in 1966 to third in 1967.

Beckert, said Leo, "worked like crazy to improve himself. Made himself into a great player. Another Eddie Stanky."

Durocher helped refine Beckert's game, and the Lip's work paid big dividends. Beckert was a four-time N.L. All-Star, and a Gold Glove winner in 1971.

In 1968 he struck out just 20 times in 643 plate appearances. A lifetime .283 hitter, Beckert batted .342 in 1971. He had hit streaks of 27 consecutive games in 1968 and 26 in '73.

*   *   *   *

Beckert's roommate during road trips was third sacker Ron Santo, who was a favorite target of clubhouse pranks. Beckert was one of Santo's worst tormentors.

During one stretch when Santo was in a slump, Beckert—together with Ernie Banks and Billy Williams—decided on a remedy to loosen up their buddy.

Beckert, Banks, and Williams found a loud-ticking timer that belonged to the team trainer. They set it for one hour, and placed the timer inside a cardboard box. They disguised the box as fan mail, and then placed it inside Santo's locker.

Later, when Santo strolled into the dressing room and got to his locker, he heard the timer.

"Hey Beck," Santo asked, "do you hear something ticking?"

"Yeah," Beckert said straight-faced. "I've been hearing that ever since I got here." Santo began rummaging through his mail until he found the source of the noise.

"Oh my, it's a bomb!" screamed Santo, heaving the ticking package out the clubhouse window onto Waveland Avenue.

Beckert, Banks, and Williams nearly died laughing. Once they came clean, even Santo couldn't keep from cracking up.

The only person who wasn't amused was the Cubs' trainer, once he learned the fate of his timer.

*   *   *   *

Leg and foot injuries curtailed Beckett's career. Traded to San Diego, he played 73 games for the Padres over the 1974 and '75 seasons and then quit baseball.

Appropriately, Beckert and Don Kessinger played their 1,000th big league game on the same date: August 21, 1971.

LOU BOUDREAU

Lou Boudreau once came out of the Cubs announcer booth to take over as manager. Born in Harvey, Illinois, Boudreau was the son of a former minor league player and a lifelong Cubs fan.

As a youth, Boudreau rooted for the Cubs and attended several games each month at Wrigley Field. His favorite players included Riggs Stephenson, Woody English, Stan Hack, and Billy Jurges.

* * * *

As a sophomore, Boudreau sparked his high school team to a state championship. He won an athletic scholarship to the University of Illinois, where he played baseball and basketball. The Cleveland Indians signed Boudreau to his first professional contract in 1938.

An excellent shortstop, Boudreau played for the Indians from 1939 through 1950 and closed out his playing days with the Red Sox in 1951-1952. He was the American League's Most Valuable Player for 1948, hitting a career-high .355.

* * * *

Boudreau also managed the Indians from 1942 through 1950, guiding the Tribe to the '48 A.L. pennant. He also managed

the Red Sox (1952-1954) and Kansas City Athletics (1955-1957) before becoming a Cubs broadcaster.

After Boudreau left Kansas City, announcer Jack Brickhouse urged him to try out for the Cubs broadcast staff on WGN Radio. Boudreau had done a little announcing during his college days, but the transition was daunting—and daring, as well.

"Until then," says Boudreau, "there'd only been a few ex-jocks in broadcasting, which shows you how far ahead of everybody Brickhouse was in 1957. Now every professional announcer has an ex-jock for a partner."

*   *   *   *

Boudreau auditioned with Brickhouse and WGN sports director Jack Rosenberg as a color man for a simulated game. Boudreau remembers worrying about making grammatical mistakes, or letting fly with some salty dugout language.

But Boudreau's audition was nearly flawless, and Brickhouse and Rosenberg liked what they heard. Boudreau was hired, and his broadcasting career began in 1958.

*   *   *   *

On May 4, 1960, the Cubs were wallowing in last place. They'd lost 11 of 17 contests when Cubs vice president Al Holland asked Boudreau to trade places with manager Charlie Grimm.

It was, said one Cubs player, "one of the weirdest transactions in baseball history."

Why Boudreau?

"I think that's obvious," owner Phil Wrigley told the *Chicago Tribune*. "Who else knows the club better than a guy like Lou who's been sitting in the press box for two years? We could have brought in a manager from somewhere else who didn't know the team, but what would have been the sense of that?"

Boudreau agreed to make the switch, and moved the Cubs out of the basement.

*   *   *   *

At the end of June, Boudreau recalled Ron Santo from the minors and installed the 20-year-old rookie in the starting lineup.

"He'd been a catcher in the minor leagues," says Boudreau, "but I moved him to third base. Don Zimmer, who was nearing the end of his playing career, had been playing that position and helped Santo make the switch—and in effect, helped Santo take Zim's job."

Santo stayed in the Cubs line-up for nearly a decade and a half.

*   *   *   *

The 1960 Cubs finished seventh, and announced the team would be guided in 1961 by a "College of Coaches"—a rotation system involving Vedie Himsl, Harry Craft, Elvin Tappe, and Lou Klein.

Boudreau declined a berth in the rotation and went back to the broadcast booth. Fans around the league teased the Cubs about the new system. On road trips, they'd taunt whomever was in charge at the time with lines like:

"When are you going to call a classroom meeting and paddle your boys?" or, "What's going to happen next week when you're not here?"

Years later, reliever Don Elston looked back on the experiment with disdain.

"There was jealousy among the coaches," Elston told the *Chicago Tribune*. "When one guy was head coach, some but not all of the other coaches did nothing to help him. They sat there waiting for their turn. It was an unhappy time."

The Cubs lost 193 games over the next two seasons and went back to a single field boss in 1963, when Chicago native Bob Kennedy took over.

*   *   *   *

Boudreau was elected to the Hall of Fame in 1970. His son Jim was a left-hander who pitched in the College World Series for Arizona State and spent a couple of years in the Cubs' chain.

Boudreau's son-in-law, former big league pitching star Denny McLain, was the 1968 A.L. MVP.

LOU BROCK

The 1964 trade that sent outfielder Lou Brock from Chicago to St. Louis is considered one of the worst in Cubs history. The truth is, Brock's performance in Chicago gave no indication of his future greatness—even when he played in the Windy City in 1959, two years before joining the Cubs.

*　　*　　*　　*

For most Chicago fans, the less said the better when it comes to the trade that sent Brock to the Cardinals along with pitchers Jack Spring and Paul Toth for outfielder Doug Clemens and pitchers Bobby Shantz and Ernie Broglio. Clemens batted .238 for Chicago from '64 through 1965. Shantz was 0-1 in 20 games as a Cub and Broglio, a 21-game winner for the Cardinals in 1960, was 7-19 between '64 and 1966.

While Toth and Spring made marginal contributions in St. Louis, Brock went on to become one of the greatest base stealers of all time. In 1985 he was inducted into the Hall of Fame.

*　　*　　*　　*

But Brock's brief sojourn with the Cubs gave no hint of what was to come.

True, he'd batted .361 for St. Cloud to lead the Northern League in 1961, his first year as a professional. But in his first two

complete seasons in Wrigley Field, he hit .243 and .269. Brock was averaging .251 when the Cubs sent him packing. Of his career total of 938 stolen bases, just 50 came in a Chicago uniform.

*   *   *   *

Once before, Brock had been a bust in Chicago. It happened two years before his pro debut.

As a Southern University sophomore in 1959, Brock's .545 batting average led the Southwest Athletic Conference. The Jaguars won the NAIA title, and Brock was named to the United States team for the Pan American Games.

The Pan Ams took place that year in Chicago, and the American squad finished third behind Venezuela and Puerto Rico. Brock had just one hit in 10 trips to the plate.

*   *   *   *

In the first two decades after World War Two, it was said that everyone in Chicago stole… except the Cubs. Brock pilfered 16 bases in his first year in Chicago, and 23 the next.

He could run all right, but nothing else seemed to go right for the youngster.

"He'd break out in a big sweat just putting on his uniform," recalled Cubs pitcher Larry Jackson. "His desire was so intense that he made things tough for himself."

*   *   *   *

"If you have watched all the Cub home games thus far," noted a Chicago sportswriter in April 1963, "you probably have come to the conclusion that Lou Brock is the worst outfielder in baseball history. He really isn't, but he hasn't done much to prove it."

*   *   *   *

Years later, Brock would look back and say the criticism was "a mite harsh," but he owned up to having trouble with lefthanders and grounders ("he hand-fought ground balls," observed one scribe).

"The coaches would get me out to Wrigley Field at 8 a.m. every day," says Brock, "practice all morning long and then—after that—I'd have nothing left for the game."

*   *   *   *

Brock did have one moment of greatness as a Cub, and it had nothing to do with running the bases.

During his 19-year big league career, Brock hit just 149 home runs. Against the Mets on June 17, 1962, however, Brock homered an estimated 475 feet into the right-center field bleachers at the Polo Grounds.

Al Jackson was on the hill for New York, and the little lefty had whiffed Brock twice that afternoon. Ernie Banks, who was Brock's roommate, had been after him to relax.

*   *   *   *

"When you walk up to the plate," Mr. Cub would tell the youngster, "there's really only three factors involved: you, the pitcher, and the ball. Once the ball is released, there's only two factors: you and the ball. And heck, Lou, the ball is just a round, hard piece of horsehide, but you are a man with a bat in your hands and good eyes in your head."

*   *   *   *

After striking out twice against Jackson in the 1962 game at the Polo Grounds, Brock was just hoping to make contact.

Jackson delivered a curve, high and outside. Brock swung and connected. He felt the bat meet the ball, and took off. Brock saw the ball streaming toward cavernous center field in the Polo

Grounds, and Mets' outfielder Richie Ashburn running with his back to the infield.

With visions of a three-base hit dancing in his head, Brock turned on the jets. When he saw home plate umpire Tom Gorman giving the home run signal, Brock thought it meant he had a chance for an inside-the-park homer. Brock circled the bases in a flash, but as he rounded home he saw the Mets catcher just standing there.

Not until after he'd crossed the plate did Brock discover he'd driven the ball into the farthest recesses of the Polo Grounds. Only two other big league batters—Babe Ruth and Joe Adcock—had ever reached that spot.

JIM BROSNAN

A pitcher for the Cubs from 1954 to 1958, right-hander Jim Brosnan authored two classic baseball books: *The Long Season* (a chronicle of Brosnan's 1960 season with Cincinnati) and *Pennant Race* (a first-person account of the Reds' first-place finish in 1961).

After retiring in 1963, he became a full-time writer.

* * * *

Known as "The Professor," Brosnan was a student of the game... and also of human nature. He once offered a classic observation on big league coaching staffs.

"All coaches," Brosnan wryly pointed out, "religiously carry fungo bats in the spring to ward off suggestions that they are not working."

THREE-FINGER BROWN

There are two monuments that commemorate the pitching career of Cubs great Mordecai Peter Centennial Brown. One is in Cooperstown, New York, sire of baseball's Hall of Fame. The other is about four hours south of Chicago in the coal mining town of Nyesville, Indiana, some 35 miles north of Terre Haute.

* * * *

Brown, elected to the Hall of Fame in 1974 with a career record of 239-139, was the nemesis of Ty Cobb and Christy Mathewson, two other Cooperstown honorees.

Cobb called Brown's curve "the most devastating pitch I've ever faced."

* * * *

A farm accident when Brown was seven years old mangled his right hand. When he tried pitching, he found his disfigured digits put an unhittable spin on the ball. Brown reached the majors with the Cardinals in 1903 and was traded to the Cubs a year later. He won 20 or more games from 1906-1911, including a 29-game season in 1908.

Brown helped the Cubs to pennants from 1906 through '08, and a pair of World Series triumphs in '07-'08. Backed by the legendary Tinker-to-Evers-to-Chance infield, Brown's

26 victories in 1906 led a Cubs staff that won 116 games—a major league record that still stands.

*   *   *   *

During Brown's era, the Giants and Cubs were fierce rivals. The great Christy Mathewson, winner of 373 major league contests, was New York's top hurler. Brown and Matty squared off 24 times. Brown won 13 of those games, including nine in a row from July 12, 1905, to October 8, 1908.

The great Mathewson heaped praise on his Chicago rival. Brown, said Matty, "is a finished pitcher in all departments of the game. Besides being a great worker, he is a wonderful fielder and sure death on bunts. He spends weeks in the spring preparing himself to field short hits in the infield, and it is fatal to try to bunt against him."

*   *   *   *

Brown won five World Series contests, including a 2-0 triumph over Detroit in the fifth and decisive game of the 1907 World Series. Prior to the Series, Cobb had boasted that he would "hit .800 against National League pitching."

The first time Cobb faced Brown, he struck out on four pitches. Cobb batted .200 in the Series. In four at-bats against Brown, he struck out twice.

*   *   *   *

Brown played for the Reds and with Federal League teams in St. Louis, Brooklyn, and Chicago from 1913 to 1915 before returning to the Cubs.

He left the big leagues after the 1916 season. For a time, he was field boss of the St. Louis team, making him the last full-time pitcher to manage a major league ball club.

*　　*　　*　　*

Teammate Jimmy Archer recalled how Brown's precision control earned the respect of a legendary N.L. arbiter.

"One time I was warming up Brown, and Bill Klem, the umpire, pushed me aside," Archer reminisced. "He put a piece of paper the size of a half dollar on the ground. 'That's the only target that fellow needs to pitch to,' Klem said. And he was right."

*　　*　　*　　*

During the winter of 1912-1913, after he'd jumped leagues, Brown took a suite at the Missouri Athletic Club in St. Louis. A fire swept through the hotel, killing several guests. At first, Brown was believed to be among the victims.

Like Mark Twain, however, reports of his death had been greatly exaggerated. Brown's wife Sallie had come to town and, since the MAC was a men-only club, they'd booked a room at the American Hotel. Brown lost his personal effects but, fortunately, wasn't around for the fire.

*　　*　　*　　*

Known as "Three Finger," "Miner," and "Brownie" around the big leagues, Brown was just plain Mort back in western Indiana. After his playing days were over he settled in Terre Haute, operating a filling station there.

Fifty years after his death on Valentine's Day 1948, the citizens of Nyesville erected a marker in Brown's honor in a cornfield on what was once his boyhood homestead.

HARRY CARAY

Holy Cow!
Love him or hate him, Harry Caray was as much a part of the Cubs as ivy vines and daytime baseball. His out-of-tune rendition of *Take Me Out to the Ballgame* during each seventh-inning stretch at Wrigley Field and his gleeful call of "Cubs win! Cubs win!" after each Chicago triumph irritated some and delighted others.

When it came to his team, Harry could never be accused of being impartial. Whether he was announcing for the Cardinals, A's, White Sox, or Cubs, Caray was his ball club's No. 1 cheerleader.

And, during his years in the Wrigley Field broadcast booth, Harry Caray was the Cubs.

*   *   *   *

Harry was the first of three generations of broadcasters. Skip Caray, Harry's son, handles Braves telecasts.

Skip's son, Chip Caray, started out with Atlanta and moved to the Cubs in 1997.

*   *   *   *

Some of Caray's most colorful lines had nothing to do with baseball commentary. The Cubs once had an attractive ball girl named Maria Collins, who posed for Playboy.

After seeing Collins in the magazine, Harry pronounced: "That's the best thing I've seen out of uniform this year!"

*   *   *   *

Caray's first marriage ended in divorce in 1949.

"I never realized how short a month is," he once quipped, "until I started paying alimony."

When Harry sent a payment to his ex-wife on the 30th anniversary of their split, he enclosed a note.

"Holy Cow!" it said. "Thirty years. How much longer does this go on?"

A week later, Caray got a note from his ex. It read: "Dear Harry, Till death do us part!"

JOSE CARDENAL

In an 18-year big league career, Cuban-born outfielder Jose Cardenal played for nine teams. He spent 1972 through 1977 with Chicago.

As the Cubs' right fielder in 1973, he led the team with a .303 average and was voted Chicago Player of the Year by Windy City baseball writers. Cardenal batted .296 during his six-season run as a Cubbie.

*   *   *   *

Cardenal was involved in a memorable "brawl" during a 1982 Spring Training game with the Giants. When the skirmish broke out, Cardenal headed straight for San Francisco's Willie McCovey.

"I want you, big man," barked the 5' 10", 150-pound Cardenal at the massive first baseman, but from a considerable distance. Cardenal then leaped up and threw a punch at his 6' 4", 225-pound opponent... and missed by about a foot.

Even McCovey had to laugh.

*   *   *   *

One year, a bizarre malady forced Cardenal out of the Cubs' Opening Day line-up: one of his eyelids was stuck shut!

DON CARDWELL

Some Cubs fans can never forgive Don Cardwell for helping the Mets blow past Chicago en route to the 1969 N.L. pennant. But long before the right-hander pitched for New York, he was a durable star for the Cubs.

The rangy North Carolinian broke in with the Phillies in 1957 and joined the Cubs on May 13, 1960, in a four-player trade that brought Cardwell and first baseman Ed Bouchee to Chicago in return for second baseman Tony Taylor and catcher Cal Neeman.

*   *   *   *

Two days later at Wrigley Field, manager Lou Boudreau sent Cardwell to the mound to start the second game of a double-header with the Cardinals. Cardwell walked the second St. Louis batter, shortstop Alex Grammas, then retired the next 23 straight Cardinals.

In the top of the ninth inning Carl Sawatski, a former Cub who'd been Cardwell's batterymate in Philadelphia, entered the game as a pinch hitter. On an 0-2 count, Sawatski blasted Cardwell's next offering deep to right.

Anticipating an extra base hit, the Sunday crowd of 33,543 let out a collective groan. The fans cheered a moment later as right fielder George Altman, running at full tilt, leaped in the air at the exit gate at the bend of the bleachers for a dramatic, one-handed catch.

One out later right fielder Joe Cunningham strode to the plate. A .324 hitter, Cunningham was all that stood between Cardwell and a no-hitter. Cunning-ham worked the count to 3-1, then sliced a low liner to left. Walt "Moose" Moryn lumbered in and made a breathtaking, shoestring catch to end the game.

*   *   *   *

The Cubs won 4-0, and Cardwell had thrown a no-hitter in his first appearance for his new team, a feat no other major league pitcher had accomplished.

"All I wanted was to get out there and win so the Cubs would be impressed with their trade for me," said Cardwell, who was mobbed by fans after the final out.

*   *   *   *

Cardwell was even more impressive in 1961, registering 15 of the Cubs' 64 wins. Traded to St. Louis after the 1962 season, Cardwell moved on to Pittsburgh and later the Mets before ending his career with the Braves in 1970.

At 33, Cardwell was the old man of a youthful Mets' pitching staff in 1969 which included Tom Seaver, Jerry Koosman, and Nolan Ryan.

*   *   *   *

Cardwell's 1960 no-hitter wasn't his only shining moment that season. His other noteworthy performance took place September 2, also at the expense of the Cardinals. Cardwell not only struck out nine batters in a 10-4 complete-game win at St. Louis, he also cracked a pair of homers.

It marked only the 24th time in 85 N.L. seasons that a pitcher had hit two homers in a single contest.

PHIL CAVARRETTA

Honesty may be the best policy, but it cost Phil Cavarretta his job as manager of the Cubs. Born in Chicago to Sicilian immigrant parents, Cavarretta starred in baseball at Lane Tech. He signed his first pro contract in 1934 at 17 years of age. He played seven games for the Cubs at the tail end of the season.

In 1935 Chicago manager Charlie Grimm, who'd platooned himself at first base the previous year, turned over the post to Cavarretta. The wispy 18-year-old hit .275 as the Cubs won the N.L. flag.

Cavarretta played on two more pennant winners in 1938 and 1945. He hit .355 in '45, becoming the Cubs' first batting champ since Heinie Zimmerman in 1912. Versus Detroit in the World Series he batted .423.

*   *   *   *

Some of the credit for Cavarretta's 1945 batting title should have gone to New York Giants pitcher Sal Maglie.

All season long, Cavarretta waged a nip-and-tuck battle for the batting crown with Tommy Holmes of the Braves. Holmes set a modern N.L. record that season by hitting in 37 straight games, a record that stood until Cincinnati's Pete Rose hit in 44 straight in 1978.

Maglie, a rookie in 1945, earned the nickname "The Barber" for the close shaves he gave any batter who crowded the plate while he was pitching. Whenever he pitched against the Braves, Maglie would send Holmes sprawling in the dirt.

Years, later, the scowling right-hander revealed that he had done all he could to help Cavarretta, a fellow *paisan*.

"If *you* were Italian," Maglie told Holmes, "I wouldn't have decked you so many times."

*   *   *   *

It was the irrepressible Charlie Grimm who gave the Cubs first sacker his nickname.

"When I first saw Cavarretta back there in the mid-'30s," Grimm recollected, "I started calling him 'Philibuck.' It just came to me and was inspired, if you can call it that, by my reaction that here was a hard-nosed athlete. Phil liked it."

*   *   *   *

Bill Nicholson, a teammate from 1939 through 1948, described Cavarretta as a "fiery ballplayer, and a good one."

"He was high strung, both on and off the field," Nicholson remembered. "It didn't take much to get him stirred up, but he was a nice fellow all the same."

*   *   *   *

After the war, the Cubs began a slow, downhill slide. They finished in last place three of four seasons between 1948 and 1951. Cavarretta replaced Frank Frisch as manager during the '51 season, and the Cubs moved up to fifth place in '52 with a 77-77 record.

Injuries, a dried-up farm system and disastrous trades (including a deal with Brooklyn in '51 that cost them their best all-around hitter, center fielder Andy Pafko) had taken a toll. With slugger Hank Sauer missing one-third of the '53 season with an injured hand, the Cubs wound up seventh.

*   *   *   *

In 1954 the Cubs went to Spring Training in Mesa, Arizona. Cavarretta saw a future star in Ernie Banks and had a few other capable players in camp. The pitching was weak, however, and after two decades in baseball Cavarretta knew what lay in store for the Cubs.

In late March, the 36-year-old player-manager gave owner Phil Wrigley a frank assessment of the ballclub. "They can't win," Cavarretta told his boss.

On March 29 the owner made a shocking move. With the Cubs in Dallas to play the Giants, Wrigley replaced Cavarretta with Stan Hack. Cavarretta, stated Cubs officials, had been guilty of "negative thinking."

*   *   *   *

Offered the managerial post at Los Angeles in the P.C.L., the disgruntled Cavarretta—who had become the first manager to be fired during Spring Training—left the squad and signed to play for the crosstown White Sox.

"I thought it was my duty to tell the truth," he told reporters.

Cavarretta was indeed telling the truth. The '54 Cubs finished seventh, 33 games out of first place. The only regular pitcher with a winning mark was Jim Davis (11-7), who joined the Cubs after Cavarretta's departure.

*   *   *   *

Cavarretta, the Cubs' last link to the glory days of Gabby Hartnett, Billy Jurges, Billy Herman, and Chuck Klein, batted .316

as a part-timer for the Sox. After retiring in 1955, he managed in the minors and scouted, and was a successful batting instructor in the Mets' system.

"Phil was the best manager I ever played for," said Frankie Baumholtz, a Cubs outfielder from 1949 to 1955. "He always spoke his piece. But he knew baseball."

CHUCK CONNORS

Chuck Connors is best remembered as television's Lucas McCain, the Winchester-toting hero of *The Rifleman,* which aired on ABC from 1958 to 1963. Before that, however, the rangy Connors was a pro athlete in two sports.

*   *   *   *

Born and raised in Brooklyn, New York, Connors was a high school baseball and basketball standout.

In November 1946 he made professional basketball history with the Boston Celtics. Warming up for a preseason game with the Chicago Stags at Boston Arena, the 6' 5", 190-pound Connors tried to dunk the ball. Instead he managed to shatter the glass backboard. It was the first time in pro basketball history that a player had smashed a backboard, and arena officials didn't have a replacement.

Celtics publicist Howie McHugh saved the day by arranging to borrow Boston Garden's backboard.

*   *   *   *

After quitting basketball in 1948, Connors joined the Brooklyn Dodgers in 1949 and had one at-bat as a pinch hitter. He grounded into a double play.

According to legend, Connors passed first base and kept on running.

"Hey, Connors," hollered Brooklyn first base coach Jake Pitler, "where ya goin'?"

Still on the run in the direction of the team clubhouse, Connors shot back: "To Montreal!"

After the game, that's exactly where the Dodgers shipped Connors—to their farm club north of the border in Quebec Province.

*   *   *   *

In 1950 the Dodgers peddled Connors to the Cubs along with fellow first baseman Dee Fondy in return for catcher Hank Edwards.

Although sorry to leave his native Brooklyn, Connors wasn't sad about getting away from Branch Rickey, the parsimonious Dodger general manager.

"Rickey had both money and players," quipped Connors. "He just didn't like to see the two of them mixed."

*   *   *   *

For most of his time in the Chicago chain, Connors played for Los Angeles of the Pacific Coast League.

In 1951 he batted .321 with 22 homers for the Angels before moving up to Chicago, where he batted .239 in 66 games.

*   *   *   *

Back with Los Angeles in 1952, Connors landed a bit part in the film *Pat and Mike,* starring Spencer Tracy and Katherine Hepburn.

The lanky Connors was bitten by the acting bug. He began entertaining teammates and opposing players alike by quoting

Shakespeare on the ballfield. In the clubhouse, he would break into dramatic recitations of *Casey at the Bat* at the slightest provocation.

After the '52 season Connors hung up his spikes, concentrating on what would prove to be a long career in film and television.

"He didn't have to play baseball anymore," quipped third baseman Randy Jackson, Connors' teammate in Chicago during the 1951 campaign, "because he became a successful actor."

JIMMY COONEY

Some 60,000 total fans flocked to Forbes Field for a Pirates-Cubs double-header on May 30, 1927. They wound up getting their money's worth:

• Five future Hall of Famers were in the starting line-ups: Pie Traynor and the Waner brothers, Paul and Lloyd, for Pittsburgh, plus Hack Wilson and Gabby Hartnett for the Cubs.

• Both contests were decided by one run in extra innings. After dropping the morning game 7-6 in 10 innings, the Bucs came back to win the afternoon contest, 6-5, in 10.

• In the first game, the Cubs broke an 11-game win streak by Pittsburgh, the eventual N.L. pennant winner.

But the most unforgettable moment came in the first game, when Jimmy Cooney of the Cubs pulled off an unassisted triple play.

*   *   *   *

Cooney's dad, Jimmy Sr., had played for Chicago in the early 1890s. Both father and son were good-fielding, light-hitting shortstops.

Jimmy Jr. joined the Cubs in 1926 after stints with the Braves, Giants, and Cardinals. In '26, Cooney's only full year with the Cubs, he topped N.L. shortstops in fielding and double plays.

*   *   *   *

In the fourth inning of the first game of the '27 double-header at Pittsburgh, the Pirates had Lloyd Waner at second base and Clyde Barnhart on first.

Paul Waner, the next batter, hit a line drive that Cooney snared for the first out. Going to his left, Cooney stepped on second to retire Lloyd Waner. Barnhart, off at the crack of the bat, was a dead duck as Cooney took a few more steps and tagged him out.

*   *   *   *

The fielding gem was Cooney's last great moment with the Cubs. Just eight days later, on June 7, 1927, he was traded to the Phillies. Woody English, a Chicago rookie in '27, took Cooney's place.

"Jimmy had some age on him," said English, explaining the deal. "He was a slick fielder, but not much of an all-around athlete. Couldn't run much."

KIKI CUYLER

Kiki Cuyler was a devout Catholic who often made the sign of the cross prior to stepping into the batter's box—a rare sight in the '20s and '30s, prior to the proliferation of Latin ballplayers.

"Judging from his record," notes one Cubs historian, "it must have worked."

*　　*　　*　　*

Cuyler, a Hall of Fame outfielder, hit .321 in 18 big league seasons, and .325 in eight years as a Cub. Cuyler's career began with the Pirates in 1921.

He came to the Cubs under unusual circumstances following the 1927 season.

*　　*　　*　　*

By the mid-'20s, Cuyler was well-established as Pittsburgh's left fielder. Two years earlier, he'd been runner-up to Rogers Hornsby in the MVT ballot.

In 1927, former Tiger shortstop Donie Bush took over as manager of the Pirates. In June, Bush moved Cuyler from the number-three spot in the batting order to second. Cuyler, a top RBI man, wasn't happy with the switch.

When he failed to deliver, Cuyler asked Bush to move him back to third. The situation led to hard feelings between the two men. When Cuyler failed to slide on a force play at second, the irascible Bush benched him.

The media and fans entered the fray, siding with Cuyler. Bush, however, wouldn't budge. Cuyler appeared in just 85 games, and during the World Series he rode the bench as the Yankees took apart Pittsburgh in four games.

After the season the Pirates shipped him to the Cubs for infielder Sparky Adams and outfielder Pete Scott.

It was one of the best trades in Chicago history. Had Bush kept Cuyler, he would have had three Hall of Fame outfielders in Cuyler and the Waner brothers, Paul, and Lloyd.

*   *   *   *

With the Cubs, Cuyler teamed with Hack Wilson and Riggs Stephenson to form one of the best-hitting outfield combinations of all time. Yet Cuyler remained aloof.

"He was a loner," observed shortstop Woody English. "He kept to himself. He liked to dance, and he'd go out, never palled around with a single player on the club. They didn't really dislike him, but he wasn't one of the boys."

*   *   *   *

Cuyler had a career-best .360 average for the 1929 Cubs led the N.L. in stolen bases three years in a row.

He moved on to Cincinnati in 1935 and finished his playing days with Brooklyn in 1938.

JIM DAVIS

J im Davis was a southpaw pitcher with the Cubs from 1954 to 1956. His playing days ended after he spent the 1957 season with the Cardinals and Giants. Davis was 24-26 with a career earned run average of 4.01, but he made the record book… the hard way.

*   *   *   *

As a rookie in '54, Davis was 11-7 for the seventh-place Cubs with a staff-leading 3.52 ERA.

He wasn't the first member of his family to pitch in the majors. Jim's uncle, right-hander Marv Grissom, hurled for five teams from 1946 to 1959.

*   *   *   *

On May 27, 1956, the Cubs were in St. Louis for a double header at old Busch Stadium. Davis was Chicago's first-game starting pitcher.

In the bottom of the sixth, Davis struck out Hal Smith for the first out. Jackie Brandt went down on strikes for out number two, and Davis fanned Cards pitcher Lindy McDaniel for what appeared to be the third out.

McDaniel, however, made it safely to first base when Cubs catcher Hobie Landrith couldn't hold on to the ball. Davis then

fanned Don Blasingame for the final out—and fourth strikeout—of the inning.

Davis was the first N.L. pitcher in half a century to strike
out four batters in a single inning. Prior to Davis, the last hurler to perform the feat was Hooks Wiltse of the Giants against
Cincinnati in 1906.

*   *   *   *

And for the record: the Cubs went on to lose to the Cardinals,
11-9.

They also dropped the nightcap, 12-2.

ANDRE DAWSON

Anyone who saw a game at Wrigley Field between 1987 and 1992 remembers the drill: The Hawk trots to his outfield post. Fans in the right field bleachers stand and bow. They add a "salaam" motion, with right arms outstretched.

Andre "Hawk" Dawson, the Cubs right fielder from 1987 to 1992, was one of the most beloved players in Chicago history. How he came to play in Chicago goes back to his high school days.

*   *   *   *

As a prep in Miami, Dawson played defensive back on the school football team. While trying to make an interception, Dawson suffered a knee injury that would bother him throughout his athletic career.

He came to the major leagues with the Expos, and Dawson won the 1977 N.L. Rookie of the Year Award. He enjoyed an outstanding 10-year run in Montreal.

*   *   *   *

Years of play on Olympic Stadium's synthetic turf caused his leg to ache, however, and by 1984 Dawson was taking pain pills. When he got out of bed on mornings after a game, Dawson had

to hobble into the shower and run hot water on his legs in order to move around.

Until the 1986 season, Dawson prided himself on his ability to play despite the agony. But that year, Dawson recalls, "I could think about nothing else but the throbbing pain in my knees. I was beginning to feel like an old man. I walked like old Festus from the TV show *Gunsmoke.*"

*   *   *   *

After the 1986 season Dawson became a free agent. His good friend and former Expos teammate Warren Cromartie, who by then played for the Yomiuri Giants in Tokyo, tried to convince Dawson to come to Japan.

"They'll pay you the real money that you deserve over here," insisted Cromartie.

But Dawson's wife Vanessa had other ideas, especially after all the years she and Andre had spent in French-speaking Quebec.

"You're crazy!" she informed Dawson. "Both of you are crazy! Playing ball in Japan? It's bad enough that we would speak differently from all the hundreds of millions of people over there, but we'd look different, too!"

*   *   *   *

And so Dawson set his sights instead on Wrigley Field, a hitter's paradise with natural grass. The Cubs seemed reluctant, so Dawson made an unprecedented offer. Send a blank contract, said Hawk, and I'll sign it; you fill in the dollar amount.

Pitcher Rick Sutcliffe offered to donate $100,000 of his own salary to sign Dawson. "We got no chance to win without him," maintained Sut. "And it would be worth it to me to get him on our club."

The Cubs signed Dawson for $500,000, less than half his salary at Montreal. Yet he couldn't have been happier.

"I was a Chicago Cub!" Dawson remembers thinking. "I wanted to jump, I wanted to scream."

When he batted for the first time in Chicago, the Wrigley Field fans gave him a standing ovation.

*   *   *   *

If the '87 Cubs couldn't win without Dawson, they didn't win with him, either. They finished last in the N.L. East.

But Dawson was a one-man show. He became the first player from a last-place club to capture the MVP Award, driving in 137 runs with 47 homers and a .287 batting average. Chicago rooters had found a new hero.

"Everything was too good to be true," says Dawson of his first year in Chicago, "especially the Cubbie fans. I could talk, mix, and have a relationship with them, something I had been unable to do in Montreal."

*   *   *   *

Dawson was part of Chicago's resurgence in 1989 under manager Don Zimmer. The Cubs improved by 16 games to finish ahead of the Mets, N.L. champions a year before. Against all odds, the "Boys of Zimmer" won the Eastern Division title.

Dawson's knee had started acting up again, and he underwent surgery in May. Despite playing in just 118 games, he still managed 21 homers and 77 RBI.

But once again, the Cubs were thwarted in post-season play when the Giants beat them in the League Championship Series.

*   *   *   *

Dawson left the Cubs after 1992 and played for Boston and Miami before retiring. Like so many other Cub greats, his days in Wrigley Field were unforgettable.

"In Montreal," he reminisced, "you never got quite the exposure you get here in the States. In Chicago, you became a household name. The fans love the ball club and are right on top of you. It makes it easy to go out and enjoy yourself."

*   *   *   *

A deeply religious man, Dawson made an impact not only on the game, but on many of his fellow players.

"He inspired others by who he is and the example he sets," declares Ernie Banks. "All who touch his life, just by his example, better who they are."

LEON DURHAM

Leon Durham played for the Cubs from 1981 to 1988. He came to Chicago after the 1980 season along with third baseman Ken Reitz and infielder-outfielder Tye Waller from St. Louis for relief pitcher Bruce Sutter.

Prior to the 1984 campaign, Durham tried two changes… with opposite results.

*   *   *   *

During Spring Training that year, Durham switched from glasses to contact lenses. He had trouble with contacts, however, claiming that he "wasn't really seeing what I should see."

Durham switched back to glasses, and felt more comfortable with them.

"I was very relaxed," he says, "and confident of what the pitchers were throwing at me."

Durham went on to clout 33 homers and knock in 99 runs that season. He wore glasses the rest of his career.

*   *   *   *

Durham also switched from the outfield to first base at the Cubs 1984 spring camp. He had suffered a series of leg injuries in 1983—due in part, Durham maintained, to lugging his 6' 3", 215-pound frame around the outfield.

Cubs' management also felt Durham's arm was below average for the outfield, and that he'd be better suited to an infield role.

"I thought Leon would be better at first base," said manager Jim Frey after incumbent Bill Buckner was swapped to Boston to make room for Durham. "And so far I've been right."

Durham concurred.

"I don't think I was that good of an outfielder," he admitted.

Durham manned first base in Wrigley Field until the arrival of Mark Grace in 1988.

*   *   *   *

Growing up in Cincinnati, Durham enjoyed watching the Reds at old Crosley Field. His heroes were Pete Rose, Frank Robinson, Vada Pinson, and Tony Perez.

He didn't get to go to the 1970 All-Star Game at Riverfront Stadium, but watched on television as Rose scored the winning run in the bottom of the 12th.

When Durham himself was elected to the N.L. All-Star team in 1982, the honor was especially gratifying.

"Chills actually went through my body" he says, "when I learned I'd been named to the National League team."

*   *   *   *

Durham got his hands on his first big league baseball at Crosley Field. He beat out 10 other youngsters in a race for the ball, making a bare-handed stop in the process.

Years later, fond memories of his boyhood days at the ballpark prompted Durham to donate $500 to athletic programs in Chicago-area schools each time he hit a home run.

FRANK ERNAGA'S BIG DEBUT

E veryone deserves 15 minutes of fame, theorized Andy
Warhol, but Frank Ernaga's renown lasted about three
innings.

*   *   *   *

At Wrigley Field on May 24, 1957, the Cubs trailed the Milwaukee Braves 1-0 going into the home half of the second inning.
Rookie right fielder Frank Ernaga, recalled from Portland of the
Pacific Coast League just four days earlier, led off the inning
against future Hall of Famer Warren Spahn.

The ex-UCLA star worked the count to 2-1 before whacking
Spahn's next pitch into the left-center field stands. Ernaga's homer not only tied the score, it put him in the record book: he was
the first Cub to hit a home run in his initial major league at-bat.

*   *   *   *

After Jim Bolger led off the fourth with a single, Ernaga batted again. This time he lined a low drive toward center that
skipped past Billy Bruton. By the time Bruton got the ball back
to the infield, Ernaga was on third with a triple. Moments later,
Ernaga scored on Cal Neeman's sacrifice fly.

The Cubs went on to win 5-1 behind 21-year-old right-hander Moe Drabowsky. Ernaga had homered and tripled in his first two major league plate appearances.

In his brief major league career, nothing before or after matched that awesome debut.

*   *   *   *

With Tulsa of the Texas League in 1956, Ernaga had 18 homers and 97 RBI. He was batting .252 for Portland when the Cubs promoted him, looking for additional bench power.

Not long after obtaining outfielder Chuck Tanner from the Braves on June 8, the Cubs dispatched Ernaga to Fort Worth of the Texas League. Ernaga's slate with the '57 Cubs showed a .314 batting average with two homers and a pair of triples.

*   *   *   *

The gaudy numbers, however, don't tell the full story. A contemporary scouting report indicated Ernaga had "plenty of power, though weak on curve balls."

Defensively, he was something of a liability.

"Shows good hands and arm," the report continued, "but covers very little ground. May be tried as catcher."

*   *   *   *

At Fort Worth, Ernaga batted .238 in 89 contests. He returned there in 1958, hitting .249 with 10 homers.

Ernaga briefly resurfaced with the Cubs in '58 and batted .125 in nine games before disappearing from the major leagues forever. His career slate shows a .278 average, two triples, and a pair of homers.

Ernaga eventually returned to Susanville, California, his birthplace, and became a building contractor.

BILL FAUL

T he Cubs have had their share of characters and oddballs… maybe more than their share. Few rank ahead of Bill Faul.

*   *   *   *

Faul was a right-handed pitcher who broke in with Detroit in 1962. Tiger teammates claimed Faul had "problems" and would occasionally go wild on the mound.

In an effort to calm himself down and concentrate on his pitching, Faul visited a psychiatrist. The doctor recommended self-hypnosis.

"But it didn't seem to work," said Detroit infielder Coot Veal. "He had good stuff, but was in a different world. He wasn't dangerous, just different. Players stayed away from him."

*   *   *   *

The Cubs purchased Faul's contract just prior to the 1965 season. In the locker room prior to his first start, Faul unnerved his new teammates when he produced a small record player and played a disc that said, over and over:

"You're going to keep the baaaaaalllllll dowwwwwwn, you're going to keep the baaaaaalllllll dowwwwwwn. You're going to pitch loooooooowwwww and awaaaaaaay, loooooooowwwww and awaaaaaaay."

*   *   *   *

As the record played, Faul went into a trance. When the record finished, Faul would snap out of it, pumped up and ready for action.

"He was ready to play all nine positions of a double-header himself," mused Ron Santo.

*   *   *   *

Faul posted a 6-6 record in his first year with the Cubs, including three shutout victories. He was gone the following year when he slipped to 1-4.

The remaining Cubs probably breathed a collective sigh of relief.

DEE FONDY

Dee Fondy was an anomaly. A big man at 6' 3", 195 pounds, he was an excellent base runner, adept at the drag bunt. Yet he didn't hit with the power of other good-sized first basemen of the '50s, like Dale Long or Joe Adcock.

A notorious streak hitter, Fondy's first major league at-bat was an unforgettable one.

*　　*　　*　　*

The Texas-born, California-bred Fondy had served as an artilleryman in Europe during World War Two, earning a Purple Heart. Fondy's professional baseball career didn't begin until 1946, when he was nearly 22 years old.

Fondy signed with the Dodgers. With Gil Hodges playing first base for Brooklyn, however, Fondy languished in the minors.

*　　*　　*　　*

By 1950, longtime Cubs first sacker Phil Cavarretta was showing signs of wear. After a broken arm shelved Cavarretta, Preston Ward inherited the job. Ward batted .253 in 80 games for the '50 Cubs, but then entered military service.

A few weeks after the season ended, the Cubs acquired Fondy and Chuck Connors, another first baseman, in a trade with Brooklyn.

*   *   *   *

The left-handed Fondy made the 1951 Cubs squad as a 26-year-old rookie. His first major league at-bat left a big impression on Cubs fans.

On a sunny but chilly Opening Day, April 17, the Cubs hosted the Reds at Wrigley Field. Chicago manager Frank Frisch started Fondy at first base, batting sixth behind Andy Pafko.

Kenny Raffensberger was the Reds starter. The left-hander was a notorious Chicago-killer who had won his last six starts against the Cubs.

When Fondy batted in the first inning, the bases were loaded with two out. Frank Baumholtz was on third, Hank Sauer on second, and Pafko aboard at first. To the delight of 18,211 fans, Fondy whacked a triple.

He followed with two singles in his next three at-bats. Fondy's 3-for-4 performance and four RBI helped the Cubs to an 8-3 victory.

*   *   *   *

Through his first 49 games Fondy batted .271. Frisch turned over first base duties to Chuck Connors and optioned Fondy to Los Angeles of the Pacific Coast League. While the future TV and film star batted just .239 for the Cubs, Fondy pasted P.C.L. pitching at a .376 clip and reclaimed his starting role in 1952.

"Fondy burned up the P.C.L.," says Randy Jackson, a Cubs third baseman in 1951, "and Connors couldn't hit major league pitching. So they swapped them in the middle of the year, and Connors did great in the P.C.L. and Fondy had a bad first year with the Cubs."

*   *   *   *

During his years in Chicago, Fondy showed signs of greatness. His best season as a Cub was 1953, when he hit .309 with
18 homers. Fondy legged out 11 triples in 53 and stole 20 bases
in 1954—the highest Cubs total since Stan Hack's 21 in 1940.

Fondy held down the first base post at Wrigley Field until May
of 1957, when he was traded to Pittsburgh. Dealt by the Pirates
to Cincinnati for Ted Kluszewski following the '57 season, Dee
retired after 1958.

*   *   *   *

As a hitter, Fondy seemed to be red-hot or ice-cold. He once
struck out six times during a July 1953 double-header, five times
in a single contest.

In 1954, with 25 games to go, Fondy was batting just .266.
He then caught fire, hitting at a .383 clip the rest of the way to
finish at .285. He averaged .286 for his eight-year big league
career, and .285 as a Cub.

Fondy held several jobs in baseball after his playing days, including a stretch as special assistant to the general manager of
the Milwaukee Brewers.

RAY FONTENOT

S ilton Ray Fontenot, a left-handed pitcher from Lake
Charles, Louisiana, came to the Cubs in December 1984
as part of a six-player deal with the Yankees. He won nine
and lost 15 in Chicago before the Cubs dealt him to Minnesota.

*   *   *   *

With the Yankees, Fontenot and teammate Ron Guidry—a
fellow Cajun—would often converse in French.

Known as a methodical, fluid worker, Fontenot had an excellent sinker, a fair curve and a good slider.

*   *   *   *

He suffered one of the most embarrassing injuries in Cubs
history. While serving as a reliever, Fontenot fell and bruised
his ribs… when he tripped on his way to answer the bullpen
telephone.

AUGIE GALAN

Asolid big league outfielder for 16 seasons, eight of them with the Cubs, Augie Galan once went an entire season without grounding into a double play.

A childhood injury nearly derailed Galan's dreams of playing in the majors, even after he'd proven himself at the highest strata of minor league baseball.

*　　*　　*　　*

In 1935, Galan was the left fielder for Charlie Grimm's pennant-winning Cubs. Galan batted .314 and led the N.L. with 133 runs scored and 22 stolen bases. In 646 plate appearances, he didn't ground into a single double play ...although he did hit into one triple killing.

Galan played the first 38 games of the 1936 season before hitting into a DP. The record still stands.

*　　*　　*　　*

Before he joined the Cubs, the switch-hitting Californian was a star shortstop for the San Francisco Seals. Near the end of the 1932 season, the Seals let Galan leave the team with three games remaining so that he could join a barnstorming squad.

Galan's replacement at short? An 18-year-old local kid named Joe DiMaggio, who was also destined to make his mark as a big league outfielder.

*   *   *   *

Although Galan had proven himself in the fast-paced P.C.L., some big league scouts were skeptical. They'd heard about a childhood injury Galan had suffered. As a boy, he'd shattered his elbow and had never gone to a doctor. The arm didn't heal properly, and Galan had trouble making throws from the hole at short.

The Yankees wanted to purchase Galan's contract from San Francisco, and sent their top west coast scout to find out if he was damaged goods. Galan, who was unable to straighten his arm, took pains to conceal the deformity.

"I couldn't let anybody know," he said years later, "because it could have meant the end of my career."

The New York scout approached Galan and asked to see his arm. Galan refused, but the scout insisted. Knowing his chances with the Yanks were cooked, Galan decided not to bare his arm for the scout.

"Well, I was dead either way," he recalled, "so I decided not to remove my coat, and maybe it wouldn't get around and somebody else would take a chance on me."

*   *   *   *

The Cubs gambled on Galan, bringing him to Chicago in 1934.

Against the Dodgers on June 25, 1937, he became the first big leaguer to homer from both sides of the plate in the same game.

*   *   *   *

Galan batted .277 for the Cubs, and .287 lifetime. He tried to enlist during World War II, but was rejected because of his arm.

"There was almost no power in my right arm," Galan said. "Even batting left, the chips I had developed caused the arm to swell to twice its size. I had to freeze the elbow a half hour before every game. By the sixth or seventh inning, the feeling would come back, and if I had to make a throw it would be like somebody sticking needles in me."

JOE GIRARDI

Catcher Joe Girardi grew up in Peoria, Illinois, rooting for the Cubs. His favorite players were Ron Santo and Jose Cardenal.

As a 3rd grader, Girardi wrote a paper about wanting to play for the Cubs. He played baseball for Spalding Institute in Peoria, and for Northwestern University in Evanston, where he earned a degree in industrial engineering.

*   *   *   *

In 1986 Chicago took Girardi in the fifth round of the free-agent draft. Three years later, his boyhood dream came true when he joined the Cubs.

A member of the Yankees from 1996 to 1999, Girardi helped New York to three World Series titles.

After the '99 season he became a free agent and came back to the Cubs.

MARK GRACE

Quick, now, what big league player had the most hits during the 1990s?

It wasn't Tony Gwynn, Wade Boggs, or Cal Ripken Jr... but Mark Grace of the Cubs. Grace, Chicago's All-Star first baseman, recorded 1,754 hits from 1990 through 1999.

Grace's 364 doubles during that span is also the highest total of any major league player.

*   *   *   *

While Gwynn's approach is methodical—the Padres' batting star keeps an extensive video library and anticipates every pitcher's next delivery—Grace is a reactionary hitter who relies on instinct. "I just react to the ball," he says, "... see it, and hit it."

Gwynn and Grace are both products of San Diego State University. They frequently worked out together during their early days in baseball despite their philosophical differences.

*   *   *   *

Selected by the Cubs in the 24th round of the June 1985 draft, Grace didn't sign immediately. While holding out, he continued to play amateur ball. That summer, Grace's stock rose higher and higher and when he finally inked a Cubs pact—just in time

for the 1986 season—he received a contract befitting a first-round choice.

In '86 Grace hit .342 for Peoria, becoming the first player to win the Midwest League batting title in his first year as a pro.

*   *   *   *

Two years after he was drafted, Grace was challenging Leon Durham, the Cubs' incumbent first baseman. Already nick-named "Amazing," Grace earned high praise from rival club officials.

"I take this job," said Don Zimmer, the new Cubs manager for 1988, "and I don't know Mark Grace. Then I go to the Win-ter Meetings, and I must have had at least two general managers from other organizations come to me and say, 'When Spring Training's over, Mark Grace will be your starting first baseman Opening Day.'"

*   *   *   *

Shortly after the first weeks of the exhibition season, it was obvi-ous that Durham's days in Wrigley Field were numbered.

"After about three weeks of spring training, I could see what everybody was telling me," said Zimmer. "I could see that Mark Grace was a hell of a player."

The Cubs tried to deal Durham, but there were no takers. Grace was optioned to Iowa of the American Association before Opening Day, and Durham started the season as Chicago's first baseman.

*   *   *   *

Grace had batted .288 in the exhibition season, but the young-ster took the demotion in stride.

"I knew from the start that as long as Leon was in Chicago, I'd be in Des Moines," Grace reflected. "But it's still a good situation for me here. I know I'm going to be playing every day and getting my at-bats. If I had stayed up there as a back-up player, I wouldn't be getting many at-bats. I'm only 23. I can be patient."

*   *   *   *

When Durham batted .219 after 24 games, the Cubs swapped him to Cincinnati and recalled Grace.

The rookie batted .296, earning N.L. Rookie of the Year honors from *The Sporting News*. Grace was the first Cub so honored since Kenny Hubbs in 1962.

STAN HACK AND THE '45 SERIES

The Chicago Cubs won the 1938 N.L. pennant, capping off one of the most dramatic seasons in history. Pittsburgh had led the league since mid-July, but the Cubs kept nipping at their heels.

Bill Lee, Chicago's stalwart right-hander, won 22 games… including four straight shutouts in September to keep Chicago's hopes alive. With Pittsburgh up by half a game, the Cubs and Pirates squared off at Wrigley Field on September 28.

*   *   *   *

The score was 5-all in the bottom of the ninth with Mace Brown, Pittsburgh's ace reliever, on the mound. As darkness gathered, the umpires announced the game would be suspended at the end of the inning.

With two out and an 0-2 count, Chicago catcher Gabby Hartnett parked Brown's next pitch into the seats. Hartnett's "Homer in the Gloamin'" gave Chicago a half-game lead. A win over the Cardinals on October 1 gave them the pennant.

*   *   *   *

Hartnett and Lee were two of the 1938 team's heroes, but the Cubs' most dependable hitter that year was Stan Hack.

A Cub since 1932 and the regular third baseman since 1934, Hack batted .320 and led the league in stolen bases in '38. In the World Series—a four-game sweep by the Yankees—the redoubtable Hack led the Cubs with a .471 average.

*   *   *   *

Aline drive hitter, "Smilin' Stan" amassed 2,193 hits in 16 big league campaigns, all with Chicago.

He was also a sure-handed fielder who once played 54 consecutive games without an error.

*   *   *   *

"Stan Hack was a topnotch ballplayer his entire career," said outfielder Bill Nicholson, Hack's longtime roommate. "A good hitter, an adequate fielder. Not a great arm, but he got it over there in time. We were close, and ate our meals together a lot of the time."

*   *   *   *

Infielder Len Merullo says Hack's favorite post-game pastime was to "sit down and have a couple of bottles of beer and talk about the game."

"He was like Wade Boggs. He hit from foul line to foul line, a line drive type of hitter. Everybody loved Stan Hack. Stan was a very, very popular player."

*   *   *   *

Phil Cavarretta remembers Hack as "a happy-go-lucky man." He enjoyed life, enjoyed playing the game.

"Stan really was never given the credit he deserves. He could field bunts as well as anybody. And he was a good hitter... I can't understand why he isn't in the Hall of Fame."

*   *   *   *

After the 1943 season, the 34-year-old Hack called it quits. In 1944, with the Cubs pinched for players due to World War II, Hack staged a comeback.

In 1945 he had a career-best .323 batting average.

*   *   *   *

Hack sparked one of the most controversial calls in the '45 World Series. At Wrigley Field for Game Six with Detroit, with two out and the score tied 7-7 in the bottom of the 12th, Hack came to the plate with pinch runner Bill Schuster on first.

Hack sliced Dizzy Trout's next pitch into left field for what appeared to be an ordinary base hit. Detroit's Hank Greenberg charged in to field the ball, with the idea of holding Schuster at second.

But then, wrote veteran baseball reporter Fred Lieb, "to the amazement and joy of the crowd, the ball hopped over tall Hank's shoulder and rolled to the hedge."

Schuster scooted home with the winning run, sending the Series to a seventh game. Greenberg was charged with an error on Hack's hit.

Greenberg, a future Hall of Famer who had rejoined the Tigers that year after wartime service in the China-Burma-India Theater, was fuming—not only about the loss, but about the official scorers' decision.

"I never had a chance at the ball," Hank told reporters. "It was three feet over my head."

The ball, wrote Lieb, "had hit a hard spot, supposedly over a drain pipe, and... Greenberg had no earthly chance to field [it]."

At about 9 p.m. that night, the scoring board of Martin Haley, Ed Burns, and Harry Salsinger reconvened. They changed the call from a base hit and an error on Greenberg to a double for Hack.

It was the first time in Series history that a scorer's call had been reversed.

*   *   *   *

The Cubs lost the following day when the Tigers mauled Hank Borowy for five first-inning runs. Hack batted .367 in the '45 Series, giving him a lifetime average of .348 in four Fall Classics.

He retired for good after the 1947 season, and managed the Cubs from 1954 to 1956.

ED HANYZEWSKI

E d Hanyzewski, a Notre Dame alumnus, signed with Chicago prior to the 1942 season and earned a berth on the Cubs' opening day roster that year. Sent to the minors for seasoning, the right-hander rejoined the Cubs in 1943, going 8-7 with a 2.56 earned run average.

He remained with the Cubs through 1946, then retired to become a policeman in South Bend, Indiana. During the fall, Hanyzewski worked as a college football referee.

*   *   *   *

Ed's last name, pronounced "Hanna-zeski," gave Dizzy Dean fits when the former pitching great turned to broadcasting.

"I like to broke my jaw tryin' to pronounce that one," said Dean of his radio days in St. Louis. "But," he added, "I said his name by just holdin' my nose and sneezin'."

BILLY HERMAN

G reatest Cubs second baseman ever? Some say Ryne Sandberg, others claim it was Johnny Evers. Many will argue for Billy Herman.

*　　*　　*　　*

There's no question, however, about the best number-two hitter in Cubs history. Leo Durocher called Herman "an absolute master at hitting behind the runner."

The Cubs starting second baseman from 1932 to 1943, Herman batted .300 or better eight times in his 15-year stay in the majors, including a .341 average in 1935.

*　　*　　*　　*

"His first two years in the league," said Giants pitching great Carl Hubbell, "he couldn't get a hit off me."

"So he set out methodically to figure me out. He did it. From 1933 on, I couldn't get him out."

*　　*　　*　　*

Herman claimed he developed bat control because he was too light to pull the ball as a youngster.

"I learned to hit to right field early," he said, "because I only weighed about 150 pounds when I broke in. In those days, teams had maybe one or two power hitters and the rest of us had to move it around."

*   *   *   *

Herman was also a superb gloveman who once set an N.L. record for putouts in one season (466). With Billy Jurges, Herman formed one of the greatest Chicago double-play combinations.

He helped the Cubs to three pennants and played in 10 All-Star contests.

*   *   *   *

Herman, however, had a less-than-glorious major league debut. He joined the Cubs from Louisville of the American Association late in 1931, and got into his first game on August 28 against the Reds at Wrigley Field.

The rookie singled his first time up, but his second at-bat was a disaster. Herman fouled off a pitch by Cincinnati's Si Johnson, and the ball struck him above the right ear. Herman had to be carried off the field.

The Cubs went on to win, 14-5, and Herman, who quickly recovered, went on to enjoy a great career.

*   *   *   *

For part of Herman's term in Chicago, Prohibition was the law of the land and Windy City gangsters grew wealthy and powerful off bootleg booze. Al Capone, Chicago's most feared mobster, liked baseball and was a frequent visitor to Wrigley Field.

"I saw him at the game many times," Herman recalled. "He was a Cubs fan.

"Those were tough days in Chicago."

*   *   *   *

Herman ended his playing days with Brooklyn and went on to manage the Pirates and Red Sox. In 1975 he was inducted into the Hall of Fame.

Tim Cohane summed up Herman's career in a 1947 magazine article: "He never was very fast. And he only had a fair arm. But he was brimful of batting and fielding talent, hustle, spirit and—most of all—brains.

"He was, as the players say, a professional."

PAUL HINES

Paul Hines scored the first run in Cubs history. It happened in Louisville on April 25, 1876, when Hines, batting cleanup and playing center field for the old White Stockings, raced home in the top of the second against the Grays for the first tally in a 4-0 Chicago victory.

*   *   *   *

Before Al Spalding took over the managerial reins in Chicago for the National League's inaugural season in 1876, he evaluated each of his players. Hines, left fielder John Glenn and shortstop Johnny Peters were, in Spalding's opinion, the only "strong players on the Chicago nine."

Spalding imported three of his old teammates from Boston—catcher Deacon White, first baseman Cal McVey and second baseman Ross Barnes, plus Philadelphia's Adrian Anson and Ezra Sutton, a third baseman.

With this revamped squad, Chicago went 52-14. Hines led the team with 21 doubles and batted .331.

*   *   *   *

From Chicago, Hines moved on to the Providence Grays in 1878. According to baseball lore, he once guaranteed a home run—in writing.

Prior to a game at Boston, Hines allegedly went to the scorer's table and marked down a home run next to his name for the fifth inning.

Hines indeed came through with a homer in the designated frame, and the feat was widely publicized.

"It marked one of the few times in early baseball," wrote historian Lee Allen, "that the populace paid any attention to the home run, a department of play in which few fans appeared to be interested."

*   *   *   *

Hines is considered baseball's first Triple Crown winner, based on his 1878 season with Providence. He hit .358 with four homers and 50 RBI.

A year earlier, during the N.L.'s second season, league president William Hulbert publicly chastised Hines. In a letter published in a Chicago newspaper, Hulbert criticized his alleged indifference, poor attitude and poor play and warned the outfielder to "attend to your business" or be fined.

*   *   *   *

While Hines may have run afoul of the N.L. president, he was friendly with another chief executive: William McKinley, the 25th President of the United States.

Not long after Hines ended his professional baseball career in 1896, McKinley hired him as postmaster in the Department of Agriculture—a job Hines held for many years.

ROGERS HORNSBY

The acrimony between New York and Chicago during the 1932 World Series stemmed from the Cubs' split of the Series shares.

Before the Series began, the Chicago players had voted a half-share of Series swag to shortstop Mark Koenig. Koenig was a former Yank who'd joined the Cubs late in the year from San Francisco of the Pacific Coast League.

His .353 average in 33 games had helped the Cubs win the N.L. flag. Yankee players griped that the Cubs were cheapskates for not voting a full share to Koenig.

At least Koenig got something. Rogers Hornsby, who began the '32 season as Chicago's manager, didn't get a penny.

*   *   *   *

Many feel Hornsby was the game's greatest right-handed hitter of all time. Grover Alexander called the native Texan the toughest batter he ever faced.

Giving the argument plenty of heft is Hornsby's lifetime average of .358, plus three seasons above .400 (.401 in 1922, .424 in 1924, and .403 in 1925, for the Cardinals).

"As a hitter," said shortstop Woody English, Hornsby's infield partner and roommate, "Hornsby stood as far back in the right-hand corner of the batter's box as he could, and he stepped directly toward home plate. He stood right on the back line and

strode right toward the front of that plate, and he'd hit the ball wherever it was pitched."

*   *   *   *

A second baseman, Hornsby spent three seasons and part of one other in Chicago.

In 1929, his last year as an everyday player, he batted .380— the highest average by a Cub in the Twentieth Century.

*   *   *   *

Hornsby managed the team from 1930 through August 1932. On April 24, 1931, the Rajah—three days shy of his 35th birthday—put on a dazzling display. He hit three homers and drove in eight runs in a 10-6 road win over the Pirates.

*   *   *   *

Yet Hornsby was disliked by opponents and teammates alike. Abrasive, belligerent and crude, he berated his own players and feuded with his bosses.

"He was a very cold man," recalled Billy Herman. "He would stare at you with the coldest eyes I ever saw. If you did something wrong, he'd jump all over you.

"He was a perfectionist and had a very low tolerance for mistakes. He was one of the greatest hitters that ever lived— maybe the greatest—but he never talked hitting with us. He just expected you to go up there and do it."

*   *   *   *

Hornsby was a favorite of Cubs' owner Phil Wrigley. But Wrigley may have been Hornsby's only fan in the Chicago organization.

Hornsby wouldn't allow reading, smoking, or drinking soda in the Chicago clubhouse.

"He didn't care about his players as people," claimed Dick Bartell, an N.L. shortstop from 1927 through 1946. Hornsby, said Bartell, was blunt with everyone, including team owners.

"Sam Breadon [who owned St. Louis] said that listening to Hornsby was like having the contents of a rock crusher emptied over his head," said Bartell.

*　　*　　*　　*

By August 1932 the Chicago brass was fed up, and Hornsby was dismissed following a widely-publicized argument with club president Bill Veeck Sr. The Cubs were 53-44 at the time. Charlie Grimm replaced the prickly Hornsby, and the Cubs went on to win the pennant.

"I put together a club that I thought would be capable of winning the pennant," said Hornsby. "We added [shortstop] Billy Jurges, Billy Herman, and [pitcher] Lon Warneke.

"Bill Veeck Sr., the president and general manager, tried to make some of my managing decisions from his office and it was obvious we didn't see eye to eye.

"We were in second place when I was fired, and it wasn't what Grimm did or didn't do that won the pennant for the Cubs. The first-place Pirates, the team to beat, lost 13 straight games."

*　　*　　*　　*

"Most of the players were pretty happy about the change," recalled Billy Herman, "especially since it was Charley Grimm who took over. Grimm was as popular with the players as Hornsby was unpopular."

When the Cubs voted on Series shares, Hornsby didn't get a red cent.

"I didn't even get any share of the World Series money I was entitled to," grumbled Hornsby. "Not a penny."

Neither the Yankees nor anyone else in baseball uttered a peep in protest.

KENNY HUBBS

A ll his life, Kenny Hubbs was a winner. The California native pitched his Little League team to the championship game of the 1954 World Series in Williamsport, Pennsylvania.

On the way back home, 12-year-old Kenny and his dad stopped off at Wrigley Field for a Cubs' game, and saw Ernie Banks hit a pair of home runs.

*   *   *   *

In high school, Hubbs played shortstop on the baseball team and quarterbacked the football team. He also played basketball, high jumped for the track squad, and served as president of the senior class.

Although he was besieged with college scholarship offers, Kenny's mind was made up. He signed with the Cubs in the spring of 1959.

*   *   *   *

Late in 1961, Hubbs debuted in Chicago. A year later, he supplanted Don Zimmer as the Cubs' regular second baseman.

That June, Hubbs began an errorless streak that would stretch to a record 78 consecutive games. He handled 418 consecutive chances without a miscue, breaking the major league standard

of 414 chances in 73 games set in 1948 by Bobby Doerr of the Red Sox.

"Kenny was built a lot like Ryne Sandberg," observed team-mate Don Elston, a relief pitcher for the Cubs in 1953 and from 1957 to 1964. "He wouldn't have hit like Sandberg, but with that glove, there was nobody I've ever seen who was any better. He made the turn well and he was so smooth."

*   *   *   *

The 20-year-old Hubbs hit .260, won a Gold Glove award and was named N.L. Rookie of the Year.

It looked like the Cubs—an improving team with Hubbs and other flashy youngsters like 22-year-old third baseman Ron Santo and 23-year-old left fielder Billy Williams—were set at second base for years to come.

"He had great tools in the field," remembered Santo, "the best I've ever seen with Ryne Sandberg. He was graceful, tal-ented, humble ... it was clear from the very first he would make it immediately."

*   *   *   *

In his second full year with the Cubs, Hubbs' batting average dropped to .235 but his fielding was still close to perfection. The Cubs improved to 82-80 in 1963, their first winning season since 1946.

Hubbs and Santo were roommates, and during the season the third baseman was surprised to learn that Hubbs planned to get a pilot's license. Hubbs had confided a fear of flying to Santo, and he hoped flying lessons would help him overcome the phobia.

*   *   *   *

On February 13, 1964, Hubbs was planning to fly a single-engine Cessna back to California from Provo, Utah, accompanied by Dennis Doyle, a lifelong pal. When the plane took off, there were snow flurries in the air and the temperature was below zero.

Moments after takeoff, the Cessna plunged into a frozen section of Utah Lake. Two days later, searchers recovered the bodies of Hubbs and Doyle.

*   *   *   *

Kenny Hubbs, who would have been the Cubs second baseman of the '60s—and perhaps one of the game's greatest of all time—died at the age of 23.

Hubbs' death set back the Cubs' development several years. Far worse, however, was the loss of one of finest men ever to don a Chicago uniform.

"He was a sparkplug who provided instant leadership and solidified our team," related Cubs pitcher Dick Ellsworth. With the arrival of youngsters like Hubbs, Santo, and Williams, Ellsworth figured the Cubs had the nucleus of a winning team.

"From the day he showed up, he was a great player and we knew he was going to be one of a kind," said Ellsworth. "We expected him to be our second baseman for at least a decade."

"To this day," says Ron Santo, "I still think about Kenny Hubbs and the kind of man he was. I miss him."

RANDY JACKSON

R andy Jackson's good looks earned the third baseman
the nickname "Handsome Ransom". Jackson broke in
with Chicago in 1950 and played for the Dodgers and
Indians before ending his career with the Cubs in 1959.

*   *   *   *

In the second inning of a game at St. Louis on April 16, 1955,
Jackson, Ernie Banks, and Dee Fondy hit consecutive home
runs in a 7-5 loss to the Cardinals.

It was the second time in team history the Cubs had clouted
back-to-back-to-back homers. On August 11, 1941, Phil Cavarretta, Stan Hack, and Bill Nicholson had consecutive homers in a 7-5 loss to the Cardinals at Sportsman's Park. The next
time it happened, May 17, 1977, the Cubs finally won, destroy-
ing Pittsburgh 23-6 at Wrigley Field. In the fifth inning of the
massacre, Larry Biittner, Jerry Morales, and Bobby Murcer hit
three homers in a row.

*   *   *   *

Jackson played in the World Series (with the Dodgers in '56)
and the All-Star Game, and also in the Cotton Bowl—for Texas
Christian University in a 34-0 loss to Oklahoma State in 1945

and in 1946 for the University of Texas in a 40-27 win over Missouri.

"I wasn't any pro prospect," says Jackson. "I was an average football player that played a lot because we didn't have that many players. I didn't play football in high school, and went out in college for something to do."

*   *   *   *

Jackson's father had played baseball at Princeton. The elder Jackson had hopes for his son, but Randy didn't play any sports in high school.

It wasn't until he got to college that Jackson took up baseball and football. He led the Southwest Conference in hitting for three consecutive seasons.

*   *   *   *

Jackson was a two-time All-Star with the Cubs in 1954-1955.

The Dodgers obtained him as a possible successor to Jackie Robinson at third base, but a knee injury in 1957 shortened Jackson's career.

*   *   *   *

In the third inning of a game with the Phillies at Shibe Park on September 28, 1957, Jackson hit a three-run homer off Don Cardwell.

After the season the Dodgers moved to Los Angeles. Jackson's home run was destined to be the last by a Brooklyn player.

FERGIE JENKINS

Bob Buhl and Larry Jackson. That's who the Cubs gave up to get Ferguson Jenkins from the Phillies on April 21, 1966. As part of the deal, the Cubs also obtained outfielder Adolfo Phillips and first baseman John Herrnstein.

Buhl and Jackson had been reliable hurlers, but at the time of the trade their best days were far behind them. They combined for 47 wins and 53 losses in Philadelphia, and by the end of the decade both were gone from the big leagues.

*   *   *   *

The Cubs acquired Jenkins because Leo Durocher wanted to get rid of Ernie Banks.

Never a Banks fan during his stay in Chicago, Leo the Lip hoped to pry loose Orlando Cepeda from San Francisco. When the Giants instead dealt Cepeda to St. Louis, Durocher asked Philadelphia about John Herrnstein, a promising first sacker.

The Cubs and Phils closed the deal, with Jenkins as an afterthought. Herrnstein played nine games for the Cubs and was traded to Atlanta less than six weeks later.

Banks stayed on first in Chicago, and Jenkins embarked on one of the great pitching careers in Cubs history.

*   *   *   *

The acquisition of Fergie Jenkins was one of the steals of the century. Jenkins, a 6' 5", 210-pound righty from Chatham, Ontario, was one of baseball's top control artists.

"What made Fergie so good was that he could locate a pitch anytime he wanted," says Ron Santo.

"He changed speeds better than anyone in the league. He didn't have the greatest fastball in baseball, but he could paint the outside corner."

*   *   *   *

His debut with the Cubs on April 23, 1966, foreshadowed great things to come.

In relief of starter Bob Hendley, Jenkins shut out the Dodgers for five and two-thirds innings. Jenkins also drove a pair of runs with a home run off Don Sutton in a 2-0 victory.

A good hitter, Fergie belted 13 career homers, including six in 1971.

*   *   *   *

On an off-day during Spring Training in 1968, Jenkins went horseback riding with team captain Ron Santo, an experienced horseman, and teammates Glenn Beckett, Bill Hands, and Rich Nye. Jenkins' mount took off suddenly and made a sharp turn, sending the pitcher sprawling on the ground.

Santo was in a panic, figuring Jenkins was seriously hurt. When Santo rode over to his fallen teammate, the agonized Jenkins told him what had happened.

"I told him to stay," moaned Fergie, rubbing his leg. "But then he just took off on me. I thought I was under control because I was yelling 'Whoa!'"

"You can yell all you want," Santo exploded, "but unless you have the reins, it won't mean a darn thing!"

Santo and the others got Jenkins to a doctor, who advised the big hurler to stay off his feet for a week.

When Leo Durocher learned of the mishap, he threw a tantrum. Durocher was sure that Jenkins would be out for the beginning of the season. Yet 24 hours after the riding accident, Jenkins was back in uniform.

"Somehow, his Canadian blood had overcome the near disaster," recalls Santo. "Fergie did start for us Opening Day that year. He won 20 games for us. He didn't miss a start."

*   *   *   *

Jenkins began putting up numbers unseen at Wrigley Field since Chicago's glory days prior to World War II. He was 20-13 in 1967, followed by seasons of 20-15, 21-15, 22-16, 24-13, and 20-12.

During those years he completed 140 of his 236 starts, hurled 24 shutouts and won the 1971 N.L. Cy Young Award. He was the bellwether of the Chicago squads of the late '60s and early '70s.

*   *   *   *

None of this would've happened, however, if Jenkins had his way.

Jenkins thought he worked best in relief. Longtime Philadelphia star Robin Roberts saw Jenkins' true potential, however, and tried to convince the Phillies to convert the young pitcher into a starter.

But Phillies brass also considered Jenkins a relief pitcher and, with young left-hander Darold Knowles blossoming in the Philadelphia bullpen, Fergie was expendable.

*   *   *   *

In the spring of '67, manager Leo Durocher and pitching coach Joe Becker convinced Jenkins to become a starting pitcher.

The switch gave the Cubs their most reliable right-handed starter since Three-Finger Brown.

*   *   *   *

"I think it was putting on the Cubs uniform that was always special to me," says Jenkins.

"I always tried to give the best performance I could, because the Cubs were the team that meant the most to me throughout my whole career."

Jenkins was inducted into the Hall of Fame in 1991.

SAM JONES

S am Jones had been a star pitcher in the Negro Leagues. He came to the Cubs in a trade with the Indians prior to the 1955 season. The right-hander had helped the Cleveland Buckeyes to the 1947 Negro Leagues World Series.

He signed with Cleveland in the wake of Jackie Robinson's ground-breaking debut with the Dodgers. With the Indians, however, Sam's path was blocked by a starting rotation that included future Hall of Famers Bob Feller, Bob Lemon, and Early Wynn, plus Mike Garcia.

*   *   *   *

The right-handed Jones, who always chewed a toothpick on the mound, immediately became the bulwark of the Cubs pitching staff. His best pitch was a sweeping curve he'd learned from the legendary Satchel Paige.

Braves hurler Lew Burdette relates a story about Jones. Del Crandall, Milwaukee's good-hitting catcher, stepped up to the plate against Jones.

"Sad Sam threw him three curves," says Burdette, "and he fell down on each one and struck out. You couldn't help but laugh."

*   *   *   *

In his first year in Chicago, Jones won 14 and lost 20 for a sixth-place team. He led the N.L. in strikeouts and walks, and he hurled four shutouts. Only Cincinnati's Joe Nuxhall, with five, had more.

"Sad Sam Jones was a nice, fun-loving guy," says Frankie Baumholtz, a Chicago outfielder from 1949 through 1955. "Despite his nickname, he always had a smile on his face. He always had a toothpick in his mouth, so they also called him 'Toothpick.'"

*   *   *   *

During that inaugural season with the Cubs, Jones was involved in one of the all-time great nail-biting games at Wrigley Field.

On May 12, 1955, he was pitching against the Pirates under overcast skies that held attendance to around 3,000. The Cubs scored in the first inning, and again in the second, fifth and sixth. They took a 4-0 lead into the top of the ninth and Jones, who'd walked four and fanned three through eight innings, hadn't allowed a hit.

Pittsburgh's lead off hitter, Gene Freese, bunted foul on the first pitch, then looked at four straight balls for a walk. Ex-Cub Preston Ward came up to bat for pitcher Vern Law. Ward worked the count to 2-2, and Freese made it to second on a wild pitch. Jones then walked Ward, and Roman Mejias came in as a pinch runner.

When Jones walked rookie Tom Saffell on a 3-1 pitch to load the bases, manager Stan Hack asked for time and walked out to the mound. The Pirates had the tying run at the plate and Dick Groat, Roberto Clemente, and Frank Thomas—the heart of their order—due up.

Hack, who had two men warming up in the bullpen, called time and headed for the mound. "One more walk," Hack scolded Jones, "and I'm taking you out, no-hitter or not!"

"When I realized I was on the verge of blowing one of the better games I ever pitched," said Jones, "I told myself, 'They aren't going to get a hit now' ... I was going to get those last three outs… and that's all I thought about."

Sad Sam threw three straight curves to Groat for called strikes. Clemente lunged at a pair of curves and fouled off two pitches before swinging at a third strike. With a 1-2 count, Jones got Thomas looking for the final out—striking out three in a row after walking the bases loaded.

The no-hitter was the first in Wrigley Field since 1917, and the first in the big leagues by an African American pitcher.

*   *   *   *

In another bad trade, the Cubs dealt Jones to the Cardinals prior to the 1957 season. He went from St. Louis to San Francisco, and in 1959 his 21 victories tied for the N.L. lead.

Pitching for the Giants, Jones threw a second no-hitter, this time against the Braves in Milwaukee on April 28, 1961.

Sad Sam ended his big league career with the Orioles in 1964.

WHITEY LOCKMAN

Whitey Lockman, a 15-year outfielder-first baseman with the Giants, Cardinals, and Reds, managed the Cubs from 1972 through 1974.

Lockman took over for Leo Durocher and was succeeded by Jim Marshall. His slate at the Cubs helm was 157 wins and 162 losses.

*   *   *   *

His best work was in '72, after he replaced Durocher. The Cubs were 39-26 under Lockman and moved from fourth to second place.

Don Kessinger praised Lockman's leadership.

"If a ballplayer can't play for Whitey," said the Cubs shortstop, "he can't play for anybody."

*   *   *   *

Lockman was involved in a revolutionary event in 1973. On May 8 in San Diego, Lockman was ejected during a 12-inning 3-2 win over the Padres. With Lockman gone, Ernie Banks, by now a full-time Chicago coach, took over the managerial reins.

Technically, this made Mister Cub the first black manager in major league history. The incident took place two years before

Frank Robinson was hired by the Cleveland Indians as the major league's first full-time African American field boss.

*　　*　　*　　*

During Lockman's tenure, Cubs players lobbied to bring wives on the road. While the idea was under consideration, the Cubs dropped six of eight contests on a West Coast swing.

"Next trip," offered one wag, "the Cubs ought to bring the wives and leave the players home."

DALE LONG

Arangy first baseman who played for six big league teams between 1951 and 1963, Dale Long hit eight home runs in eight consecutive games with Pittsburgh in May 1956. Only one other player—the Yankees' Don Mattingly in 1987—has equaled that power display.

But the 6'4", 205-pound Long performed another unusual feat in 1958, this time as a Cub.

*   *   *   *

Scouted in high school by Casey Stengel, Long once passed up an offer to play for the National Football League's Green Bay Packers.

He debuted with the Pirates in 1951, and came to Chicago with outfielder Lee Walls in exchange for Gene Baker and Dee Fondy in May 1957. Ideally suited to the Friendly Confines, Long smashed 55 homers and batted .274 in two-plus seasons as a Cub.

*   *   *   *

During the first game of a double-header with the Pirates at Wrigley Field on August 20, 1958, skipper Bob Scheffing—himself an old Cubs catcher—inserted the left-handed Long behind the plate.

Years earlier, Pittsburgh general manager Branch Rickey had taken the unusual step of trying Long as a receiver. Long had even caught for one inning during a 1954 Pacific Coast League contest, when he played all nine positions for the Hollywood Stars.

Long took the field with chest protector, shinguards, his cap turned backwards, and—since no lefty catchers gloves were available—his first baseman's mitt.

Long became the major leagues' first southpaw backstop in more than five decades.

*   *   *   *

On September 21 Long went behind the plate again, this time in the ninth inning of a home game with the Dodgers. How'd he do in his two-game big league catching career?

"Not bad," he boasted. "I picked a runner off first. Actually, I've never figured out any reason why a lefty couldn't play short or third, either."

PEANUTS LOWREY

Harry "Peanuts" Lowrey, a child actor-turned baseball player, was an outfielder for the Cubs from 1942 through 1949.

Even after he made the majors, Lowrey continued to get bit parts in Hollywood.

*　　*　　*　　*

Lowrey got into 27 games with the Cubs in 1942. A year later he replaced Dom Dallessandro as Chicago's center fielder.

Lowrey went off to war in 1944, but was back for the pennant-winning 1945 season. With Andy Pafko now in center, Peanuts shifted to left and batted .283.

He hit .310 against the Tigers in the World Series.

*　　*　　*　　*

Charlie Grimm claimed Peanuts Lowrey was his son's favorite player. The boy followed Lowery everywhere around the ball-park.

Grimm played first base while Lowrey manned left field for Chicago. Yet whenever anyone asked Charlie's son about his favorite Cub, his answer was always the same: Peanuts Lowrey.

"He didn't idolize me," lamented Jolly Cholly. "He idolized Peanuts."

*   *   *   *

Traded to Cincinnati in June 1949 as part of the deal that brought Hank Sauer to the Cubs, the 5'8", 170-pound Lowrey moved on to the Cardinals in 1950. He spent his final big league season with the Phillies in 1955.

Lowrey coached in the big leagues for 20 seasons, and was part of Leo Durocher's staff in 1969.

"The Cubs didn't blow it in '69," he insisted, "the darn Mets kept winning."

*   *   *   *

A native of Culver City, California, Lowrey stayed active in motion pictures during his playing days. He was an extra in *Pride of the Yankees* (1942), *The Stratton Story* (1949), and *The Winning Team* (1952), the film about Cubs' pitching great Grover Alexander.

Curiously, the credits for *The Winning Team* include quite a few past, present and future Cubs. Listed as a technical advisor is Jigger Statz, Alexander's Cubs teammate from 1922 to 1925.

Among the other extras are Lowrey, Hank Sauer, outfielders George Metkovich (who played briefly for Chicago in '53) and Irv Noren (1959-60), plus infielder Gene Mauch (a Cub in 1948-49).

*   *   *   *

The script of the *The Winning Team* called for Lowrey to plunk Ronald Reagan in the head with a baseball. In one scene Reagan, playing Alexander, is forced at second base and Lowrey beans the future president with his throw to first on an attempted double play.

"I'm supposed to hit him in the head," Lowrey related. "Well, they got this two-by-four plank with a hole in it, and right behind that is the camera. I'm supposed to throw the ball right at this hole, which I do, and when it gets there they stop the cameras."

Lowrey said the ball that he threw at Reagan was actually made of cotton.

"He goes down and lies there," Lowrey continued. "I turn him over and I say, 'Sorry, Alex.' Then I'm supposed to look real soulful."

*   *   *   *

So what was it like working with a future president?

"We'd have parties at night," Peanuts recalled, "and Reagan would come with his girl, Nancy Davis... They're married now. All of us thought he was a fine guy."

BILL MADLOCK

Bill Madlock grew up in Decatur, Illinois. He had around 150 college scholarship offers—for basketball. Two schools, one in Trinidad, Colorado, the other in Keokuk, Iowa, offered him baseball scholarships.

*   *   *   *

In 1970 Madlock signed his first professional contract with the Washington Senators. The franchise relocated to Texas in 1972 and Madlock joined the Rangers in 1973 after a 22-homer, .338 season at Spokane.

Cubs scout Gene Handley spotted Madlock at Spokane and was impressed by his compact swing. After the '73 season, the Cubs traded Fergie Jenkins to Texas for Madlock and infielder Vic Harris.

*   *   *   *

The original package was Madlock, Harris, and rookie catcher Jim Sundberg for Jenkins, catcher Randy Hundley, and out-fielder Gene Hiser.

Cubs manager Whitey Lockman had second thoughts about the exchange, however, and wanted to sleep on it. A day later, the Rangers had cooled off on the deal.

The two teams finally reached an agreement and, in 1974, Madlock supplanted Ron Santo at third base in Wrigley Field.

*   *   *   *

Madlock's .313 was the highest average by a Cub third baseman since Stan Hack's .323 in 1945. He won back-to-back N.L. bat titles in 1975-1976.

Was Madlock a natural hitter?

"I didn't have this knack for going to all fields until I hit the major leagues," he claims. "In my last year of Triple-A ball, I considered myself a pull hitter... but when I got up here and saw how these guys pitch, I shortened my stroke and started going to all fields."

Madlock claims he wielded a potent bat as a youngster.

"In Little League I hit .700 or .800," he recollects. "Then in my last year in high school, in American Legion ball, I hit about .430."

Was it coaching?

"No, man... you know how it is in Legion ball. The coach is usually your mailman or something and they usually only get there in time for the games. I just worked on hitting by myself."

*   *   *   *

The Cubs dealt Madlock to San Francisco after the 1976 season. He also played for the Pirates and Dodgers, retiring after the 1987 season with a career .305 batting average.

He hit .336 in an even 400 games as a Cub.

ED MAYER

L eft-hander Ed Mayer pitched in 22 games for the Cubs in 1957 and l958, splitting four decisions. One of the bespectacled Mayer's victories was a win over Dodger great Sandy Koufax.

*   *   *   *

On May 30, 1958, the Cubs took two games from Los Angeles at Wrigley Field, winning 3-2 and 10-8. In the second game, Mayer and Koufax both came on in relief. The Cubs touched the future Hall of Famer for two runs in the bottom of the ninth for the victory.

The win was Mayer's last. Chicago farmed him out to the Pacific Coast League in June. He bounced around until 1959, but never returned to the majors.

*   *   *   *

Those two stints with the Cubs remain one of the highlights of Mayer's life.

"When I put on that Cub uniform and walked on the diamond at Wrigley Field, that was the biggest thrill of my life," he says. "They often make fun of the Cubs. But from my point of view, it was great being a Cub. It was a beautiful park, wonderful fans, great city."

The personalized license on Mayer's car reads "OLD CUB".

LINDY McDANIEL

From 1955 through 1975, forkball specialist Lindy McDaniel pitched for the Cardinals, Cubs, Giants, Yankees, and Royals.

McDaniel joined the Cubs in 1963, replacing Don Elston as the bullpen stopper. In three full seasons with Chicago, he saved 39 games.

A control pitcher, McDaniel didn't have a great fastball but was adept at working out of a jam. His forte was the forkball, a pitch McDaniel learned from Pirate reliever Roy Face.

*   *   *   *

During a 1963 game against the Giants, McDaniel looked like Cy Young and Babe Ruth rolled into one.

At Wrigley Field on June 6, 1963, the Cubs and Giants were tied at 2-2 in the top of the 12th. With one out, the Giants loaded the bases against Barney Schultz, and Chicago skipper Bob Kennedy summoned McDaniel from the bullpen.

The right-hander promptly picked off Willie Mays at second base, and then quashed the San Francisco rally by striking out Ed Bailey.

McDaniel wasn't done yet. In the bottom of the inning, he stepped up against southpaw Billy Pierce. On a 2-2 count,

McDaniel slammed Pierce's next delivery into the left field stands for a 3-2 Cubs win.

*   *   *   *

The triumph was the Cubs' 11th in 13 games and put them in a three-way tie for first place with St. Louis and San Francisco.

It marked the first time Chicago stood atop the league since May 1958.

BILL NICHOLSON AND WARTIME BASEBALL

Wartime Player. That label hung like a cloud over many of baseball best players 1942 through 1945. The United States entered World War II in December 1941. When big league players entered military service, their places on the rosters were filled by minor leaguers. When those men were drafted, players from further down the depths of the minors took their place.

With Ted Williams in the Marine Corps, Bob Johnson—a solid major leaguer in his day, but by then 38 years old and past his prime—patrolled left field for the Red Sox.

While Pee Wee Reese was in the navy, Eddie Basinksi took over as Brooklyn's shortstop.

At Yankee Stadium, Tuck Stainback became New York's center fielder after Joe DiMaggio went off to war.

When peace returned in 1945, so did Williams, Reese, DiMaggio and the rest of the stars. Many of the players who filled during their absence quietly drifted back into obscurity.

*   *   *   *

At one time or another during the war years, 27 Cubs traded baseball flannels for military uniforms. They were:

• *Pitchers:* Dale Alderson, Hi Bithorn, Bill Fleming, Emil Kush, Walt Lanfranconi, Red Lynn, Russ Meers, Vern Olsen, Johnny Schmitz, Lon Warneke.

• *Catchers:* Marv Felderman, Mickey Livingston, Clyde McCullough, Bob Scheffing, Joe Stephenson, Bennie Warren.

• *Infielders:* Cy Block, Al Glossop, Lou Stringer, Bob Sturgeon, Eddie Waitkus.

• *Outfielders:* Dom Dallessandro, Charlie Gilbert, Peanuts Lowrey, Lou Novikoff, Whitey Platt, Marv Rickert.

*   *   *   *

Some big leaguers were draft-exempt for family reasons, or because they were too old or physically unfit for military service. The 1945 Cub pitching staff included 36-year-old Claude Passeau along with Paul Derringer and Ray Prim, both 38.

Forty-three-year-old Johnny Moore, a Chicago outfielder in the late '20s and early '30s who hadn't played in the majors since 1937, was pressed into service for seven games during the '45 campaign.

*   *   *   *

Sometimes players who were too young for military service donned major league uniforms. During the 1944 season, Joe Nuxhall of the Cincinnati Reds pitched in his first game as a 15-year-old.

Players like pitcher Hal Newhouser of Detroit and Yankee second baseman Snuffy Stirnweiss, who came into their own during the war years, are sometimes dismissed as Wartime Players—men who excelled against watered-down competition.

That "Wartime Player" tag early kept Newhouser (who won 207 games between 1939 and 1955) out of the Hall of Fame.

*   *   *   *

Despite the vagaries of wartime baseball, the Cubs waged a tight battle with the St. Louis Cardinals for the 1945 N.L. title.

"That wasn't an easy season," maintains Phil Cavarretta. "Even though it was during the war, there were a lot of good players still around, and more were coming home from the war."

*   *   *   *

Some critics dismiss Bill "Swish" Nicholson, the Cubs' power-hitting right fielder of the 1940s, as a Wartime Player. A refugee from Connie Mack's Athletics (Nicholson was 0-for-12 for Philadelphia in 1936), Nicholson refined his talents at Chattanooga under the tutelage of Lookouts' manager Kiki Cuyler, an ex-Cub.

Nicholson developed into one of the Southern League's most feared sluggers and in June 1939—tipped off by Cuyler—the Cubs purchased Nicholson's contract.

*   *   *   *

It was the fans in Brooklyn—the same folks who dubbed Cardinals great Stan Musial "Stan the Man"—who gave Nicholson the nickname "Swish."

Every time the muscular ex-dairy farmer cut loose with a powerful practice swing, the awed Flatbush crowds would respond with a respectful cry of "Swish!"

*   *   *   *

It was the crosstown rival Giants, however, who accorded Nicholson the greatest show of deference. With the Cubs trailing in the seventh inning of a July 23, 1944, contest, New York manager Mel Ott ordered his pitcher, Andy Hansen, to walk Nicholson with the bases loaded.

Nicholson had been on a rampage, hitting four consecutive homers over two games. In a 40-hour span he'd clubbed a total of six round-trippers. Ott wasn't taking any chances, and took the bat right out of Nicholson's hands—even if it cost him a run.

The strategy worked. The base on balls to Nicholson forced in a run, but the Giants went on to win, 12-10.

*   *   *   *

Nicholson also received a compliment from an army paratrooper. Just before he went overseas, the serviceman sent the Chicago outfielder a letter.

"I've always admired your playing," wrote the soldier, "and I wonder if you'd be so kind as to send me a Cubs cap. I'd like to wear it into battle."

Nicholson made sure the G.I. got his cap.

*   *   *   *

Prior to Pearl Harbor in 1940 and '41, Nicholson had chalked up impressive 25- and 26-homer seasons. He belted 29 home runs with 128 RBI in 1943, followed by a 33-homer, 122 RBI campaign in 1944.

Nicholson lost the '44 N.L. MVP award to St. Louis Cardinals shortstop Marty Marion by a single vote.

*   *   *   *

Swish was also a capable fielder with a decent throwing arm. He was also a smart base runner, as future Hall of Fame second baseman Red Schoendienst found out the day he made his major league debut.

On Opening Day in 1945, Nicholson scored the winning run in the bottom of the ninth on a single by Don Johnson. Nicholson beat the throw home by the rookie Schoendienst, who was playing left field.

*   *   *   *

Oddly, Nicholson batted only .243 for the pennant-winning Cubs in 1945, with 13 homers. During the off-season, he worked at a Maryland defense plant. He underwent an army physical exam in '45, but was never called for military duty.

Nicholson would later recall that during the '45 season he "felt bad all the time. No pep." He still managed to drive in eight runs in the World Series, won by Detroit in seven games.

Five years later, when he played for the Phillies, doctors discovered Bill's problem. He was a diabetic, and the ailment prevented him from playing in the 1950 Series with the Yankees.

*   *   *   *

The '45 Series was Bill's last, just as it was for the Cubs—at least in the Twentieth Century.

Swish Nicholson, downgraded by some as a Wartime Player, ranks among the Cubs' all-time leaders in a half-dozen offensive categories.

LOU NOVIKOFF

Lou Novikoff was a four-time minor league batting champ who played for the Cubs from 1941 to 1944. Born in Arizona, Novikoff spoke nothing but Russian until he was about 10.

Dubbed "The Mad Russian," Lou was proud of his ethnic heritage and owned a Russian wolfhound. He once broke out of a slump after his wife fed him Russian-style ground beef rolled in cabbage leaves and served on a bun.

*   *   *   *

Novikoff was a notoriously bad outfielder. He blamed some of his defensive problems on Wrigley Field's ivy-covered walls, believing the foliage was actually poison ivy.

Novikoff also claimed he had trouble playing left field at Wrigley because the foul lines were crooked.

After the Cubs shipped him to the minor leagues, Lou complained that the outfield in Milwaukee (then part of the American Association) had too many bumps.

*   *   *   *

After retiring from baseball, Novikoff was elected to the Hall of Fame... not the baseball shrine in Cooperstown, but the Softball Hall of Fame in Rockford, Illinois.

Softball was actually Novikoff s first love. He once struck out 22 batters in an eight-inning game, and played until he was 53 years old.

MILT PAPPAS

Right-hander Milt Pappas won 209 big league contests between 1957 and 1973 for the Orioles, Reds, Braves, and Cubs.

He started the 1965 All-Star contest for the A.L., and after the season was part of one of the most controversial trades in history. Pappas went to the Reds in a four-player deal that brought Frank Robinson to Baltimore.

Robinson proceeded to win the 1966 A.L. MVP Award, sparking the Orioles to a four-game World Series sweep of the Dodgers.

*   *   *   *

In 1970 Pappas, by then 31 years old, joined the Cubs from Atlanta.

The Detroit native was 51-41 in three-plus seasons in Chicago, winning a career-high 17 games in 1971 and '72.

*   *   *   *

By 1972 the Cubs were starting to slip. Leo Durocher quit as manager in late July, handing over the club to director of player development Whitey Lockman. The Cubs revived, at least temporarily, and finished second, 11 games behind Pittsburgh in the N.L. East.

In 1973 the Cubs finished under .500 for the first time in seven seasons. They wouldn't be winners again until 1984.

But one afternoon in '72, Pappas gave Chicago fans something they'd never forget when he came within one pitch of a perfect game.

*   *   *   *

On September 2 at Wrigley Field, Pappas took the mound against the Padres. The Cubs gave him plenty of support, scoring two runs in the first, another pair in the third and four more in the eighth.

Meanwhile, Pappas' slider was unhittable. Heading into the last inning, he'd retired 24 Padres in a row.

John Jeter led off the ninth for San Diego and hit a short fly into center. Center fielder Billy North broke back, lost the ball in the sun, and then fell. As the crowd gasped and Pappas' heart sunk to his toeplate, Billy Williams came streaking over from left field to make a fine running catch. Fred Kendall, the next batter, grounded out to shortstop Don Kessinger.

With the pitcher due up, San Diego skipper Don Zimmer called on Larry Stahl, a .226 hitter. Stahl swung and missed the first pitch. Pappas' next delivery was wide. Stahl missed again on the next pitch, and the Wrigley Field fans were on their feet. No Cubs pitcher had ever thrown a perfect game.

Pappas' next two pitches were close but, said home plate ump Bruce Froemming, both were outside. With a full count, Pappas delivered. Stahl watched.

From third base, Ron Santo saw what looked "like a knee high strike" for what he thought was the third out.

Yet Froemming barked "Ball four!" and Stahl became the first San Diego baserunner. Pappas had missed perfection by inches. It was a heartbreaking moment for Milt, for the Cubs and for the crowd of nearly 13,000 on hand that day.

Moments later, Pappas salvaged a no-hitter when he retired ex-Cub Garry Jestadt on a pop-up caught by second baseman Carmen Fanzone.

*   *   *   *

Afterward, Cubs catcher Randy Hundley mused on how close Pappas had come to pitching a perfect game.

"They were so close," said Hundley, "I don't know how Stahl could take them."

Pappas shook off the near miss.

"I always said I'd rather be lucky than good," he philosophized, "and today I was lucky."

Pappas' performance delighted manager Whitey Lockman.

"I've been in professional baseball thirty years," he enthused, "and this is the first time I've been on the winning side of a no-hitter. I couldn't believe the thrill."

*   *   *   *

The day of his no-hitter, Pappas almost called in sick.

The 1972 season had been a tough one for Milt. He'd broken a finger during Spring Training. His elbow had given him trouble throughout the season, requiring repeated cortisone shots. Early in the season he'd missed a few starts with a bad back.

In early September, he was suffering from a bad cold.

Feeling miserable, Pappas was ready to call the ballpark to say he wouldn't be coming to work. But his wife, Caroline, convinced him to give it a try.

The Padres were sorry she did.

*   *   *   *

Pappas had a near-miss in one other category.

During his 17-year career, he won 209 games. Ninety-nine of those wins were in the N.L.

Just one more would have made Pappas one of a handful of pitchers with a 100 victories in both leagues.

Bob Ramazzotti

Infielder Bob Ramazzotti spent all or part of seven seasons in the major leagues, including a hitch with the Cubs from 1949 to 1953.

To Randy Jackson, "Ram" was the Roommate From Hell.

* * * *

A 5' 8½", 175-pounder from Pennsylvania, Ramazzotti was a former Dodger whose pro career started in 1940. After missing 1942 through 1945 due to military service, he spent all of 1946 with Brooklyn as a backup at third and short.

In May 1949 the Dodgers sent him to Chicago for infielder Hank Schenz. For a stretch in 1951, Ramazzotti took over at shortstop after a broken leg shelved Roy Smalley.

The following year, Ram played 50 games at second and batted .284 despite spending time on the disabled list. A hand injury limited Ramazzotti to 39 at-bats in '53, his last year in the majors. He batted .230 lifetime, including .236 for Chicago.

* * * *

Randy Jackson, the Cubs' third baseman during the early '50s, roomed briefly with Ramazzotti during road trips and couldn't wait to get away from him.

"He was a wonderful guy," Jackson recollects, "but he smoked Italian cigars that just curled your hair. I didn't smoke, so I told him he'd have to get someone else."

CHARLIE ROOT AND BABE'S "CALLED SHOT"

T he great Babe Ruth hit 714 home runs during his career, and 15 more in 10 World Series. None was more controversial than Ruth's home run off Chicago right-hander Charlie Root in Game Three of the 1932 Fall Classic at Wrigley Field.

*   *   *   *

Baseball legend says that Ruth strode toward the plate with one out in the fifth inning, the jeers and taunts of the multitude floating down like spent shrapnel. There was bad blood between the Cubs and Yanks in that World Series and, according to myth, the only people not booing the Bambino that day were Ruth's Yankee teammates and the umpires.

The score was 4-all with the Yanks leading the Series, two games to none. Ruth had knocked a three-run homer in the first off Root, and nearly 50,000 Cubs fans were all over the Bambino like Sammy Sosa on a hanging curve.

Even baseball commissioner Kenesaw Mountain Landis, him-self fluent in barbaric dialect, was taken aback by the language.

*   *   *   *

From there, fact and fantasy blend. Even film doesn't prove or disclaim what happened next. On a 1-2 count, Ruth swung and connected. The ball sailed straight out toward the flagpole in center field and sank into the bleachers. Ruth had homered into the deepest regions of Wrigley Field.

*   *   *   *

But had Ruth called his shot?

A few reporters, most notably John Drebinger of the *New York Times*, wrote that Babe had pointed to the exact spot where he hit his home run.

Most other scribes, however, made no mention of such an incident. Even Ruth's biographer, Robert Creamer, cast doubts upon the veracity of the "Called Shot."

*   *   *   *

No way, said the Chicago players.

Had Ruth pulled a stunt like that, they insisted, Charlie Root—remembered by one contemporary as "one of the roughest, toughest competitors who ever lived" and a "hard-nosed, hard-assed pitcher"—would have tried to stick the next pitch in the Babe's ear for grandstanding.

*   *   *   *

The stocky Root is the winningest pitcher in Cub history, with 201 career victories. He helped Chicago win four pennants, and was still pitching in the major leagues at age 42.

When he left the Cubs after the 1941 season, Root returned to the minors and kept on pitching until he was 49.

*   *   *   *

Years later, a long-forgotten homemade film of the episode surfaced. In it, Ruth appears to make some kind of gesture with his hands.

But was he pointing to a spot in center field? Several Yankee players swore he did, and the Babe—ever the showman—always milked the story without giving a straight answer.

*   *   *   *

Was Charlie Root someone the Bambino would try to show up?

"Root would have murdered him," claimed Chicago infielder Woody English.

"He [Ruth] didn't point," insisted second baseman Billy Herman. "Root would have had him with his feet up in the air."

"I'd have knocked him on his fanny," growled Root.

But the legend of the Called Shot has transcended myth and hardened, for many, into fact. As longtime *Washington Post* sportswriter Shirley Povich noted, "Who could ever forget the scene, even if he never saw it?"

*   *   *   *

Perhaps Cubs catcher Gabby Hartnett offered the most logical explanation. Hartnett maintains that after Root got two strikes on the Babe, Ruth held up a finger toward the jeering Cub dugout and said, "It only takes one to hit it."

No matter what, Ruth's homer signaled the Cubs' downfall. Lou Gehrig followed with another home run, and the Yanks went on to win, 7-5. The Yanks won again the following day to complete the sweep.

*   *   *   *

All but forgotten amid the controversy over the Called Shot is fact that Root surrendered Babe Ruth's last home run in World Series play.

VIC SAIER AND
MRS. O'LEARY'S COW

Wrigley Field, the home of the Cubs, opened in 1914 as Weeghman Park. Restaurateur Charles Weeghman built the ballpark at Clark and Addison for his Chicago Whales club of the Federal League.

Weeghman purchased the Cubs after the Federal League's demise. He uprooted the team from the West Side Grounds at Polk and Lincoln (now Wolcott), the Cubs' home park since 1893, and brought them to the park that bore his name.

*   *   *   *

Prior to the formation of the National League in 1871, Chicago had a team in the National Association, an early professional circuit.

The thriving city was proud of its ballclub, and an area beside Lake Michigan was set aside for the team's new home at Randolph, Michigan, and Madison Streets. Known as Lake Park, the ballfield was closer to the water in those days (over the years, the shoreline has been extended further eastward via landfill projects).

In October 1871, Mrs. O'Leary's cow allegedly started the fire that consumed 2,600 city acres. Lake Park was destroyed

by the conflagration. Without a place to play, the Windy City's baseball team disbanded.

Professional baseball didn't return to Chicago until 1874.

*   *   *   *

Chicago's N.L. franchise called several locations home, including the 23rd Street Grounds (23rd and State, 1876-1877); Lakefront Park (south of Randolph Street between Michigan Avenue and Illinois Central railroad tracks, 1878-1884); West Side Park (Congress and Throop Streets, 1885-1892); and the West Side Grounds (1893-1915).

*   *   *   *

The Cubs's first game in the new park took place April 20, 1916.

Vic Saier, who had taken over at first base from Frank Chance after the 1911 campaign, was the hero in that contest. The 24-year-old Michigander hit a sacrifice fly in the bottom of the 11th, driving in the winning run in the Cubs' 7-6 triumph over Cincinnati.

*   *   *   *

A Cub from 1911 to 1917, Saier's career was curtailed by a back injury. The lifetime .263 hitter finished up with Pittsburgh in 1919.

Saier, whose 21 triples topped the N.L. in 1913, has one other distinction: his five career home runs against Christy Mathewson (including four in 1914) are the most off the Hall of Fame pitcher.

RYNE SANDBERG

For several years, two of Chicago's greatest sportsmen wore number 23: Michael Jordan of the Bulls and the Cubs' Ryne Sandberg.

Both retired at a young age, both made brief comebacks and then quit for good, at an age when many of their contemporaries were still playing every day.

*   *   *   *

Like Michael Jordan, Sandberg was an all-out competitor.

When Jordan, observed Sandberg, decided he was "mentally tired out getting to that level [of intensity] every time out, he walked away." And, added Ryne, "in that sense, so did I."

*   *   *   *

What a legacy Sandberg left behind! What Billy Herman was to Chicago in the first half of the century, Sandberg was to the latter-day Cubs: a brilliant second baseman who could do it all. His .285 lifetime batting average and 282 homers tell only half the story.

Sandberg was one of the all-time great fielders at second base. He once played 123 consecutive games without an error, and he

shares the big league record for the highest fielding percentage
by a second baseman (.989).

*   *   *   *

Sandberg, a native of Spokane, Washington, came to the Cubs
from the Phillies in January 1982 along with Larry Bowa for
Ivan DeJesus.

It's hard to believe now but, when Ryne came to Chicago
he was a man without a position. Sandberg had signed with
Philadelphia as a shortstop and had also played third and second
in the minors.

The Cubs had Bowa at short, Ken Reitz at third, and Bump
Wills at second. During his first Spring Training with the Cubs,
Sandberg spent time at each of those positions, and in center
field as well. "I had three different gloves in my locker," he recalled, "and I didn't know what to think."

*   *   *   *

Toward the end of spring camp, manager Lee Elia gave Sandberg the word: Reitz was going to be released, and Sandberg was
now the Cubs' third baseman.

Ryne responded with a .271 average. He fielded beyond expectations, making just 11 errors all year.

In September, however, general manager Dallas Green
abruptly informed Sandberg he was moving to second base.

*   *   *   *

Sandberg took a crash course on how to play second base from
an unlikely tutor: Cubs pitching coach Billy Connors. Despite
his job description and portly build, Connors proved to be a
capable teacher.

"He showed me, with that bad body of his, how to turn the double play and then jump afterward," says Sandberg.

Sandberg's biggest problem was trying to hold a straight face every time Connors tried to turn a pivot in less-than-balletic movement.

*　　*　　*　　*

While Connors didn't look like the ideal infield instructor, he turned out to be an excellent teacher. Just a few days after the fielding lesson, Pete Rose of the Phillies observed Sandberg's work around the bag and predicted Sandberg would be an All-Star at second base.

Sandberg turned out to be even better than that, earning the N.L. MVP in 1984. That year he batted .314 with 200 hits, including 36 doubles, 19 triples, 19 home runs, and 32 stolen bases. He barely missed becoming the first big leaguer to collect 200 hits, 20 doubles, 20 triples, 20 homers, and 20 stolen bases.

*　　*　　*　　*

Until 1984, Sandberg saw himself as a singles hitter. It was Jim Frey, who managed the Cubs from 1984 to 1986, who convinced him he could be a power hitter.

"I just thought he had too much talent not to take advantage of it, too much talent to remain a line-drive hitter," says Frey, who claims he had no quarrel with Ryne's hitting style.

Frey just wanted Sandberg to know that he had the potential, at 6'2" and with ample body strength, to be a line drive hitter with power.

"I wasn't trying to make him a home run hitter," insists Frey. "What I told him was that on certain pitches I knew he could handle, he should be looking to drive the ball for extra bases, instead of just settling for singles."

Sandberg listened to Frey's suggestion, and doubled his extra-base hit production from 37 in 1983 to 74 in 1984.

*   *   *   *

During the summer of 1969, the year Sandberg celebrated his 10th birthday, he would head for Fairgrounds Park in his native Spokane to watch the local Indians of the Pacific Coast League. Spokane was the Triple-A affiliate of the Dodgers, and 19-year-old Bill Buckner was a highly-regarded outfielder-first baseman.

Thirteen years later, following the trade with the Phillies, Sandberg and Buckner became teammates.

"I never let Buckner forget that I used to watch him play when I was a kid," chortles Sandberg.

*   *   *   *

In 1970, Sandberg began following the career of Larry Bowa, then a rookie shortstop with the Phillies. The youthful Sandberg idolized Bowa, and became his teammate when he joined Philadelphia in 1981.

Bowa was traded to Chicago with Sandberg prior to the 1982 season. Playing third for the Cubs that season, Sandberg found himself in the same infield with two of his boyhood heroes: Buckner on first and Bowa at short.

*   *   *   *

Sandberg's first year with the Cubs started out like a nightmare. The youngster had just one hit in his first 32 at-bats. He hung in there, however, and finished at .271.

Throughout Sandberg's ordeal, Bowa never lost faith in his infield partner. The veteran kept telling the other Cubs that Sandberg would be able to do everything that Mike Schmidt could do, except hit with Schmidt's awesome power.

Sandberg's toughness in the face of his early-season adversity really impressed Bowa.

"No knock on Schmitty," Bowa said, "but he might have panicked if he'd gone though anything like that as a rookie. Ryne Sandberg never came close to panicking."

*   *   *   *

Derwent Sandberg, Ryne's father, was a real baseball fan. Ryne claims he was named after Ryne Duren, a hard-throwing Yankee relief pitcher in the late 1950s and early '60s.

"My dad had taken my mother to... see the Yankees play when she was pregnant with me," says Sandberg, "... and the name just stuck."

According to Sandberg, his brother Del was named for former big league outfielder Del Ennis.

"Yeah," Sandberg says with a grin, "my dad was quite a baseball fan."

RON SANTO AND THE '69 CUBS

D uring an era of excellent third basemen—Brooks Robinson of Baltimore, the Braves' Eddie Mathews, Frank Malzone of Boston, the Cardinals' Ken Boyer and his brother, Clete Boyer of the Yankees—Ron Santo stood out.

Even Cubs skipper Leo Durocher, with whom Ron had a stormy relationship during their seven years together in Chicago, praised Santo.

"When I took over the club," said Durocher, "I looked upon Santo as one of my greatest assets. He was the best-fielding third baseman in the National League, and he knocked in his 100 to 110 runs a year."

*   *   *   *

A Cub from 1960 through 1973, Santo ended his playing days with the White Sox in 1974. He batted .277 with 342 homers and was an excellent glove man who set several fielding records.

When his career ended, the fiery Seattle native became a Cubs color commentator on WGN. Like Ernie Banks, Santo is as much a part of the Windy City as the Sears Tower or deep-dish, thick-crust pizza.

Yet he came close to playing for the Dodgers early in his career.

*   *   *   *

During the 1961 season, Santo's second in the majors, the Cubs were playing Los Angeles. The Dodgers' third base coach was Leo Durocher, who would become Santo's manager in Chicago four years later.

Just before the game, Durocher told Santo he was headed for stardom.

"By the way," added Leo, "you might be wearing a Dodger uniform tomorrow."

Trade rumors began to swirl. Word was that L.A. wanted Santo badly. Third base had been a revolving door for the Dodgers since Billy Cox's departure after the 1953 season.

According to the scuttlebutt, Los Angeles would give up pitcher Stan Williams, outfielder-first baseman Ron Fairly, and power-hitting outfielder Frank Howard for Santo.

*   *   *   *

Fortunately for Chicago fans, the trade never took place. The Dodgers won pennants in 1963 (platooning veteran Jim Gilliam at third with rookie Ken McMullen) and '66 (with Gilliam and John Kennedy sharing the hot corner).

The Cubs' best finish in the ensuing years was second in the N.L. East in 1969.

*   *   *   *

Any regrets? No way, insists Santo.

"There's no place you can go in the United States," he says, "any city or team, where, if you lose, they still get the support the people give you here. The fans here are the best."

*   *   *   *

Cubs fans' loyalty was severely tested in '69 when the Mets over-took the Cubs for the Eastern Division title and went on to win the N.L. pennant at the World Series. Over the years, the Cubs' '69 collapse has sparked more theories than an Oliver Stone film.

- Durocher didn't provide the right leadership and twice went AWOL from the team.
- The Cubs quit hitting down the stretch.
- Durocher wore out his regulars.
- The Cubs didn't have enough bench strength.
- Durocher's hostile approach toward his own players back-fired.
- The Cub players were too concerned with off-field enter-prises.
- Et cetera, et cetera, et cetera...

*   *   *   *

The fact is, the Mets outplayed the Cubs down the stretch. Some claim the summer of '69 produced two miracles: the lunar land-ing and the Mets winning the N.L. pennant.

Nonsense. The Apollo expedition and the '69 Mets were both the end product of diligent preparation, execution and leadership. The man who provided the Mets' leadership was Gil Hodges.

"The New York Mets were the worst team in the league," wrote outfielder Curt Flood in his autobiography.

"When some of the youngsters showed signs of becoming first-rate professionals, Gil Hodges was named manager and they became serious."

*   *   *   *

The '69 Mets were a terrific team.

So were the '69 Cubs.

Did Bobby Thomson's homer make the 1951 Dodgets any less of a great ballclub? Chicago's lineup of Randy Hundley, Ernie

Banks, Don Beckert, Don Kessinger, Santo, Billy Williams, and Jim Hickman was one of the most potent in history.

Fergie Jenkins, Ken Holtzman, Bill Hands and Phil Regan could command millions of dollars today on the free-agent market.

*　　*　　*　　*

But the Mets won, and that's baseball.

The real tragedy is that Ron Santo nor Gil Hodges—two central figures in that great '69 season—have been repeatedly ignored in Hall of Fame balloting.

*　　*　　*　　*

What made Santo's achievements all the more incredible is the debilitating ailment that dogged him throughout his career.

Honored in ceremonies at Wrigley Field during August 1971, Santo revealed that he was a lifelong diabetic. He made arrangements for all proceeds from Ron Santo Day to be donated to the Diabetes Association of Chicago.

*　　*　　*　　*

Santo wasn't immune to an occasional mental lapse. During the 1969 season, Dick Selma approached him with a trick play. With two out and a full count on a good hitter and runners on first and second moving with the pitch, Selma said he would go into the stretch, take his foot off the rubber, and then lob the ball to Santo at third.

The move was technically a balk, but Selma figured he might be able to catch the umpires off guard and nail the runner going into third. If he didn't, reasoned Selma, the runners would move up on the balk call, and Selma could then dispose of the good hitter at the plate by putting him on first base by throwing a ball on the next pitch.

Selma and Santo agreed on a signal. If the Cubs found themselves in the right circumstances, Selma would look at Santo and yell, "Two out! Knock it down!"

This disingenuous comment, of course, is basic baseball strategy: guard the line with a runner in scoring position; let nothing hit to the corners get through for extra bases.

Santo and Selma came up with Santo's countersign, which would be a simple "Yeah!" With that, Santo would creep toward the baseline to be ready for Selma's throw.

One night in September, Selma ran the count to 3-2 on Philadelphia's Dick Allen with two out and runners on first and second. Selma looked over at the intense Santo, who was guarding the line.

"Two out, knock it down," yelled Selma, waiting for the countersign.

"Yeah!" shot back Santo, staring straight ahead at Allen in the batter's box.

Selma went into the stretch. As the runners started moving, he took his foot off the rubber. Selma whirled and lobbed the ball toward third. There was no balk call.

The ball sailed into foul territory. Santo was nowhere near the bag. One runner scored, the other took third, and the Phils went on to win.

Afterwards, a furious Leo Durocher ordered coach Joey Amalfitano to find out why Selma had thrown to third. Selma explained the trick play, including the sign and countersign. Next, Amalfitano confronted Santo, who said they'd talked about the play earlier in the year.

"Know what the sign is?" Amalfitano asked.

Santo pondered the question for a few seconds, then replied: "Yeah. He tells me to knock the ball down."

"Did you answer him," asked the coach.

"Holy cow!" exclaimed Santo, finally realizing he'd completely spaced it. "I answered him!"

HANK SAUER

Before Henry Aaron claimed it, the nickname "Hammerin' Hank," belonged to Hank Sauer, the Cubs' slugging outfielder from 1949 to 1955.

The rawboned 6'2", 200-pound Pittsburgh native was the second member of his family to play in Cubs livery.

*   *   *   *

Sauer broke into organized baseball in 1937 as a first baseman in the New York Yankees chain. He reached the majors with Cincinnati in 1941, playing nine games in the outfield. He got into seven more in 1942 as a first basemen.

After spending all of 1943 with Syracuse of the International League, Sauer joined the Coast Guard. He was out of baseball until Word War II ended in August 1945. He rejoined the Reds, playing in 31 games.

*   *   *   *

Dispatched to the minors prior to the '46 season, Sauer spent the next two years in Syracuse. He was the I.L.'s most valuable player in 1947, batting .336 with 50 home runs and 141 runs batted in.

The following year Sauer took over as the Reds' left fielder. He evolved into one of the majors' top sluggers, producing 35 homers and 97 RBIs.

*   *   *   *

In June 1949 the Reds dealt Sauer to Chicago in a four-player swap. Soon, Hammerin' Hank would pick up another nickname: Mayor of Wrigley Field.

A favorite of Chicago fans, Sauer averaged better than 30 homers a season in his first six years as a Cub, including a career-high 41 in '54.

When the pipe-smoking Sauer would return to his fielder's post after each round-tripper, Wrigley Field bleacher fans would strew the outfield with packets of tobacco.

*   *   *   *

Sauer's prominent proboscis made him a favorite target of bench jockeys around the league.

Leo Durocher, who claimed Sauer's nose resembled an automobile hood ornament, was one of Hank's worst tormentors. Every time Sauer stepped up to the plate against one of Durocher's teams, Leo would yell, "Hey, Pontiac!"

Sauer would have to call time and step out of the box to regain his composure.

*   *   *   *

During the 1950s, Sauer was involved in two acrimonious controversies.

He was elected by fans to the 1950 N.L. All-Star team along with outfielders Enos Slaughter of the Cardinals and Pittsburgh's Ralph Kiner. But Brooklyn's Burt Shotton, manager of the N.L. squad, wasn't happy about having three left fielders in the starting line-up.

Shotton announced plans to start his own center fielder, Duke Snider, with Sauer going to the bench.

*   *   *   *

Shotton's decision set off howls of protest in Chicago, where the All-Star contest was to take place at Comiskey Park. *Chicago Tribune* sports editor Arch Ward, the man who helped launch the annual midsummer classic back in 1933, blasted Shotton. The Dodger skipper, claimed Ward, was "telling 781,553 fans who supported Sauer they are wrong and he is right." Shotton eventually relented and Sauer was the starting right fielder in the N.L.'s 14-inning 4-3 triumph.

At the All-Star game at Philadelphia two years later, Hank's homer off Cleveland's Bob Lemon gave the N.L. a 3-2 win in a five-inning, rain-shortened contest.

*   *   *   *

After the season, the announcement of Sauer as the N.L. MVP for 1952 touched off a firestorm that made the '50 All-Star game controversy seem like a picnic.

Sauer had tied for the N.L. homer lead with 37, and his 121 ribbies led both leagues. The MVP ballot showed 226 points for Sauer, who received eight of a possible 24 first-place votes.

Phillies pitcher Robin Roberts, a 28-game winner, earned seven first-place votes and a 211-point total. Several Eastern writers claimed Roberts deserved the award, and demanded a recount.

*   *   *   *

In the *Chicago Sun-Times*, columnist Edgar Munzel defended the Mayor of Wrigley Field's MVP credentials.

"What anguished screams are emanating from the east," wrote Munzel, "because of the selection of Hank Sauer over Robin Roberts... It's pure sour grapes that should be crushed underfoot. In my estimation, the choice of Sauer was one of the soundest ever made ..."

*   *   *   *

The Cubs sent Sauer to St. Louis after the 1955 season in an unpopular trade.

He played for the Giants in 1957, their last year in New York, and moved west to San Francisco with the team for 1958, his final season.

*   *   *   *

Ed Sauer, Hank's younger brother, was also a major leaguer. Ed played for the Cubs from 1943 to 1945 and spent time with the Cardinals and Braves in 1949.

SAMMY SOSA

Cubs right fielder Sammy Sosa demolished more than just N.L. pitching during 1998. He also destroyed a baseball shibboleth that stereotypes Dominican players good-field, no-hit middle infielders.

*   *   *   *

Over the years, the Dominican Republic has produced hard-hitting outfielders like George Bell and the Alou brothers, Felipe, Jesus and Mateo, and multi-position thumpers like Rico Carty and Pedro Guerrero… not to mention hard-throwing hurlers like Juan Marichal and Joaquin Andujar.

Ossie Virgil, the first Dominican-born big leaguer, wasn't a second baseman or a shortstop, but a catcher.

But then came Manny Alexander. Mariano Duncan. Tony Fernandez. Julio Franco. Pedro Gonzalez. Alfredo Griffin. Julian Javier. Manny Lee. Nelson Norman. Rafael Ramirez. Rafael Robles. Amado Samuel. All middle infielders, and all from the sugar-producing municipality of San Pedro de Macoris in south-eastern Santo Domingo.

*   *   *   *

Right-handed hitting Sammy Sosa also hails from San Pedro de Macoris. He was discovered by Omar Minaya, then a scout for the Rangers and today one of baseball's top executives.

In those days, Samuel Peralta Sosa was known as "Mikey," a nickname bestowed by his grandmother. When he wasn't shining shoes or selling oranges, little Mikey played baseball—usually with a broken broomstick for a bat and a ball made of soap wrapped in a sock.

*   *   *   *

Sosa signed with Texas in 1986 and, three years later when he joined the Rangers at age 19, his 6'0", 150-pound frame appeared better suited for shortstop than right field. Scouts raved about his great speed and range, his arm and his power.

In July 1989 Texas dealt Sosa to the White Sox in a five-player trade. The Cubs acquired Sammy and pitcher Ken Patterson in a trade for George Bell on the last day of March in 1992.

*   *   *   *

Sosa split the '92 season between the Cubs and Iowa of the American Association. He hit 33 home runs in 1993, his first full season with the Cubs.

He followed with homer totals of 25 in strike-curtailed 1994; 36 in 1995; 40 in 1996; and 36 in 1997.

*   *   *   *

By 1998 Sosa had filled out to a muscular 210 pounds. That summer, he and St. Louis first baseman Mark McGwire hooked up in one of the greatest home run duels of all time.

Sosa and McGwire became only the third and fourth sluggers to surpass the 60-homer mark. McGwire finished with 70, while Sosa hit 66. Both men bettered the 37-year-old major league mark of 61 by Roger Maris of the Yankees.

Sosa and McGwire staged another homer-fest in 1999. The pair again topped the 60-mark, with McGwire coming out on top, 65 to 63.

*   *   *   *

But for chance, Sosa may have been playing in Philadelphia or Toronto. When Sosa was 15, he signed a contract with the Phillies. The contract was illegal, however, since professional baseball rules prohibit players under 16 from turning pro.

When the mistake was discovered, the contract was voided. Soon afterwards Sosa began working out at a Blue Jays camp in the Dominican Republic. Spotting Sosa arriving daily at the rival Blue Jays' field, the quick-witted Omar Minaya developed a plan.

"I had someone wait for him at the bus stop by the Jays' camp," confesses Minaya, "and when he got off the bus we shipped him three hours across the island and signed him to a contract with the Rangers."

*   *   *   *

Four years after snatching Sosa away from the Jays, Minaya projected Sosa as a power hitter. "He's going to hit 30 home runs," Minaya told a newspaper reporter.

Thirty home runs?

Even if he was a tad weak on his projections, Minaya sure knew talent when he saw it.

AL SPALDING

Anyone who set foot on a schoolyard playground during the middle years of the Twentieth Century remembers playing with hollow, bright pink rubber balls. Known as "Spaldeens," those balls were as common to generations of young Americans as bubblegum, baseball cards, and braces.

"Spaldeen" was a corruption of the name of the firm that made the balls—the A.G. Spalding sporting goods company, which also produced the official baseball of the National League.

*　　*　　*　　*

Sports historians will also recognize the name Spalding from the series of baseball guide books. The Spalding baseball guide series provided an annual recapitulation of the previous year's season, complete with statistics and commentary.

The man behind this conglomerate was Illinois native Albert G. Spalding (1850-1915), a skilled businessman and promoter who organized the world's first baseball tour in 1888-1889.

*　　*　　*　　*

Spalding was also manager, club secretary, president and, eventually, owner of Chicago's N.L. franchise. The multi-talented Spalding was even a member of the 1900 U.S. Olympic shooting team.

In his younger days, Al Spalding was an outstanding baseball pitcher. He earned the win in Chicago's first game, a 4-0 win over Louisville on April 25, 1876.

The right-hander was also the winning pitcher in Chicago's first home game on May 10, 1876, a 6-0 triumph over Cincinnati at 23rd and State Streets.

*   *   *   *

Al Spalding, a skillful politician and diplomat, and an excellent organizer as well, was elected to baseball's Hall of Fame in 1939.

He was also responsible for one of baseball's earliest fiascos. In 1882 Spalding came up with an idea for color-coded uniforms—not by team, but by position!

According to Spalding's scheme, the color of each player's cap and shirt would identify where he played on the diamond. The color code was as follows: baby blue, pitchers; scarlet, catchers; scarlet and white, first basemen; orange and black, second basemen; blue and white, third basemen; maroon, shortstops; gray, right fielders; red and black, center fielders; white, left fielders.

All players wore white belts, pants, and ties.

So how were fans supposed to figure out a player's team? By the color of his socks.

Fortunately, Spalding's experiment didn't last beyond the 1882 season.

EDDIE STANKY

One of the toughest, smartest players of his time, Eddie Stanky reached the majors with the Cubs in 1943. Nicknamed "The Brat", Stanky also played for the Dodgers, Giants, Braves, and Cardinals in an 11-year career, and also managed St. Louis, the White Sox, and the Texas Rangers.

Leo Durocher appreciated Stanky's drive and determination. When Stanky played second base for Leo in Brooklyn, Durocher lauded the 5'8", 170-pound pepperpot.

"Look at 'The Brat'," said Durocher. "He can't hit, can't run, can't field. He's no nice guy, but all the little guy can do is win."

Durocher compared Stanky to Mel Ott, the slugging outfielder who was managing the Giants at the time. Leo pointed out that Ott, on the other hand, was a nice guy, but finished second.

Somehow, these words morphed into "Nice guys finish last"—something Durocher never actually said. Yet when Leo penned his autobiography, he entitled it *Nice Guys Finish Last*.

*   *   *   *

Peanuts Lowery was on hand during the feisty rookie's early days with the Cubs. He remembered Rip Sewell of Pittsburgh beaning Stanley, who went down in a heap.

"We all ran out, of course," Lowery recalled. "Stanky looked awful woozy and the doctor, after some first aid, started asking him what day it was, how many fingers was he holding up and so forth."

The plucky Stanky bounced up and shook off the ministrations of the doctor and his teammates.

"Nuts to that stuff, Doc!" spat Stanky. "I'm all right."

Stanky refused to come out of the game, got up and trotted off to first base. On the very next pitch, he took off for second and slid into the bag.

"He hit shortstop Huck Geary so hard," claimed Lowery, "he broke the guy's leg!"

HARRY STEINFELDT

These are the saddest of possible words:
"Tinker-to-Evers-to-Chance."
Trio of bear cubs, and fleeter than birds,
"Tinker-to-Evers-to-Chance."
Ruthlessly pricking our gonfalon bubble,
Making a Giant hit into a double—
Words that are weighty with nothing but trouble:
"Tinker-to-Evers-to-Chance."

*B*aseball's *Sad Lexicon,* Franklin P. Adams' ode to the Cubs' great infield ran in the *New York Evening Mail* in July 1910 and became a baseball classic.

Although not mentioned in Adams' poem, Harry Steinfeldt played third base alongside Joe Tinker, Johnny Evers, and Frank Chance from 1906 to 1910.

*   *   *   *

A St. Louis native who originally hoped to make his mark in theater, Steinfeldt played in four World Series with the Cubs and batted .471 (8-for-17) in Chicago's four-game sweep of Detroit in 1907.

*   *   *   *

Steinfeldt broke in with Cincinnati in 1898 and was a steady, if unspectacular, mainstay in the Reds' infield through 1905. His 32 doubles led the N.L. in 1903, a year he batted .312.

Injuries limited Steinfeldt to 99 games in 1904 and the Reds, figuring Harry's best days were behind him, dealt him to Chicago for third baseman Hans Lobert and pitcher Jake Weimer in March 1906.

*   *   *   *

The change of scenery rejuvenated the 28-year-old infielder. Steinfeldt hit a career-best .327 in his first year in Chicago and helped the Cubs win 116 games.

His 176 hits and 83 runs batted in topped the N.L. During Harry's five years of service in Chicago, the Cubs won four pennants and two World Series.

"Steiny" once played an entire 15-inning game without handling a single chance at third base.

*   *   *   *

Harry's presence helped solidify the Cubs as the favorite team of one segment of Chicago's population.

With players like Steinfeldt, Solly Hofman, Johnny Kling, Jack Pfiester, Ed Reulbach, Frank "Wildfire" Schulte, Jimmy Sheckard, and Heinie Zimmerman on the roster, the Cubs were the darlings of the city's German-American community.

*   *   *   *

Steinfeldt was traded to the Boston Braves after the 1910 season and played just 19 games in 1911 before bowing out of the majors.

He was the first member of the glamorous infield to pass on. A few years after retirement, he became ill, and in time had to be confined to a sanitarium. Released in August 1914, Steinfeldt returned to his home in Bellevue, Kentucky, just across from Cincinnati. He died there soon after, at age 36.

*   *   *   *

Harry Steinfeldt deserved better treatment than omission from *Baseball's Sad Lexicon*.

Grantland Rice, after all, paid homage to the entire Notre Dame backfield of Crowley, Layden, Miller, and Stuhldreher, and the thought of the Apocalyptic Horsemen without mention of Pestilence or Famine is unthinkable.

The following lines are dedicated to the memory of the Cubs' stalwart, albeit snubbed, infielder:

> *Here's evidence justice will sometime miscarry,*
> *"Tinker-to-Evers-to-Chance."*
> *The Cubs' infield ode fails to mention poor Harry,*
> *"Tinker-to-Evers-to-Chance."*
> *Chicago's third baseman, just as sublime,*
> *As Chance, Evers or Tinker… most of the time.*
> *Left out because Steinfeldt's unwieldy in rhyme,*
> *"Tinker-to-Evers-to-Chance."*

RIGGS STEPHENSON

Some say superb fielders are ignored when it's time for Hall of Fame balloting. Cooperstown, they maintain, favors offensive players. Maybe so. But how, then, do you account for Riggs Stephenson?

*   *   *   *

Stephenson, a star fullback for the University of Alabama, reached the major leagues with Cleveland in 1921 as a second baseman. An arm injury from his football days hampered Stephenson's throwing, but not his bat.

He averaged .371 in 74 games for the Indians in 1924.

*   *   *   *

Stephenson went to the minors to become an outfielder. When Riggs played for Kansas City and Indianapolis in the American Association, Joe McCarthy managed Louisville. And when McCarthy became Chicago's manager in 1926, he demanded that the Cubs acquire Stephenson's contract.

From 1929 to 1931, the Cubs boasted one of baseball's finest outfields with Kiki Cuyler in right, Hack Wilson in center, and Stephenson in left. Stephenson never hit below .319 for the Cubs except for 1934, his final big league season, when he batted just 74 times in 38 games. Starting in '26, Stephenson hit

.338, .344, .324, .362, .367, .319, .324, and .329. In two World Series, he batted .378—.319 against the Athletics in '29, and .444 against the Yankees in '32.

Never a power hitter, Stephenson's top homer mark was 17 in '29. He led the N.L. with 46 doubles in '27.

*　　*　　*　　*

Umpire Ernie Quigley was Stephenson's fraternity brother. Whenever Quigley called a strike on Stephenson, Riggs would gently chide him, saying "That was a little outside, wasn't it, Ernie?"

One day, after Stephenson commented after a close pitch, Quigley replied: "My boy, I'd rather call them on you than on anyone else."

"Yes," shot back Riggs, "but if you keep calling them like that on me, I won't be around here very long!"

*　　*　　*　　*

Teammate Woody English said he couldn't understand how Kiki Cuyler could be elected to the Hall of Fame, while Stephenson had been passed over.

English said that if Stephenson came to the plate in the bottom of the ninth with the bases loaded and the lead run aboard, "we'd put our gloves in our pockets and go up the runway to the clubhouse. He would drive that winning run in time after time."

*　　*　　*　　*

Stephenson's .336 career batting average with Chicago is the highest of any Cub player. The lifelong Alabaman had good memories of Cub fans.

"They were very nice to me," he recalled. "I couldn't have played in a better place."

RICK SUTCLIFFE

Twice in Chicago history, American League castoffs have pitched the Cubs into post-season play.

In late July 1945, right-hander Hank Borowy came over from the Yankees. Borowy's 11-2 record down the stretch helped the Cubs win the N.L. pennant. A 10-5 record in New York gave the Fordham University product 21 wins on the season.

*   *   *   *

Thirty-nine years later at Wrigley Field, lightning struck again. Midway through 1984, the Cleveland Indians were ready to unload Rick Sutcliffe, a 6'7", 215-pound right-hander.

Sutcliffe had won 17 games for Los Angeles in 1979, and four years later had matched that figure with the Indians. The Tribe traded Sutcliffe, reliever George Frazier and catcher Ron Hassey to the Cubs for outfielders Joe Carter and Mel Hall, along with pitchers Don Schulze and Darryl Banks.

*   *   *   *

The change of scenery worked like a tonic on Sutcliffe. Struggling at 4-5 with Cleveland, the former N.L. Rookie of the Year went 16-1 for the Cubs. During one stretch he won 14 consecutive decisions.

The Cubs charged to the N.L. East title, appearing in post-season play for the first time since '45. Sutcliffe, with a combined record of 20-6 with the Indians and Cubs, became the first pitcher since Borowy to win 20 games after changing leagues in mid-season.

*   *   *   *

Rick's heroics earned him the '84 N.L. Cy Young Award. In 1989 his 16-11 slate helped the Cubs win another division title.

Sut remained in Chicago through 1991 and retired after the 1994 season after doing time with Baltimore and St. Louis.

*   *   *   *

One of the big redhead's most unforgettable moments as a Cub happened against the Phillies on July 29, 1988.

On a steamy night at Veterans Stadium, the Cubs took a 3-2 lead into the top of the seventh. Sutcliffe, a good hitter, opened the inning with a double to left center. After Shawon Dunston flied out, Sutcliffe rumbled into third on Manny Trillo's deep drive to right.

Phillies pitcher Kevin Gross walked the following batter, Mitch Webster. On his next delivery, Gross threw to first and caught Webster off base. Seeing an opportunity, Sutcliffe—who would never make anyone forget Lou Brock—took off for home.

Phils first baseman Ricky Jordan, stunned by the sight of the mammoth Sutcliffe churning toward the plate, threw the ball into the Cubs dugout. Sutcliffe scored, and the umpires waved Webster around.

Webster was credited with a steal of second and Jordan was charged with a throwing error. Sutcliffe, too, got a stolen base on the play.

"You guys shouldn't be surprised," said a straight-faced Sutcliffe afterwards. "I stole a base last year, too."

*   *   *   *

Sutcliffe became the first Cubs pitcher in 69 years to steal home.

The last to do it? Another terror of the basepaths, Jim "Hippo" Vaughn.

BRUCE SUTTER

Bruce Sutter was an outstanding athlete at Donegal High School in Mount Joy, Pennsylvania. He was the football team's quarterback, he captained the basketball squad and pitched for the baseball team.

In 1972 Sutter signed with the Cubs. Soon afterward, he suffered an elbow injury that required off-season surgery.

* * * *

Sutter reported to Quincy of the Midwest League in 1973. His arm was still tender, however, and Sutter was reluctant to throw any kind of breaking pitch. He was relying strictly on fastballs, and the Chicago brass figured he was, at best, a marginal prospect.

That changed after Fred Martin visited Quincy. Martin, the former Cubs pitching coach, was by then a roving minor league pitching instructor. Martin talked Sutter into trying the split-fingered fastball. That pitch would turn Sutter into one of the game's most effective relief pitchers.

* * * *

Sutter joined the Cubs after compiling a 1.75 ERA over his next two-and-a-half seasons. His split-finger, which dropped suddenly when it reached home plate, was nearly unhittable.

Sutter rapidly developed into one of baseball's most effective closers. He was the winning pitcher in the 1978 and 1979 All-Star Games. Sutter won the N.L. Cy Young Award in '79.

*   *   *   *

After that season, Sutter asked for a $700,000 salary. The Cubs countered with a $350,000 offer. The matter went to arbitration, and the judgement was in Sutter's favor.

Baseball's landscape was changing rapidly. Just a few years earlier, Sutter's salary had been in the $20,000 range. Bill Wrigley, a scion of the family that had owned the Cubs for decades, saw the writing on the wall.

In June 1981, Wrigley sold the team to the Chicago Tribune Company for $20.5 million.

*   *   *   *

Sutter helped the Cardinals win the 1982 World Series, and finished his career in 1988 after a stint with the Braves. Yet Wrigley Field would always have a special place in his heart.

"Cubs fans are exceptional, whether you're in first place or last place," maintains Sutter. "They are the most loyal fans in the United States. I enjoyed Chicago a lot."

TONY TAYLOR

Tony Taylor, a 19-year big league second baseman, began his career with Chicago in 1958. He was the Cubs second baseman from '58 through May 1960, when he was swapped to Philadelphia along with catcher Cal Neeman for pitcher Don Cardwell and first baseman Ed Bouchee.

*   *   *   *

In 2,195 big league contests, the Cuban native hit just 75 home runs, 15 of them in a Chicago uniform.

The Cubs' bullpen deserves credit for one of them.

*   *   *   *

At Wrigley Field on July 1, 1958, Taylor and Ernie Banks both had a pair of home runs against the Giants. One of Taylor's homers was a smash just inside third base that bounced into the Cub bullpen and then into a rain gutter at the base of the left field grandstand wall.

Taylor's drive scattered the Cubs' bullpen corps. As San Francisco left fielder Leon Wagner rushed toward the scene, the Chicago players peered intently under the bullpen bench as if the ball were still there. Wagner scrambled around the bench

looking for the ball, when it was actually 40' or 50' farther down the line in the gutter.

By the time Wagner found the ball, Taylor was around the bases. The Cubs won the game, 9-5.

TINKER TO EVERS TO CHANCE

Together, shortstop Joe Tinker, second baseman Johnny Evers and first baseman Frank Chance started for the Cubs for eight full seasons. They collaborated on their first double play on September 15, 1902.

During their tenure the Cubs won pennants in 1906, 1907, 1908, and 1910, and World Series titles in '07 and '08. All three took turns as manager of the Cubs, and the trio was elected to baseball's Hall of Fame in the same year.

Franklin P. Adams' famous poem earned them another slice of immortality. It's easy to think of Tinker, Evers, and Chance as a single entity, a homogenous, open-the-box-and-snap-together unit.

Nothing could be further from the truth.

*   *   *   *

Frank Chance played for Chicago from 1898 to 1912. Chance was a dental student at the University of Washington when he was discovered by Bill Lange, Chicago's star outfielder of the 1890s.

A catcher, Chance languished on the bench until 1902. Since Chance suffered frequent injuries behind the plate, manager Frank Selee suggested a move to first base. Chance wouldn't hear of it, and threatened to quit when Selee ordered him to

make the switch. Chance relented, however, and developed into one of the deadball era's top first basemen. His best year was 1903, when he batted .327 and stole 67 bases.

*   *   *   *

Tough, smart and a fierce competitor, Chance succeeded Selee as manager in 1905. Dubbed "the Peerless Leader," he was a demanding field boss who led the Cubs to four pennants and a pair of World Series victories. His 1906 team won an amazing 116 regular-season games, a mark that still stands. Chance was also a hard-knuckled disciplinarian who pummeled opposing players (and his own men as well) if he thought they had it coming.

Chance left Chicago on a sour note. When owner Charles Murphy criticized Chance's players for carousing during the 1912 season, Chance lambasted Murphy as a cheapskate. Soon after, Chance was gone from the Cubs. He later managed the Yankees and Red Sox.

*   *   *   *

Johnny Evers (pronounced like "weavers") was known as "The Crab" for the way he scuttled around second base ... as well as an abrasive disposition that rivaled Ty Cobb's. Like Cobb, Evers had no qualms about spiking opponents who got in his way.

A native of Troy, New York, Evers came to Chicago in 1902. He was a quick thinker and a sure-handed second baseman, but a light hitter. Still, Evers could rise to the occasion. In both the 1907 and 1908 World Series he batted .350.

*   *   *   *

In 1913 he took over from Chance as Cubs manager. Like Chance, however, Evers quarreled with Charles Murphy and was soon gone. In 1914 he managed Boston's "Miracle Braves" to an N.L. pennant and a World Series title. He returned briefly to Chicago in 1921 for another stint as Cubs manager.

Like most of the Cubs players, Evers had a great respect and admiration for Frank Chance.

His relationship with shortstop Joe Tinker was another matter.

*   *   *   *

Like Evers, *Joe Tinker* came to Chicago in 1902. And, like Evers, he was considered an artist in the field, but a weak hitter—yet one who came through in the clutch, just like his keystone partner.

In 1908 Tinker hit the first home run by a Cub in World Series play. Against the great Christy Mathewson of the Giants, he had a lifetime .291 average. In his time, Tinker was ranked second at shortstop only to Pittsburgh's Honus Wagner.

*   *   *   *

Tinker was an aggressive competitor, as were Chance and Evers. He may not have been as quick with his fists, but Tinker could hold his own in any rumble.

After a game with Cincinnati, Dick Egan of the Reds challenged him. Tinker, who had already dressed, removed his coat and squared off. The fight lasted five minutes, and Tinker completely thrashed Egan.

After the fight, said witnesses, Tinker's hair wasn't even mussed.

*   *   *   *

The Cubs sent Tinker to the Reds in an eight-player deal in December 1912. Tinker jumped to Chicago of the Federal League for the 1914 and 1915 seasons, then returned to the Cubs as player-manager in 1916.

Like Chance and Evers, Tinker's first hitch with the Cubs ended acrimoniously. He asked to be traded when Evers was named manager.

*   *   *   *

The two had rarely spoken to each other since September 1905, when they got into a fight during an exhibition game in Bedford, Indiana. The problem centered around a ride from their hotel to the ballpark. Tinker had left by himself in a hack, leaving Evers and others standing at the curb. Evers wasn't happy about it. When he finally made it the park, Evers told off Tinker.

Tempers simmered until the middle of the game, when the pair locked horns right on the diamond. Teammates broke up the fight, but Evers was still fuming over the curbside snub. A day after the fight, Evers told Tinker they'd be better off just doing their jobs, but not speaking to one another unless it was absolutely necessary.

"That suits me," is what Tinker is said to have replied.

"It was unfortunate," Evers said years later. "I figured that if he wanted that way, he could have it."

*   *   *   *

And that's the way it continued, season after season, through four pennants and two championship seasons. Tinker and Evers played side by side for the next five seasons, avoiding each other as much as possible.

After their playing days, the hard feelings softened. At Cooperstown in 1946, Evers and Tinker stood together one more time as they were inducted into the Hall of Fame.

"Joe was there when I walked in," said Evers. "We hadn't seen each other for years. And do you know what we did? We rushed together, threw our arms around each other and cried like a couple of kids."

Chance, who died in 1924 at age 47, was inducted posthumously.

"I'm glad we made it all together," said Evers. "Chance should have been elected long ago. I wish he were alive to feel as happy about it as I do. I'm glad for Tinker, too."

*   *   *   *

When a Chicago newspaper reporter researched the number of twin killings by the celebrated trio, he came up with some astonishing numbers. Between 1906 and 1909, they combined for just 54 double plays—29 initiated by Tinker, the rest by Evers. Comparison with modern double play figures, however, doesn't work.

In an era when stolen bases and sacrifice bunts were the order of the day—and when pitchers put more trust in fly-ball outs, rather than grounders on rough infields—double plays were much more scarce.

Evers died less than a year later, and Tinker passed on in 1948. Together with Chance, they live on as the most celebrated infield in baseball history.

CHUCK TOLSON

After breaking in with the Indians in 1925, first baseman Chuck Tolson moved on to Chicago the following year and played for the Cubs in 1926-1927 and 1929-30. In 1927 Tolson was the N.L.'s top pinch hitter with 14 hits in 40 at-bats.

One year later, he made Cubs history while batting in a pinch.

*   *   *   *

In the seventh inning of a game with Pittsburgh at Forbes Field on May 1, 1927, Chicago manager Joe McCarthy sent Tolson up to hit against right-hander Ray Kremer with the bases loaded.

Tolson responded with a home run, becoming the first Cub ever to pinch-hit a grand slam. Tolson had just four homers in his 144 big league contests, but was 23-for-74 lifetime as a pinch batter.

*   *   *   *

Tolson's grand slam heroics, however, went for naught. The Cubs lost, 7-6, in the bottom of the ninth when Charlie Root walked the bases full and Pittsburgh's Paul Waner singled home the tying and winning runs.

Hippo Vaughn

J im "Hippo" Vaughn, a 6'4", 215-pound Texan, pitched 13 years in majors, including a hitch with the Cubs from 1913 to 1921. He won 20 games or more five times for Chicago. In 1918 he led the N.L. with 22 victories and a 1.74 ERA, and helped the Cubs to a pennant.

*   *   *   *

Vaughn, whose nickname stemmed from his lumbering gait, is best remembered for a May 2, 1917, contest at Weeghman Park (as Wrigley Field was known until 1926), when he hooked up with Fred Toney in one of the greatest pitching duels in history.

"I'd always given Toney's team, Cincinnati, a fit, so this day they laid for me," Vaughn said years later. The Reds loaded their line-up with right-handed batters against the southpaw Vaughn, even benching left-handed hitting Edd Roush, a future Hall of Famer.

*   *   *   *

For nine innings, Vaughn and Toney threw hitless ball. The game was scoreless with the Reds coming to bat in the top of the 10th.

"I knew I was tired," said Vaughn, "but I felt that I still had my stuff."

Vaughn retired the leadoff man but the next batter, Larry Kopf, got the game's first hit. One out later, Hal Chase hit a fly ball that Chicago center fielder Cy Williams dropped. After Kopf went to third on the error, Chase stole second. Cincinnati's Jim Thorpe, the great track and field star of the 1912 Olympics, sent a swinging bunt toward third.

"I knew the minute it was hit that I couldn't get Thorpe at first," said Vaughn. "He was as fast as a race horse."

Vaughn tried to nail Kopf at the plate, but the throw hit catcher Art Wilson's chest protector and dropped to the ground. Chase tried to score on the play, but Wilson tagged him out. Toney set down the Cubs in order in the bottom of the 10th to preserve his no-hitter.

"I don't believe he ever beat me again," Vaughn said of Toney years later. "We met a lot of times, and most of the games were close, but he had licked me for the last time."

*   *   *   *

Vaughn is best remembered for the near double no-hitter. All but forgotten, however, are Vaughn's pitching heroics in the World Series. He won one game and lost two against the Red Sox in 1918, with an earned run average of 1.00.

The World Series of 1918 took place in early September. The United States had entered World War I, and the government had issued a "work-or-fight" order that threatened to put every able-bodied major leaguer either at work in a defense plant or in uniform.

The government gave the major leagues until the end of August to finish the season, and another couple of weeks' grace to play the Series.

*   *   *   *

The Cubs, who finished the season 84-45, opened the Series at home against the Red Sox. Vaughn gave up just one run in the fourth inning on a walk and two singles. It was the lone score in a 1-0 Red Sox triumph.

After the Cubs evened the Series, Vaughn started Game Three at home on September 7. Boston won another squeaker, this time by a 2-1 margin behind Carl Mays.

Three days later in Boston, the Cubs had their backs to the wall. The Red Sox had won the fourth game, and one more Boston victory would have ended the Series. Once again, Cubs manager Fred Mitchell went with Vaughn. Vaughn responded with another stellar performance. This time, the big right-hander threw a 5-hit shutout to beat Boston's Sam Jones, 3-0.

It was all for naught, however. The following day, the Red Sox won 2-1 to take the Series. And the Boston pitcher who beat Vaughn in the 1-0 game? He was a 23-year-old southpaw named Babe Ruth.

JEROME WALTON AND DWIGHT SMITH

The longest Cubs hitting streak between 1900 and 1999 is 30 games, by:
   A. Rogers Hornsby
   B. Stan Hack
   C. Billy Williams
   D. Ryne Sandberg
   E. None of the above

The answer is E. The longest Cubs hit streak during the 20th Century belongs to Jerome Walton, a right-handed hitting outfielder for the Cubs from 1989 through 1992.

Bill Dahlen, a 19th Century star, had hitting streaks of 28 and 42 in 1894.

Prior to Walton, the top hit skein by a Cub in the 1900s was 28 by Ron Santo in 1966.

*   *   *   *

Outfielders Jerome Walton and Dwight Smith hooked up in Chicago in 1989. They batted in the top two spots in the Cub line-up, earning the nickname "The Daily Double".

During spring camp that year in Arizona, Smith couldn't find himself. He batted .259, made three errors and was farmed out.

"You'll never see that Dwight Smith again," he vowed.

*   *   *   *

Walton made the jump from Double-A Pittsfield in '89 as a 23-year-old. He began the season in center field, but a hamstring injury cost him 30 games during May and June.

The 25-year-old Smith, in the meantime, tore up the American Association at a .325 clip and was recalled after 21 games.

When Walton came off the disabled list in June, the two took over the top two spots in the batting order. Walton manned center, with Smith in left.

*   *   *   *

While Smith was outgoing and a clubhouse comic, Walton was more reserved. He soared like a meteor in '89, but flamed out just as quickly.

Walton batted .293 in his first season, and won N.L. Rookie of the Year honors. Smith hit .324 in 109 games.

*   *   *   *

After winning the Eastern Division title in '89, the 1990 season was a bust for the Cubs as they dropped into a tie for fourth place. At one point the entire Chicago outfield—Walton, Smith, and right fielder Andre Dawson—was on the DL.

Walton and Smith were disappointments. Walton tailed off to .263 in '90, however, and his average plummeted to .219 in 1991. After hitting .127 in 30 games for Chicago in '92, Walton was gone from Wrigley Field.

*   *   *   *

Smith slumped to .262 in '90. Although he batted .276 in '92 and an even .300 in '91, he never lived up to the promise

he showed as a rookie. After a .262 average in 1993, he was dispatched to the California Angels.

BILLY WILLIAMS

Billy Williams is the man who forced Ernie Banks out of left field in Wrigley Field. Ernie Banks? *Left field???* In 1961, when his legs began to wear out, Chicago's College of Coaches tinkered with the idea of making a left fielder out of Ernie.

*   *   *   *

The '61 season was Billy Williams' rookie year. He'd been with the Cubs for a couple of cups of coffee in 1959 and 1960.

A .323 average and 26 homers for Houston of the American Association, coupled with a brilliant Spring Training performance in '61, brought the sweet-swinging Alabaman to Chicago for good.

*   *   *   *

Shunted between right and left field, Williams muddled through the early going. Vedie Himsl, the head coach at the time, shifted Banks from short to left on May 23. From then through the middle of June, Williams spent most of his time riding the bench.

He did go 5-for-8 as a pinch hitter, however, and in mid-June general manager John Holland sent word to the dugout: get Williams in the lineup every day, for at least a month.

*   *   *   *

On June 16, the Cubs opened a three-game series at San Francisco. Banks—who hated playing the outfield—was shifted to first. Andre Rodgers played short, George Altman was in right and Williams took over in left.

Billy responded with a grand slam homer in the Cubs' 12-6 win. He had 10 hits in his next 19 at-bats, and was in the lineup for good. He batted .278 with 25 homers and 86 RBI, earning the N.L. Rookie of the Year Award.

*   *   *   *

Williams hit 20 or more homers for 13 consecutive seasons. He had 30 or more five times during that stretch, including a career-high 42 in 1970.

In a line-up that included Banks, Ron Santo, Glenn Beckert, Don Kessinger, and Randy Hundley, Williams sparked the Cubs' renaissance in the late '60s and early '70s. A perennial All-Star, he was named Major League Player of the Year by *The Sporting News in* 1972.

*   *   *   *

During his early years with the Cubs, Williams would toss his glove into the stands after the last game of the season. "To make some kid happy," he explained. Williams would then break in a new glove during Spring Training.

After Fergie Jenkins joined the Cubs, Williams would turn over his old gloves to him. Jenkins collected equipment for distribution to needy youngsters.

"A few years ago," Billy relates, "I got one of my gloves back. I now keep it in a Plexiglas box."

*   *   *   *

Williams conducted an unusual ritual when he came in from the field knowing he'd be coming up to bat. He would chew half a stick of gum and, as he'd walk around the catcher on his way to the plate, he would spit out the wad and swing at it.

Williams' theory was that if he could hit a little piece of gum, he should be able to hit a baseball.

*   *   *   *

One of Williams' greatest feats was a playing streak of 1,117 games. The streak began September 22, 1963, and lasted until September 3, 1970. It set an N.L. record (since topped by Steve Garvey) for consecutive games played.

After the 1974 season the Cubs dealt Williams to Oakland, where he played two more seasons, mostly as a designated hitter. In 1987 Williams was inducted into the Hall of Fame. He eventually returned to the Cubs as a batting instructor.

*   *   *   *

Sportswriter Bill Gleason paid homage to Williams in his *Chicago Sun-Times* column. "He combines the dignity of Ernie Banks," wrote Gleason, "the determination of Santo, and the competitive fires of Hundley, and he plays every day, every night."

NED WILLIAMSON

Babe Ruth of the Boston Red Sox hit 29 homers in 1919, a new major league mark. The record he broke was 27, by Chicago infielder Ned Williamson in 1884. But talk about cheap home runs! In 1884 Chicago's home field was Lakefront Park. There, the right field fence was 230 feet from home plate. Until 1883, any ball hit over the wall in right was a ground rule double. The rule changed in 1884, and any ball over the right field fence was a homer.

*　*　*　*

In the second game of a double header on May 30, Williamson hit three home runs in Chicago's 12-2 victory over Detroit. Williamson's triple-homer performance was the first-ever by a big league player.

Of his 27 homers in 1884, all but two came at Lakefront Park. The following year, when the Chicago squad moved to West Side Park, Williamson's homer total dropped to three.

*　*　*　*

Primarily a third baseman-shortstop, Williamson spent 13 years in the majors. From 1878 through 1883 he hit eight homers.

From 1885 to 1890 he had 28. Of his 67 career home runs, 43 percent came during that 1884 season at Lakefront Park.

*   *   *   *

In his time, Williamson was as popular with the fans as Ernie Banks would be decades later.

Cap Anson called him "the greatest all-around ballplayer the country ever saw," and said Williamson was "a big, good-natured and good-hearted fellow."

*   *   *   *

Williamson was an excellent fielder. He was also—to Anson's chagrin—a *bon vivant* who took full advantage of Chicago's social opportunities.

He was also a superstitious man. Whenever he needed a turn of luck, Williamson would find a pebble and place it under the foul side of third base.

*   *   *   *

Williamson suffered a knee injury in France during Al Spalding's world tour in 1888-1889. He never fully recovered, and was gone from the big leagues after the 1890 campaign.

Williamson died in 1894 at age 38. "He could do more with a baseball," wrote sportswriter C.G. Perkins, "than anybody I ever saw, and I have seen them all."

HACK WILSON

Hack Wilson drove home 1,063 runs during his 12-year big league career. He picked up his last one in 1999. Pretty impressive for a guy who died in 1948.

*   *   *   *

Wilson was one of the most exciting players in Chicago history. Built like a fireplug at 5'6" and 190 pounds, Wilson had powerful arms and shoulders that enabled him to hit 56 home runs in 1930—an N.L. record that stood until 1998.

*   *   *   *

Wilson played for the Cubs from 1926 through 1931. He averaged .307 in Chicago, including a career-high .356 in 1930, and helped the Cubs to the 1929 N.L. flag. Despite his odd build—a barrel-thick body on stumpy legs—Wilson was a capable center fielder.

"Wilson," said John McGraw, who managed Hack when he played for the Giants from 1923 through 1925, "is the greatest judge of fly balls I have seen since Tris Speaker."

*   *   *   *

Hack was also one of the great carousers in baseball history. Trying to curb Wilson's thirst for bootleg liquor, Cubs manager Joe McCarthy conducted a legendary experiment.

Marse Joe once placed two glasses on a clubhouse table. One filled with water, the other with Prohibition booze. He placed a worm in the glass of water, where it wriggled happily. McCarthy removed it, and then dropped it into the booze. The worm promptly died. McCarthy asked his players to draw a conclusion. Wilson spoke first.

"If you drink whiskey," Hack piped up, "you won't get worms."

*   *   *   *

In a 14-8 win over the Boston Braves on May 23, 1926, Wilson became the first player to hit a homer off the Wrigley Field scoreboard, then situated at ground level.

That night Hack was arrested for violating the Volstead Amendment while drinking beer at a friend's apartment.

Another time, Hack tried to duck the authorities during a raid but got stuck in a bathroom window.

*   *   *   *

Bill Veeck, who later owned the Cleveland Indians, St. Louis Browns, and Chicago White Sox, joined the Cubs front office in 1933. He recalled how Cubs trainer Andy Lotshaw tried to sober up Wilson before one contest.

Lotshaw placed Wilson in a big tub of water with a 50-pound cake of ice. Wilson kept trying to escape, and Lotshaw kept dunking the inebriated slugger's head into the frigid water.

"Every time Hack's head would bob up," mused Veeck, "Andy would shove it back down under the water and the cake of ice would come bobbing up. It was a fascinating site, watching them bob in perfect rhythm ..."

According to Veeck, Wilson played that day and hit three homers in a single game for the first and only time in his career.

*   *   *   *

Wilson was the N.L. MVP for 1930, when he drove in 190 runs—a record that stood for the rest of the 1900s.

The 1931 season was a different story. Rogers Hornsby took over as Chicago manager in '31, and the N.L. introduced a new, less lively baseball. Complaining bitterly about the new ball, Hack slumped to .261 with 13 homers in 112 games.

*   *   *   *

The no-nonsense Hornsby, meanwhile, wasn't happy with Wilson's extracurricular escapades. After benching Wilson in August, Hornsby inserted a pitcher in left field during one game while consigning Hack to the bullpen, where the disgruntled slugger warmed up pitchers.

After an altercation with sportswriters a few days later, the Cubs suspended Wilson for the remainder of the season.

*   *   *   *

Chicago unloaded Wilson after the '31 season. Three years later, he was gone from the majors. At various times, he tended bar, worked as a bouncer, freight-handler, and stevedore.

He was working as a laborer when he died in Baltimore at age 48. Wilson's body lay unclaimed until N.L. president Ford Frick paid for a coffin and his funeral.

*   *   *   *

When members of the Society for American Baseball Research reviewed Wilson's 1930 season, they discovered a discrepancy. Wilson, it turns out, had batted in one more run than the official records indicated, for a total of 191.

The SABRites passed along their findings to Major League Baseball. After a recommendation from MLB historian and longtime *Chicago Sun-Times* sports writer Jerome Holtzman, Wilson received credit for the extra RBI.

WRIGLEY FIELD

During the '50s, one of the most popular table games was Cadaco's All-Star Baseball. The game came with three-and-a-half inch discs that bore the names of major league stars. Printed on each disc's border were numbers that corresponded to hits or outs (1 = home run; 2 = ground ball; 3 = fly out; etc.).

Inside the game box was a flat-surface playing field and a stand-up scoreboard. On the flat surface were metal spinners, over which player discs were placed during an at-bat. After a spin, the tip of the spinnet pointed to a number on the disc, determining the outcome of each play.

*   *   *   *

When assembled, the playing surface presented a beautiful sight—a vast expanse of green baseball field, confined by ivy-covered walls. An old-fashioned scoreboard sat atop the center field bleachers. The photograph was taken during an actual game, and the pitcher on the mound was just beginning his kick as the hitter in the batter's box was starting to coil. The view was from the press box.

Immediately below, behind short, red-brick walls, were the fans—so close to the action on the field, it looked like they could toss a bag of peanuts to the player in the visiting team's on-deck circle. The only thing missing was the smell of the hot dogs... and the wind.

*   *   *   *

The ballpark depicted was, of course, Wrigley Field. Cadaco All-Star Baseball came out when most telecasts were still in black and white. For a considerable number of post-World War II baseball fans growing outside Chicagoland, the game board provided the first chromatic view of a sports arena that does double duty as an *objet d'art*.

Yankee Stadium is majestic. Dodger Stadium is lavish. The home fields of the Mets and Phillies looks as if they were wrought by the same dull cookie cutter, and the Seattle Mariners' former home at the Kingdome was a monstrous birth.

Wrigley Field is as lovely an antiquity as the Parthenon, the Taj Mahal or the Baths of Caracalla. The Cubs' home field is art. Not graceful, serene and perfect, like a Raphaelite composition, but comfortable, charming and very American, like something out of Norman Rockwell.

*   *   *   *

Second only to Boston's Fenway Park in terms of longevity, Wrigley Field is a throwback to the days before America swallowed the hype; to a time when baseball was still a sport, and teams were as much a part of the neighborhood as the cop on the beat mom-and-pop grocery stores.

And the history! Restaurant chain owner Charles Weeghman built the park in 1914 for his team, the Chicago Whales of the Federal League. When the Feds folded after the 1915 season, Weeghman acquired the Cubs.

He moved them to Weeghman Field, as it was known, in time for the 1916 season. By 1927, the ball park was rechristened Wrigley Field, to honor the Cubs' new owners.

*   *   *   *

It was here that Hippo Vaughn of the Cubs and Cincinnati's Fred Toney hooked up in the famous "double-no hitter" of 1917. In 1932, Babe Ruth hit his final World Series homer in the Friendly Confines.

Wrigley Field was night baseball's last holdout. No night games took place there until August 9, 1988, when the Cubs beat the Mets, 6-4.

*   *   *   *

That inaugural night game had actually been post-poned for 46 years. The first major league night game was in 1935, and six years later the Cubs decided to add lights to Wrigley Field. Installation was to begin on December 8, 1941.

On December 7, the Japanese attacked Pearl Harbor and a day later the United States declared war on Japan. Owner Phil Wrigley scrapped the idea of adding lights to the ball-park, and donated the light towers to the Great Lakes Naval Air Station.

The Wrigley Field lights didn't make it back after the war. For the next 45 seasons, the Cubs continued to play all home games in daylight.

*   *   *   *

The scoreboard situated atop the center field bleachers was constructed in 1935 under the direction of Bill Veeck, at the time an up-and-coming Cubs' executive. The scoreboard is 27' high and 75' long. It is operated by hand. It wasn't until

1982 that any electronic device was installed in the score-board.

It was also Veeck who purchased the original vines of ivy for Wrigley's walls in 1937.

The flag that flies over the center field pole tells neighborhood fans how the Cubs have done in a game. A blue flag with a white 'W' indicates a victory, while a white flag with a blue 'L' signals a defeat.

Ernie Banks' uniform number, 14, is imprinted on the flag that flies from the left field foul pole. Over on the right field foul pole, a flag flies with Billy Williams' No. 26.

*   *   *   *

Chicago's fans are as unique as the facility. Most players who spend the bulk of theit career playing in Chicago conclude that Cub fans are among baseball's most knowledgeable and most loyal.

Wrigley's denizens may also be the only fans for whom a play was written. *Bleacher Bums,* described as a "nine-inning comedy," was conceived by actor Joe Mantegna and written, in part, by Mantegna and Dennis Franz of *NYPD Blue* fame. *Bleacher Bums* takes place in Wrigley's right field bleachers during a 1977 game between the Cubs and Cardinals.

The characters are based on actual fans and incidents. Anyone who's sat in the bleacher seats during a Cubs home game will easily recognize Greg, Zig, Richie, Marvin, Cheerleader, Decker, and the others.

*   *   *   *

Cub rooters regenerate annually, as old fans pass on and young fans take their place. Baseball parks, however, only grow older. When vintage ballparks like Tiger Stadium are abandoned, baseball purists sadly shake their heads.

We pour concrete over a dirt path in the name of progress, they seem to say, and while it may be more efficient, we've lost something we'll never have again.

Somewhere in this favored land, there's got to be room for at least one unpaved country road. And true baseball fans everywhere hope—against all odds and logic, perhaps—that when another century dawns on Chicago, Wrigley Field will still be there on Addison Avenue, unchanged and beautiful as ever.

ZIP ZABEL

Talk about long relief! On June 17, 1917, the Cubs hosted Brooklyn at the West Side Grounds. With two outs in the first inning and the Dodgers up by a run, Zack Wheat buzzed a line drive that split a finger on the pitching hand of Chicago starter Bert Humphries.

Manager Roger Bresnahan had to put in an emergency call to right hander George Washington "Zip" Zabel.

*   *   *   *

All but forgotten today, Zabel pitched three seasons in the majors, all with the Cubs, from 1913 through 1915. But against the Dodgers on that late spring day in '15, Zabel set a big league record that may never be broken.

Zabel blanked the Dodgers until the eighth, when they tied the contest at two-all. He held them scoreless until the 15th, when Brooklyn eked out another run. But in the bottom of the frame, Vic Saier's homer into the right field bleachers kept the marathon going.

Finally, in the bottom of the 19th, Cubs shortstop Bobby Fisher scored the winning run from second base on a throwing error by Brooklyn second sacker George Cutshaw.

*   *   *   *

The final score was 4-3, and Zabel was the winning pitcher. Zip struck out six batters, gave up six hits and one intentional walk in the three-hour, 15-minute contest. But that day he earned a place—very likely permanent—in the record book.

His 18 and two-thirds innings were the longest relief job in major league history.

BOB ZICK

By late July 1954 the Cubs were in the doldrums once again. The pitching was particularly atrocious, and for help the front office summoned Chicago native Bob Zick, a right-hander, from Beaumont of the Texas League.

*   *   *   *

According to legend, Zick dutifully reported to manager Stan Hack when he joined the team and introduced himself, saying, "I'm Zick."

"Oh, yeah?" deadpanned Hack, whose Cubs were en route to a sixth-place finish and a 72-82 record. "I don't feel so good myself."

PART II

Chapter 1

WAIT 'TIL THIS CENTURY

A whole century—yes, 100 years, count 'em, 100—has come and gone since the Cubs played in their first World Series. Since irony is right up there with frustration as the hallmark of this Chicago sports saga, history records that the all-conquering Cubs got conquered in that crosstown classic of 1906 by the White Sox, known as the "Hitless Wonders."

A century later, new generations of Cubs fans had to bite their lips and sob into their suds while watching those same Sox storm into the 2005 World Series. The thought that, with a little more luck, a lot less injuries, and a clutch hit here and there might have led to a Cubs-Sox rematch was scant consolation.

It would have been worth waiting 99 years, maybe even 999 years, to see this ever-ferocious rivalry unfold on an all-Chicago stage. Those North Side partisans deserve such a reward for their patience, tolerance, and unshakeable faith that some day, somehow, the Cubs will not only return to the World Series, but actually win it.

SOX-CESS? BAH!

Most Cubs fans believe that a Chicago World Series not involving Wrigley Field is a non-event. While much of the city got caught up in the frenzy when the White Sox brought the big show back to town for the first time since 1959, bedrock Cubs diehards weren't singing "Na-na, hey-hey-goodbye!"

Even their disdain was tinged by anger at the Cards, the National League foe they love to hate.

"I'd only root for the White Sox if they play St. Louis in the World Series," vowed Christina Weiss, singing the blues and bleeding her Cubbie blue.

"Without the Cubs in it, I can't care about this World Series any more than if it was the Diamondbacks against the Royals," said Tonia, another unhappy voice in the crowd at Bernie's saloon, a Derrek Lee homer's distance from the Wrigley ramparts.

IN DUSTY WE...TRUSTY?

For those true believers and thousands more like them, what happens south of Madison Street—the dividing line between Cubs Nation and Sox Sentiment—means little. Only when the annual Cubs-Sox interleague clash shifts to U.S. Cellular Field, home of the White Sox, do they even find their way to the Chicago ballpark without ivy-bedecked walls. Regardless, the fact that the Sox got to the World Series just two years after the Cubs fell agonizingly short of fulfilling their fans' fantasies in 2003, brought North Siders' also-ran rage to the boiling point.

So the burning, stomach-churning question is both simple and searing for the Cubs and their suffering fans: When's our turn?

Everybody thought it would happen quickly when Dusty Baker came to Chicago, toothpick in mouth and hope in hand, to take over the managerial reins in 2003. His friendly smile and contagious optimism was a tonic and his reputation as a players' manager—whatever that means—created a soothing atmosphere in the Cubs' clubhouse.

Johnnie B. Baker, Jr. said all the right things about "Not coming here to lose" and so on that Cubs fans heard from Don Baylor and other managers, all the way back to the infamous revolving college of coaches in the '60s. Somehow, he seemed more believable, possibly because everybody wanted so desperately to believe in him. While the Cubs drove toward the National League's Central Division title in 2003, before delirious packed houses in Wrigley Field, Dusty got elevated overnight to demigod status. Victory-starved Chicagoans shrugged off the memory of Baker's San Francisco Giants blowing the 2002 World Series to the California Angels with a collapse in the last two games.

The notion that it could happen again, even more horrendously, never entered the minds of Cubs fans or the Chicago media that daily painted Baker as a cross between Casey Stengel and Tommy Lasorda. With young fireballer Mark Prior pitching the way everybody hoped Kerry Wood could, the Cubs seemed invincible—well, almost. The euphoria was so blinding that Baker virtually escaped criticism for a move on July 11 that was to haunt the Cubs three months later in the NL Championship Series.

PRIOR WARNING

Many highly-touted young prospects come to the big leagues with "can't-miss'" labels on their suitcases. All too often, the baggage in their heads prevents them from living up to the hype in the pressure-packed daily grind of pro sports. Mark Prior seemed ready to break the mold when the Cubs unveiled their top 2001 draft pick only a year later, after just nine starts in the minors. The right-hander's blend of blazing speed, crackling curve, and winning attitude made him an 18-game winner in 2003, seemingly on the fast track to the Hall of Fame.

"Mark would have been bored in the minor leagues," said Larry Rothschild, the Cubs' pitching coach. "He belongs up here."

The legendary Rod Dedeaux, Prior's baseball coach at USC, found that out while his young ace was blowing away over-matched college hitters. He sent a congratulatory note when Prior won his first start for the Cubs on May 22, 2002, and also phoned former USC standout Tom Seaver, a 311-game winner in the majors, and now in the Hall of Fame.

"Tom said, 'Tell the kid nice going, and he only needs 310 more to catch me,'" Dedeaux chuckled.

DELAYED PAIN

Dreams of World Series glory were far from Prior's mind when he faced Atlanta on that July afternoon in Wrigley Field. The budding superstar got knocked out of his first All-Star slot by a violent collision with Braves second baseman Marcus Giles that put him on the disabled list until August 4. Prior landed on his shoulder, but it seemed like a narrow escape that left Cubs fans breathing heavily. Almost as astonishing was the way Prior talked Baker into letting him get up and keep pitching, to lose a 9-5 decision. It could have been a disastrous, perhaps even career-threatening, situation, although Prior racked up a gaudy 10-1 record and 1.52 ERA in 11 starts after his enforced layoff.

"Mark's a gamer, and he wanted to go back out there," Baker said.

Some Cubs fans thought allowing Prior to play Russian roulette with his unlimited potential was foolhardy. Their voices got drowned out by the roars greeting the 22-year-old phenom's dominance down the stretch. When Prior beat the Florida Marlins, 12-3, in Game 2 of the NLCS, Cubs backers figured his next start would be in the 2003 World Series.

HOLY CHOKE!

Curses! Foiled again! Blame it on the Billy Goat Curse, the fickle finger of fate or the greedy fingers of Cubs fan Steve Bartman. One way of looking at the worst late-season foldup by a team notorious for such choke jobs was that Bartman's lurch for a foul fly that Cubs left fielder Moises Alou might or might not have caught provided America's lovable losers with a handy alibi for another crushing defeat. Realists among the legions of downcast Cubs fanatics faced the fact that their best three starters—Carlos Zambrano, Prior, and Kerry Wood—were rested and ready after the Cubs had the Fish on the hook-3-1. All three failed.

Just like 1984, this bewitched, bothered, and bewildered team had three shots at one win to end its self-imposed, 58-year World Series boycott. Instead of Bartman's presence, moist-eyed fans knew the disappearance of a few batmen in the Cubs' line-up and pitchmen on the mound meant more in the end.

MAYBE HE'S A SOX FAN

Heartbroken Cubs fans looked for solace from each other after the Cubs lost to the Marlins, 9-6, on October 15, ending their dream of a 2003 World Series in Wrigley Field. One of them, Mike McFaul, realized nothing on earth could save his heroes, so he went straight to the top. While downcast fans straggled out of the darkened ballpark, McFaul held up a cardboard sign, lettered with black tape. It said only, "God help us."

"Prior and Wood losing at home was worse than Rick Sutcliffe losing (the 1984 playoff pennant clincher) in San Diego," McFaul lamented. "We just can't get into the World Series."

HISTORY LESSON

Dusty Baker was baffled by the way Cubs fans seemed resigned to the inevitable after the visiting Marlins erupted for eight runs in the eighth inning to knot their frantic pennant showdown at three games each.

"Anybody who thinks the Cubs are out of this series doesn't know my team," the manager snapped. "We need our fans to give us that extra edge. Here we are at home for Game 7, winner take all, with Kerry Wood ready to go. I don't understand this talk about history or curses or whatever causing us to lose last night."

But the last night Baker mentioned was only the prelude to the real last night for the 2003 Cubs. What happened at the end of Game 6 brought the ghosts of 1969, 1984, 1989, and 1998 tumbling out of the closet, along with seven-straight World Series setbacks, from 1910 through 1945, on the Cubs' long trail of misery. The pall of gloom blanketing Wrigley Field deepened when the Marlins' Miguel Cabrera rocked Wood for a three-run homer in the first inning. Even though Wood's homer helped the Cubs rebound for a 5-3 lead, the foreboding hung around. Sure enough, Wood couldn't hold it and Florida went to the World Series for the second time in the franchise's brief history.

It didn't cheer up Cubs fans a bit to reflect that, since the NL expanded to Miami in 1993, the Marlins had won two pennants (1997, 2003)—and went all the way both times. The Cubs remain the only 1876 NL charter franchise still operating in the same city. Aging Wrigley Field tottered gracefully into the 21st century, longing to be crowned by a World Championship flag.

NO CHOKING MATTER

"Plain and simple, I choked," Kerry Wood said. "I let the team down, and I let Chicago down."

The hard-luck pitcher took his loss in the decisive game of a bitterly-fought playoff series as much to heart as the Cubs fans still milling around Wrigley Field. The Marlins were in, the Cubs were out, and the cycle of frustration remained unbroken. Wood had little on the ball except the cover, yielding seven runs and four costly walks in 5-2/3 innings. When he came to the Cubs in 1998, the sturdy right-hander's brilliance soon got eclipsed by an unending string of elbow, arm and shoulder ailments.

Regardless, the agony of this 2003 playoff defeat hurt more. The look on Wood's face made that clear.

"It's sad to hear Kerry say that," said Cubs pitcher Matt Clement. "He got us here by beating Atlanta in our division playoff."

In another touch of irony, nice guy Clement soon felt the same frustration in Chicago. The Cubs let him go, and he helped the Boston Red Sox into the 2005 AL playoffs, only to get shelled by the White Sox in their AL division series opener.

FATE WORSE THAN ...

Kenny Lofton stuck around only long enough to help the 2003 Cubs make the playoffs, but he could read the handwriting on the wall. When their seemingly unstoppable charge to the World Series suddenly deflated like a punctured tire, the well-traveled veteran outfielder sensed it must have been written in the stars.

"Fate wasn't with the Cubs," Lofton said. "I figure the plan was set for this team a long time ago."

BARTMAN VS. BASEBALL

Moises Alou said it best: "When we win next year, the fans will forget about all this. I don't blame the guy (Steve Bartman) for trying to catch the ball. That's what fans do."

Alou was patrolling left field for the Cubs the night they were on the verge of winning the NL pennant before an ecstatic Wrigley Field throng. Fans in that ivy-covered museum of masochism get used to seeing Cubs outfielders fail to make the catch, but these were extraordinary circumstances. With the Cubs ahead 3-0 and hopes, dreams, and beating hearts of the crowd following the flight of Luis Castillo's eighth-inning foul fly as it angled toward the left-field stands, the stage was set for high drama.

Instead, it turned into low comedy, quickly followed by another baseball tragedy, the sort the Cubs have specialized in since their World Series defeat in prehistoric 1945. Bartman, wearing a headset over his Cubs cap, reaches for the ball just inside the low wall and muffs the catch. So does Alou, although neither man is charged with an error. What Cubs fans soon want to charge Bartman with is murder of their World Series fantasies.

But the Cubs promptly commit suicide, imploding under the stress. Prior's bellow of "Fan!", pointing at the cringing Bartman, proves to be the Cubs' last hurrah in 2003. He can't get anybody else out and both he and his lead vanish under the Marlins' eight-run onslaught, fueled by shortstop Alex Gonzalez' error. The best-of-7 series is tied 3-3, but real Cubs fans go home knowing the season is over.

KASS COUP SCOOP

Nobody knew who Steve Bartman was until he became the most notorious Cub hexer since William "Billy Goat" Sianis's goat. When the goat was refused admission to Wrigley Field for a 1945 World Series game against the Tigers (naturally), Sianis slapped a curse on the Cubs. It was still intact when Bartman got the Cubs' goat by renewing the warranty for who knows how long.

John Kass, *Chicago Tribune* political columnist and diehard White Sox fan, was the only media person who talked with Bartman that night.

"Bartman was trying to hide in his seat, rocking back and forth, with people all around, cursing, throwing things and threatening to tear him apart," Kass related. "He just covered his ears and sat there until security came and hustled him out of the park. It was wonderful."

WHAT KIND OF BREAK?

Some, not many, Cubs fans, had compassionate thoughts about the Bartman Bungle. The majority agreed with one beer-soaked Wrigley spectator's primal scream at the cowering Bartman.

"You're lucky we're better than Boston fans, or you'd be dead now," the fan sputtered while he was being ejected.

Most of the onlookers would gladly have given Bartman a break, depending on which of his arms or legs they could reach. More reasonable types, including Cubs fan Jason Sucia, agreed that the players who couldn't rebound from that traumatic Game 6 loss were more to blame than Bartman.

"Anyway, that poor guy shouldn't have to live in fear," Suscia said.

Classy Cubs catcher Damian Miller didn't want to hear about this being the latest chapter in the long-running Cubs curse.

"The only curse on us in this series was the Florida Marlins," Miller pointed out.

Understandably, Bartman became a recluse, declining interviews and refusing to take part in the ceremonial destruction of the baseball he didn't catch, at Harry Caray's Chicago restaurant. While Cubs fans brooded through a winter of discontent, the Bartman ball, purchased for a whopping $113,000, got blown up. A tent outside the restaurant was sold out for the event, which raised more than $1 million for Ron Santo's favorite charity, the Juvenile Diabetes Foundation.

That exorcism didn't remove the curse for the following two seasons, at least. Neither did Bartman's only public utterance: "I'm truly sorry from the bottom of this Cubs fan's broken heart," his statement said.

VILLAIN TO HERO

If Cubs fans needed a real scapegoat, instead of the hapless Bartman, to blame for the World Series that got away in 2003, plenty of suspects were available. They all wore Marlins uniforms, including first baseman Derrek Lee. A 3-for-25 bust through most of the NLCS struggle with the Cubs, Lee's bat came to life when it counted most, with the bases loaded in the fateful eighth inning of Game 6.

His two-run double knocked out Cubs starter Mark Prior, tying the score at 3-3. The Marlins poured across five more runs to win 8-3, putting everything on the line one final time. That old courtroom question, "Where were you on the night of October 15?" pointed to Wrigley Field, with Lee as the culprit one more time. He singled home the go-ahead run off weary, fading Kerry Wood in the fifth inning, and the Marlins were on their way to the pennant.

But Cubs general manager Jim Hendry did his homework, tracking Lee's potential. He gave up first baseman Hee Sop Choi in a three-way trade to put Lee's booming bat and gobbling glove into the 2004 lineup. It proved to be a move that gave Cubs fans hope that his club's dreary start to the 21st Century might brighten up before long

ANOTHER SWEET SWING

The torch was passed in 2005, when Derrek Lee joined the list of Cubs who've worn National League batting crowns. That hadn't happened for a quarter-century, way back when Bill Buckner led the league with a .324 average in 1980. Lee, one of only six Cubs ever to become the NL's top gun, also made a run at the Triple Crown before falling short of that rare feat. He still had a sensational season, pacing Cubs hitters with a .335 mark, 46 home runs, and 107 RBI.

"You can tell when the word gets around the league," said Billy Williams, the Sweet Swinger who was the 1972 NL batting champ at .333. "Scouts picked up in a hurry on Derrek's power to all fields. Pitching coaches and managers were saying

'Don't let Lee beat us.' They tried to pitch around him a lot, but when the Cubs needed a clutch hit, he was the man."

Lee was a hit with Cubs fans in more ways than one. Besides dazzling them with glove and bat, the six-foot-five, right-handed swinger smiled, signed autographs, posed for pictures, and talked to the media—win or lose. He played with the kind of intensity and lack of ego that quickly filled the North Side superstar gap left by Sammy Sosa's departure.

"I never expected to win a batting championship," said Lee, only a .266-career hitter before his breakout 2005 campaign. "I'm more concerned with helping the Cubs put the intensity to match our talent on the field.

"It takes a lot of both to make the playoffs every year."

He knows Cubs fans would be happy to see that happen any year.

REAL-LEE GOOD

Derrek Lee piled up some spectacular numbers in 2005, emerging as one of baseball's best hitters. But, just like the Cubs, he couldn't get over he hump in a few categories. Going 0-for-8 at season's end prevented Lee from becoming the first Cub to compile a 200-hit season since Ryne Sandberg in 1984. The fancy-fielding first baseman also finished with 99 extra-base hits, falling just short of joining an elite group of major leaguers who got 200 hits, scored 100-plus runs and compiled 100 or more extra base hits and RBI in a single season. Babe Ruth did it once and Lou Gehrig twice.

"Derrek bailed us out so often, we were rooting for him to do it," said Greg Maddux, speaking for the appreciative Cubs pitching staff. Billy Williams, another Cub who knows how to hit, summed up Lee's feats succinctly.

"When you're hitting that consistently, your biggest problem is getting through all that traffic on the way to the ballpark without an accident," Williams said.

'A' FOR AGONY

When an eight-run, eighth-inning punch from the Marlins set the Cubs up for a 2003 playoff knockout, their frustrated fans figured it couldn't get any worse.

Wrong.

In the hysterical history of Chicago baseball, there's sure to be something even more catastrophic. For the Cubs, it was inning seven, Game 4, of the 1929 World Series. With an 8-0 lead over the powerhouse Philadelphia Athletics, the Cubs seemed a cinch to square the Series at 2-2, assuring that it would go back to Wrigley Field.

Whoops!

The A's brought the dozing crowd in Philly's bandbox Shibe Park back to life and put Cubs fans in a coma by erupting for 10 runs in that historic seventh inning, still a World Series record. Instead of Moises Alou failing to catch a game-turning fly ball 74 years later, this prelude to disaster was Cubs center fielder Hack Wilson, trying in vain to surround a deep drive by Mule Haas. Blinded by the sun, or perhaps a hangover, Wilson never saw the ball. It turned into a three-run inside the park homer, the pivotal play in the A's incredible 10-8 victory.

Before the home team wrapped up the Series with another winning comeback the following day, a kid in the stands asked Cubs manager Joe McCarthy for a baseball. Marse Joe, later the mastermind of a Yankees dynasty in the '30s, had a ready reply.

"Young man, just go out to center field and stand behind Hack Wilson," he said. "You'll get all the baseballs you want."

MAGNIFICENT MADDUX

Greg Maddux never thought 15 was his lucky number. The veteran right-hander's streak of winning at least 15 games ended at 17 when he lost his last two decisions in 2005 to finish with a 13-15 record. And less than 14 victories left Maddux tied with Hall of Famers Walter Johnson and Warren Spahn, who also chalked up at least that many for 17-straight seasons. A gem of consistency, Maddux joined the charmed circle of 20-game winners twice in his brilliant career, and on five other occasions, missed that total by just one.

Cubs fans still lament the failure to match Atlanta's salary offer in 1993, letting Maddux spend the prime of his career as the Braves' ace. Mad Dog got a big welcome and instant forgiveness for his 11-3 career mastery of the Cubs when he came back to Chicago in 2004, winning his 500th game and registering his 3,000th strikeout for the team he started with.

"Greg not winning 15 this year is more an indication of the way we played behind him," said Cubs catcher Michael Barrett, summing up the 2005 summer flop on the North Side.

Maddux, the consummate professional, reacted with his trademark composure.

"Fifteen is only a number," he said. "My goal every season is to win 20 games and help my team get into the playoffs."

RYNE'S SO FINE

Maybe the highlight of the Cubs' season in 2005 came on January 4, exactly three months before Opening Day. That's when the Baseball Writers Association of America did what it should have done two years before—voted Ryne Sandberg into the Hall of Fame, taking his place among the best who've ever played in the major leagues. I had never seen—and still haven't—a better second baseman, so Ryno's name was on my ballot from the first day he became eligible—in 2003. He lit up Wrigley Field, day or night, with such brilliance that even the powerful Yankee-Red Sox bloc of BBWAA voters finally had to agree.

Sandberg's sustained excellence for 15 seasons with the Cubs spoke much louder than he did in the clubhouse. But baseball passes statistics from generation to generation, and Ryno's consistent numbers could not be ignored. Along with talent, he had a brand of class that stood out clearly, sticking with one team while many of his contemporaries scrambled to find new uniforms and bigger paychecks every year. And despite the Chicago media's endless quest to fix blame for the Cubs' prolonged World Series drought, few fingers got pointed in Sandberg's direction.

But while fans in American League cities might have overlooked Sandberg's skills, the men he played with and against did not. Houston's Jeff Bagwell, who finally got into the 2005 World Series after 14 futile years with the Astros, gave his longtime opponent the respect he deserved.

"Sandberg set the bar at a higher level for second basemen," Bagwell said. "He redefined that position."

HALL OF A SPEAKER

Ryne Sandberg's Hall of Fame credentials were beyond dispute before his plaque was hung in the Cooperstown, New York, baseball museum on July 31, 2005. But the brief speech he gave at the induction Ceremonies made it clear how a quiet kid from Spokane, Washington, became a big-league star and a Chicago sports icon.

"Baseball fit me, because it was all about doing things right," Sandberg told the crowd gathered near the entrance to the shrine of America's pastime. "I had too much respect for the game to play it any other way. Harry Caray and Don Zimmer compared me to Jackie Robinson. Can you think of a better tribute?"

Sandberg also lauded Cubs fans, his wife, Margaret, "The love of my life," and ex-teammate Andre Dawson.

"Nobody did it better than the Hawk, and I hope he's up here (in the Hall of Fame) some day," he said.

Later, Sandberg told the media, " Learning how to bunt and turn the double play is more important than locating that red light on the (TV) camera. I'd like to see more of a team concept. When I played, respect for the game of baseball was mandatory. It's something I hope we will see again."

PUT A CORK IN IT

That's what Sammy Sosa suggested for Cubs fans. It was his way of wishing the corked bat caper would just go away. For years, the slugger reveled in the way right-field Wrigley bleacherites greeted his pregame romp and wave to them. It was the King saluting his subjects—a ritual that said "Play Ball!" as much as Wayne Messmer's booming baritone, belting out the National Anthem in the Friendly Confines.

All that changed on June 3, 2003, and not for the better. Sosa's bat shattered when he grounded out and umpire Tim Mc-Clelland picked up the pieces, discovering illegal cork nestled into the wood. Things got ugly from then on, with Sosa's heated denial that he corked his bats followed by a blast at the Chicago media for allegedly convicting him without a trial. Sammy Sunshine grew increasingly sullen and withdrawn when the rest of his bats were found to be cork-free, but the cloud of suspicion refused to go away.

So ended Sosa's decade-long Wrigley Field honeymoon. If the Cubs had not collapsed in the 2003 NLCS, letting the World Series slip through their fingers, all might have been forgiven, if not forgotten. Instead, the Sosa pot kept boiling through the following season, overflowing with frustration when the Cubs blew a wildcard playoff berth in the final week. Such comedy capers as Sosa leaving the park before his final Cubs game ended, and the destruction of his noisy boom box (perhaps by a corked bat?) made it apparent that he had to go.

So Sammy did, for a mediocre, injury-riddled 2005 stint in Baltimore, under more suspicion, this time about alleged steroid use, tainting the memory of Sosa's historic 1996 home run duel with Mark McGwire. Sosa hit 545 homers for the Cubs, but speculation about cheating haunted him, ex-Cub Rafael Palmiero, Barry Bonds and other musclebound power hitters.

NO GRACE PERIOD

The corked bat episode that got Sammy Sosa suspended in 2003 drew some rebukes from other players.

Mark Grace, who feuded with Sosa behind the scenes before leaving the Cubs in 2001, got in a few jabs.

"Instead of hitting 500-foot homers, I guess Sammy wants to hit them 550 feet," Grace said "That's weird."

And Yankees manager Joe Torre, one of baseball's most respected voices, joined Sosa's critics.

"Considering all he's accomplished, it's a dirty mark," Torre said. "It's embarrassing for a player that good and this kind of thing is unfortunate for the game."

A DUSTY TRAIL TO ...?

"Life is full of disappointments," Dusty Baker said after harsh reality exploded his fantasy of a World Series for Wrigley Field in his first season as the Cubs' manager.

"In Dusty We Trusty, " the battle cry of ecstatic fans during that almost-magical season, got rusty after the 2003 playoff debacle. Those same diehard fans expected their team to bounce back high and hard after that bitter experience. Sadly, they just missed the postseason pandemonium in 2004, and the playoff train left the station early in '05, with the Cubs watching it roar past in baffled anger. Such excitable types as Carlos Zambrano couldn't handle the frustration, hanging his emotion out in public, just like many of the 3,099,992 unhappy Wrigley customers.

"There's no Baseball 101 manual I can give the players," Dusty said, defending himself against growing dissent from fans and media. "Losing humbles you some, but I believe when the Cubs win one World Series, we'll go on to win three."

A scapegoat was required for the Cubs' dismal 79-83 record, after two-straight winning seasons under Baker. As usual, it was the manager, although Baker didn't take kindly to the storm of criticism about his handling of the talent-laden 2005 Cubs. Injuries, square bounces by round baseballs, and just plain bad luck all played their part. Still, these Cubs played bad fundamental baseball, often couldn't buy a clutch hit, and made their supporters shudder whenever Baker went to the bullpen. Even Ron Santo, the biggest Cubbie Blue booster of them all, had to face the truth.

"We led the NL in average, but we were last in RBI with runners in scoring position," Santo told his radio audience. "Our defense and fundamentals were lacking. We need a couple of reliable relief pitchers, more speed and better defense."

In short, the need for some fast rebuilding faced GM Jim Hendry. For Cubs fans, some things never seem to change. When Herman Franks managed them in 1978, his stock phrase was, "We're rebuilding."

So I trudged across the Wrigley turf to the visitors' clubhouse and asked Lou Brock what it was like before the Cubs traded him to the Cards in 1964.

"They were rebuilding," Brock replied.

OZ TRUSTS DUSTY

It didn't do much for rabid Cubs fans' morale when they learned the 2005 World Series would be played on Chicago's South Side, instead of their beloved Wrigley Field. Imagine their surprise when White Sox manager Ozzie Guillen defended his embattled friend, Dusty Baker.

"He was the best manager ever in 2003," Guillen said. "Last year and this year, you guys [Chicago media] ripped the bleep out of him. I know the media here, and that's why I don't care what they say."

Chapter 2

THE LAST QUOTER

The Chicago Cubs walked the walk into the promised postseason land just three times in the final 55 years of the 20th Century. The new millennium began with the most crushing collapse of all—their 2003 playoff foldup, just five outs away from a long-overdue National League pennant. So it was easy for anguished fans to forget the Cubs' winning tradition.

Cubs? Win? Yes, indeed. From 1906 through '45, the Cubs won 10 NL pennants (way back then, they called it the "gonfalon") and enjoyed two World Series victories in 1907 and '08, but who's counting?

Regardless, in those 60-plus futile seasons their fans endured during baseball's longest famine, aside from the fast-fading feasts of 1984, 1989, and 1998, the Cubs still talked the talk. Oh, brother, as Jack Brickhouse used to say, did they ever!

So there's no better way for Cubs junkies to get a daily fix of Wrigley Field fever—and fervor—than by talking about their beloved bunglers. Or by listening to the Cubs talk about themselves, rehashing and reliving every agonizing minute of this frantic trip through good times (few) and bad (as usual) for the Little Team that Very Seldom Could.

Lots more than half the fun in all those frustrating summers is the endless array of might-have-been, should-have-been, could-have-been and why-not theories, fantasies, alibis, and arguments over the plight of our loveable losers. My bulging file of Cubs quotes, almost as entertaining as sun-deviled Cubs infielders in pursuit of a windblown Wrigley popup, provides plenty of insight but few solutions.

Understandably, this baffling mystery has spread from a hallowed patch of turf on Chicago's North Side to Cubs diehards across the country and around the world. What keeps killing the Cubs? Here are a few hundred suspects.

LESSONS FROM LEO

Few managers in baseball history stirred up more conflicting emotions than Leo Durocher. During his stormy sojourn (1966-72) as fiery field boss of the Cubs, Leo the Lip aroused adulation bordering on worship among fans and fury that sometimes boiled over in the clubhouse. His shouting matches with such emotional players as Ron Santo and Joe Pepitone, among others, came perilously close to mayhem at times.

Even the nicest of Cub nice guys, Ernie Banks, drew his share of scorn from the manager, who was credited as declaring (although he actually didn't), "Nice guys finish last." So did shortstop Don Kessinger, a genial Southerner who survived the Durocher era to go down as one of the all-time top Cubs at his position.

"When Leo came to Chicago, the first thing I heard him say was, 'We've got to find a shortstop,'" Kessinger recalled. "He said I couldn't hit, field, or throw."

A sensitive man, Kessinger at times was nearly in tears, because he took to heart some Durocher tirades that most veteran players merely shrugged off. Although he disliked Leo's methods, Kessinger soaked up lots of baseball acumen from the brash manager, who broke in during the Roaring Twenties with the legendary Bronx Bombers—the Yankees of Babe Ruth. When Kessinger took over as manager of the White Sox in 1979, the mild-mannered skipper remembered what he had learned from the crusty baseball icon.

"When I made a move, I used to stop and think, 'Hey, I learned that from Leo,'" Kessinger recalled.

BRIAN, CAN YOU PITCH?

Brian Urlacher flashed his speed in Wrigley Field before the Bears' top 2000 draft pick made his first NFL tackle. As soon as he got tapped to play in Soldier Field, the All-America linebacker from New Mexico U. hot-footed it to the North Side to throw out the first pitch before the Cubs lost to the Florida Marlins on April 16, 2000.

"I grew up rooting for the Cubs, and seeing a game in this park is a dream come true," said Urlacher, a New Mexico native. "Shane Andrews [another of the 80 or so pretenders who've had a cup of coffee at third base for the Cubs since Ron Santo departed in 1974] is still an idol at home."

'69 ON OUR MINDS

The September swoon of the 1969 Cubs is the stuff of legend, still sticking in their faithful fans' craws more than three decades later. It sent shockwaves through Chicago, especially on the North Side, where Wrigleyville went into virtual mourning.

There were worse disappointments to come, especially in 1984, when the Cubs finally snapped the Billy Goat jinx that had kept them out of postseason action since 1945. Weeks, even months later, a joyous banner still hung above the entrance to the firehouse at Waveland and Sheffield Avenues, across the street from Wrigley Field: "Official Firehouse of the 1984 World Series."

It was not to be, because the Cubs staged a colossal collapse in San Diego, falling one game short of their goal after storming to a 2-0 lead in the best-of-five series. The oh-so-close firehouse banner swayed sadly in the winter wind swirling through the deserted ballpark, a harbinger of even quicker Cubs playoff exits in 1989 and '98.

SELMA THE SAVIOR

Over the years, millions of words and billions of Cubs fan laments keep postmortem-ing and second-guessing those foldups. In seeking to sort it all out and explain the inexplicable, they always come back to the same plaintive wail: "Why? Why? Why?"

Cubs fans know they might as well try to turn the Hawk—the icy blast off the Lakefront that transports Chicago to a February suburb of Siberia—into a balmy breeze to explain the unfathomable. Amid the pile of hand-wringing lamentations, this conversation with quirky ex-Cubs pitcher Dick Selma, from his home in Mexico, emerged as my favorite memory of 1969, that sensational summer that made the fatal fall hurt much more.

Free-spirited reliever Selma appointed himself the official cheerleader of the left field Bleacher Bums in 1969. His towel-waving antics began one day when the Cubs fell behind in

Ernie Banks, flanked by his wife and another Hall of Famer, Hoyt Wilhelm, shakes off the disappointment of 1970 season with a cheerful prediction for '71. It didn't happen, but that never deters Mr. Cub from issuing the same rosy forecast every year.

Wrigley Field. Selma yelled to the bleacher creatures from his bullpen perch, "It isn't over yet. Make some noise!"

The Bums erupted, Ernie Banks homered, and the Cubs won. From that moment on, superstitious Cubs manager Leo Durocher barked orders to "Get 'em stirred up!" Selma gleefully obliged, and a Cubs tradition was born, overflowing into a season-long jubilee of songs, cheers, chants and zany antics by the Bleacher Bums, adorned with yellow hard hats and led by bullhorn-wielding Ron Grousl.

"When Leo saw what I was doing and how the Bums reacted, he told me to keep doing it every day," Selma recalled. "Despite how things turned out, the way those fans lived and died with us made that one of the best times in my life."

After the ecstasy turned to agony, trampled under a 41-12 closing stampede by the New York Mets, Selma departed with fond memories of the National League pennant that got snatched away. They include the following excerpt from a letter written to him by a Bleacher Bum's mother:

"You kept my son off the street and in the bleachers. His hero is Billy Williams, instead of Fidel Castro. Ron Santo's autograph is worth more to him than a stolen hubcap. And how can an LSD trip beat a trip to Wrigley Field?"

KERRY WOOD, BUT CUBS WOULDN'T

The fallout from more than a half-century of franchise failures still haunts competitors like combative Cubs pitcher Kerry Wood. The fireballing right-hander fought back from a career-threatening injury, submitting to Tommy John elbow surgery on April 8, 1999, and missing that entire season to recuperate.

But Wood's blend of overpowering stuff and will to win couldn't prevent the Cubs from barging into the new millennium with the same old results, losing 97 games in 2000, falling apart after making some early noise in 2001 and turning 2002 into total disaster. After a 3-0 loss in St. Louis on May 13 greased the skids for manager Don Baylor's firing, Wood's frustration boiled over in a profanity-laced postgame tirade.

"We're dead," Wood admitted angrily. "The Cubs are playing like we're already out of the [NL Central Division] race. I'm tired of this same old stuff about 'Keep your head up and we'll get 'em tomorrow.' It's not happening."

Things got even worse from there. When dependable starter Jon Lieber—the first Cub 20-game winner (20-6 in 2001) since Greg Maddux went 20-11 in 1992—departed with arm trouble, the inevitable result of too many elbow-straining sliders, the

Cubs hit bottom. To those ever-hopeful fans, Wood's outrage brought back echoes of futility from the past.

MURCER PLEADS FOR MERCY

Bobby Murcer was supposed to out-Sammy Sosa in 1977, when the Cubs acquired the supposed slugger from San Francisco in a bad trade that shipped recalcitrant third baseman Bill Madlock to the Giants. Murcer arrived amid much fanfare from general manager Bob Kennedy and field boss Herman Franks. He contributed modest team-best totals of 27 homers and 89 RBI in his debut, while the Cubs improved by six games that season, inching up to .500 at 81-81. They promptly sank again in '78, and Murcer went back to the Yankees, where he earlier had been touted as the next Mickey Mantle.

Murcer found handy scapegoats to explain his so-so performance—the rest of the Cubs and the San Francisco fog.

"When you're around dead people, you play like you are dead," Murcer moaned. "In Chicago, there was all that day ball. It was so cold and windy in San Francisco, you didn't like playing ball. Both places, I never felt I belonged."

Franks, not much of a humorist, got a laugh out of that complaint.

"I see where Murcer made a bad throw that cost the Yankees a game last night," the rotund Cubs manager said. "Funny he should talk about us now."

PHONEY EXCUSE

Shortly before his roller-coaster tenure with the Cubs ended in 1972, manager Leo Durocher provided a painful glimpse in-

side the confusion that prevented his sagging squad from finding some fresh bodies. Calls to general manager John Holland
from other teams seeking deals went unanswered shortly before
the trading deadline. Holland was meeting with his embattled
manager in Durocher's clubhouse office.

"If they'd put the calls down here on my line, we might have
been able to make a trade," Leo the Lion mumbled, his roar
muffled by almost seven years of inability to lead the Cubs into
the playoffs.

But the communications gap within the Cubs organization
went deeper than that. Leo had moved, without giving Holland
his new phone number.

"I don't know any more than you do," Holland told frustrated sports scribes, scrambling to contact the elusive Durocher.

But the Billy Goat hex, slapped on the Cubs by Chicago
character William Sianis when the Cubs refused to let his pet
goat enter Wrigley Field with him for the 1945 World Series,
apparently afflicted the front office as well as the team. Sianis's
nephew, Sam, still runs the Billy Goat Inn, made famous on
Saturday Night Live ("Chizborger! Chizborger!") as a hangout
for such thirsty Chicago newspaper types as the legendary Mike
Royko.

Mysteriously balky telephones also got general manager Jim
Frey's goat while he was trying to beat the 1989 trade deadline.

"The phones went out for four hours, and I couldn't talk to
anyone," Frey grumbled.

LOU LOSES

A winner on the field and in the broadcast booth, former Cubs
manager Lou Boudreau got caught with the team in the 1977
power blackout that turned off the lights in New York and much
of the Eastern seaboard. Easy-going Lou found a way to make
light of the situation, along with his own well-earned reputation

as another of Chicago handicapper Dave Feldman's legion of "BDHs"—broken-down horseplayers.

"I lost all my money," Boudreau said of the peril lurking on New York's pitch-black streets. "But it was this afternoon, at the race track."

Meanwhile, Cubs catcher Steve Swisher confessed that he found somebody willing to spend the dark night with him.

"Unfortunately, it was a guy," Swisher said. "This is some city."

A FAMILIAR TARGET

During his productive 19-year playing career with a half-dozen American League clubs, ex-Cubs manager Don Baylor grew used to wearing a bull's-eye on his uniform. Baylor chalked up the big-league record for getting hit by pitches a total of 267 times.

It hurt a lot more when Baylor became the chief target of criticism for the injury-riddled Cubs foldup in 2002. As usual in such situations, the players survived, but the manager didn't. While he was struggling through his rocky 65-97 inaugural year as Cubs field boss in 2000, Baylor lamented the way batters nowadays tend to charge the mound, triggering a brawl, when pitchers try to work inside.

"When I got hit you could even the score by taking out somebody on the other team with a hard slide," Baylor said. "Now you have to stay three feet away from fielders.

"Frank Robinson stood on top of the plate, and he got hit plenty. If pitchers are throwing at your head, it's just part of the game. I hope we don't turn into the NBA, where the coach has to keep his players on the bench when a fight starts."

That never was a problem for Leo Durocher, who often told his pitchers "Stick it in his ear," if an opposing hitter's bat got too hot. Even after he retired, Durocher watched TV games with disdain when umpires warned pitchers not to throw too close to batters.

"I agree with Larry Goetz, a tough old umpire, about beanballs," Durocher said. "He told me he couldn't look inside a pitcher's head to tell whether he was throwing at anybody. He was right. The hitters have to protect themselves."

RAY KNOWS THE WAY

Ray Burris saw his share of losing under four different Cubs managers from 1973-79. They produced a .500 record just once in that span (81-81 in 1977), but Burris was their leading winner twice, with back-to-back 15-victory seasons in 1975-76.

So the veteran right-hander knew what Herman Franks was up against in 1981, when that ex-Cubs manager replaced Bob Kennedy as general manager. A straight shooter, right-hander Burris came into Wrigley Field with the Montreal Expos to sum up the situation.

"Maybe the Cubs are the worst team in baseball, but I hate to see what they're going through right now," Burris told me. "Does that mean the fans should go out and shoot them? Can the Cubs go down to Western Avenue and pick up 25 new players?

"Take a young pitcher in this park, where the ball jumps when the wind's blowing out. If he gets rocked in a few starts, the fans get on him, the media writes and talks like he's a dog and he gets no support from the front office. I know, because all that happened to me here."

POISON-TO-POISON CALL

Bob Rush was an effective Cubs pitcher from 1948 through 1957. Like all starters, though, he went to the Wrigley Field mound without good stuff one afternoon, and line drives soon began chopping shrubbery off the ivy-covered walls. Manager Phil Cavarretta stood it as long as he could before making a long, slow trip from the dugout, while the Cubs bullpen sprang into action.

"I have to take you out," he told Rush. "Our outfielders are getting poison ivy."

GOING BACKWARDS

Injuries left the Cubs in a jam throughout their season-long plummet in 2002, but it happens to them a lot. Even a traffic jam put catcher Joe Girardi in a jam during his first tour of duty with the Cubs. Already idled by back problems, Girardi got caught in typical postgame gridlock on Clark Street. While waiting for it to get unsnarled, he felt more back pain. Instead of going on the road with the team, Girardi had to stay home—and out of traffic.

GAME OF REAL LIFE

Along with the rest of America, the Cubs paused on September 11, 2002, to pay tribute to victims on the first anniversary of the terror attacks. And, like the rest of us, they faced the reality that such things can happen here.

"It would be very difficult to detect one person carrying something into a crowded ballpark," said pitcher Kerry Wood. "I'm not worried about myself, but I think everybody's concerned about their family and wondering how secure we are anywhere in the country."

Sammy Sosa, a native of the Dominican Republic, used his role as the team leader to speak out for America. He lifted the spirits of Cubs fans and TV viewers after homering on September 27, 2001, the first Wrigley Field game since the terrorist attacks on New York and Washington, D.C.

"God wanted me to show my appreciation for America," Sosa said of the way he carried two small American flags, handed to him by first base coach Billy Williams, on his trip around the bases. "I did it out of respect for America, which means a lot to me."

COSELL VS. CARAY

Howard Cosell, the biggest thing in sports broadcasting when he was the ringmaster for Frank Gifford, Dandy Don Meredith, and others on Monday Night Football telecasts, was no fan of Harry Caray.

"There is no excuse for Caray's cheerleading," Cosell fumed after watching Harry turn Comiskey Park into Carayland, USA during a televised White Sox game. "I was amazed when I heard him leading the fans in singing 'Take Me Out to the Ball Game.' Caray's broadcasts are on the grade-school level.

"It's true all sports announcers are housemen to an extent, but some more than others," Cosell continued, warming to his diatribe. "I once had high hopes for [former Chicago sportswriter and TV sportscaster] Brent Musberger. I thought he would be the next Howard Cosell, but he has become a high school cheerleader. He's not as bad as Harry Caray, though."

Fortunately for Cosell's massive ego, he was not asked to comment later on the way Caray wrapped Wrigley Field fans around his finger and became America's favorite cheerleader after moving to the Cubs' TV booth in 1982.

QUICK DOUBLE-DIP TRIP

Seemingly endless games have become a problem in the major leagues, especially in Chicago. Although the White Sox seem to specialize in three-and-a-half-hour marathons, the Cubs now take longer to totter through nine innings as well. It's hard to imagine that on September 4, 1957, the Cubs not only followed Ernie Banks's favorite rallying cry—"Let's play two today"—but did so in double-quick fashion.

They reeled off the first Wrigley Field game against the Cincinnati Reds in a mere hour and 37 minutes before slowing somewhat through a two-hour, 20-minute nightcap. Still, the whole afternoon in the Friendly Confines took just three hours and 57 minutes.

MAYDAY? NO, MAY NIGHT

The Cubs' first ever Wrigley Field night game was supposed to be on 8/8/88, but maybe the Billy Goat hex applied to arc lights as well as day games. Persistent rain forced the Cubs to call it off and try again against the Mets on August 9. It rained on their parade again 10 years later, pushing that first pitch back to 9:17 p.m. on April 30, 1998, the latest ever Wrigley Field starting time. The game didn't finish until the next month—at 12:15 a.m. on May 1.

HOOTON NO HISTORIAN

Burt Hooton didn't give a hoot about the possibility of equaling Johnny Vander Meer's feat—back-to-back no-hitters. The Cincinnati lefty did it in 1938 against the Boston Bees (later the Milwaukee/Atlanta Braves) on June 11 and the Brooklyn (now Los Angeles) Dodgers on June 15. Hooton, a 22-year-old Cub rookie, made the quantum leap from the University of Texas to the bigs by no-hitting the Phillies 4-0 in Wrigley Field on April 16, 1972.

The media crush in those days was nothing like the mob hounding players and jamming clubhouses after games now, especially with shoulder-mounted TV cameras. Even so, Hooton got grilled exhaustively after making the Phils knuckle under with his pet pitch, a dazzling knuckle curve. He was astonished that anyone would expect him to do it again in his next start, a Shea Stadium outing against the Mets.

"I never heard of Vander Meer," the exasperated Hooton said. "The reporters were looking at me like I was some kind of fool because I didn't know who he was. I'm not up on baseball history, and pitching two no-hitters in a row never crossed my mind."

Not to worry. Hooton did not twirl another no-no. The chunky right-hander went 10-14 for the Cubs in the rest of the 1972 season and failed to win consistently until he got traded to the Dodgers, three years later.

MR. CONSISTENCY

Jon Lieber, Opening Day starter for the Cubs in 2001 and 2002, paid the price for his consistent brilliance. The Cubs declined to pick up his 2003 contract option, making the sturdy right-hander a free agent. The strain of working more than 200

Ferguson Jenkins (hands on hips) takes a detour en route to the Hall of Fame while the Cubs pitcher hears a lecture from umpire Chris Pelekoudas. Later in that same 1969 season, the Bleacher Bums got revenge on Pelekoudas by making him run all the way out to the left field wall.

innings for three straight years, including an NL-high 251 in 2000, finally took its toll on Lieber's pitching arm. He was missed on the mound and in the clubhouse, but made a comeback with the Yankees and Phillies.

"My job is to take us into the seventh inning with a chance to win the game," the unassuming Lieber kept telling us after his typical no-nonsense starts. He got the ball and threw it, keeping the Cubs' defense alert and opposing runners off the bases with masterful control. Lieber went 20-6 in 2001, joining Greg Maddux (1992), Rick Sutcliffe (1984) and Rick Reuschel (1977) as the Cubs' only 20-game winners since Fergie Jenkins did it for six straight seasons. (1967-72).

TUFF ACT TO FOLLOW

Opening Day at Wrigley Field is a blue-letter day in Chicago, as in Cubbie Blue. Maybe the most spectacular moment was Willie Smith's two-run pinch homer in the 11th inning on April 8, 1969, giving the Cubs a 7-6 victory over the Phillies. That put Leo Durocher's confident club in first place, where they stayed for the next 155 days, touching off a matching wave of hysteria and an epidemic of pennant fever that spread from coast to coast, like a giant (not San Francisco Giant, of course) tsunami.

But for sheer power, not even Sammy Sosa could match the three-homer 1994 Opening Day outburst by unheralded Cubs center fielder Karl "Tuffy" Rhodes. He astonished the jam-packed Wrigley Field throng by starting the Cubs' first turn at bat with a homer off Mets ace Dwight Gooden. Warming to his task, he connected off Gooden in each of his next two trips.

"I've never seen somebody come out of the gate like that," said Cubs manager Tom Trebelhorn.

Neither had Cubs fans, joyously preparing to anoint lefty swinger Tuffy their new Teddy, as in Ted Williams. Alas, it didn't last, and neither could the lead provided by his trio of round-trippers. The Cubs lost that opener 12-8. Rhodes's magic bat faded soon after, like many of the baseball flowers that bloom in the spring, or until pitchers get loose when the weather warms.

As the old story goes, rookies begin calling home when cut-down date arrives at big-league training camps to voice the same plaintive wail: "Put another bean in the pot, Ma. The pitchers are starting to throw curves."

Rhodes wasn't a rookie, and he had a few more bright moments, notably a pair of homers against the Astros on April 28 at the Astrodome. But Tuffy batted a meek .201 from May 1 to the end of the 1994 season, collecting only 38 hits in 189 trips. Still, unlike many "can't-miss" hotshot Cubs prospects over the years, Rhodes had his big moment in the sun—actually, three of them in a row at that electrifying home opener.

Chapter 3

YOU CAN'T BEAT FUN GUYS AT THE OLD BALLPARK

Of all the endangered species in baseball, the certified screwball ranks right up there with the two-hour game, the $2 beer and the .200 hitter making less than $2 million per year. It's big business now, much too big for monkey business (except in Anaheim) or showbiz antics to intrude on the money machine that raked in $3.7 billion for all 28 major-league clubs in 2003. That included even the cash-strapped Puerto Rico Expos.

There are a few exceptions, notably Barry Bonds's leisurely saunter from the plate after rocketing one of his moonshots into McCovey Cove at Pac Bell Park. But neither that nor Sammy Sosa's trademark homer hip-hop is considered hot doggery, with or without mustard and relish. That's because (a) both were superstars, more gigantic than the Giants and more colossal than the Cubs, and (b) Early Wynn and Don Drysdale are dead. If

Hall of Fame catcher Johnny Bench tracks this popup by Larry Biittner. One of many nice guys to play for the Cubs, Biittner is best remembered for losing a ball in his cap after sprawling in vain to make the catch.

those two combative right-handers were still around, Bonds and Sosa would be smart to wear a suit of armor on their next trip to the plate after homering off them.

Most baseball brawls nowadays erupt when a batter charges the mound in righteous wrath at a pitch that veers slightly off the inside corner. The game's etiquette and individual testosterone levels then demand that dozing bench players awaken and join the melee, along with bullpen exiles, reluctantly interrupting their national pastime—girl-watching in the stands. Somehow, I doubt that Harry Caray's ritual chant ("You Can't Beat Fun at the Old Ballpark") included these occasional rugby scrums.

But there always will be a place for another Dizzy Dean or Mark "The Bird" Fydrich, if clones of those delightful screwballs ever make it to the big leagues. Chances are their agents, lawyers, accountants, and financial advisors will convince them that skylarking is bad business.

So I scrutinize rosters every spring, in a vain search for the next Jay Johnstone. This light-hearted goofball was fun to be around, pulling pranks to enliven every clubhouse and ballpark he entered. As a reward, Johnstone got abruptly released by the Cubs in 1984, because general manager Dallas Green, in grim pursuit of the Cubs' first postseason berth for 39 years, wasn't about to tolerate such nonsense as horseplay or smiling on the job.

JAY BRIGHTENS THE DAY

I didn't have to read Jay Johnstone's book, chock full of gags, practical jokes and one-liners, to realize I was dealing with a fun-loving guy. The former Cub and White Sox part-time outfielder and full-time prankster always has a glint in his eye, the one that keeps seeking another victim.

Regardless, it's impossible to get mad or stay annoyed with jovial Jay, even after your cap has been nailed to the dugout wall, your shoes filled with shaving cream or your locker packed with water-filled balloons. Johnstone was constantly on the lookout for gullible writers, too, so he figured he'd found a ripe pigeon—me—when our paths crossed in Comiskey Park while Jay was adding his colorful brand of color commentary to a televised White Sox game and I was trying to write a version coming somewhat closer to what really had happened.

We had been on friendly terms since 1972, when astute Sox general manager Roland Hemond swung a deal to bring the lefty swinger—and thinker—to Chicago. And when Jay got released without warning by the Cubs in 1984, after lightening their spirits and loosening up the rookies, I commiserated with him. But this was years later, and Jay had fresh mischief in mind, especially since illegal corking of bats by some players, notably Cleveland sourpuss Albert Belle, was a hot topic at the moment.

"Hey, Bob, you ought to go see [Sox trainer] Herm Schneider," Jay said. "He's in the clubhouse, talking about how Frank Thomas sneaks into the training room to put cork in his bat."

"Sure, Jay," I replied, fully aware he'd be disappointed when he picked up the paper the next morning, vainly seeking a screaming headline about the fictional bat-corking scandal.

That's just Jay's way. He and pitcher Jerry Reuss, a fellow free spirit, once delighted a Dodger Stadium crowd by trading their uniforms for goundskeepers' garb, joining the crew to sweep the infield between innings. He was the same old clubhouse cutup with the Cubs, easing the pressure of their 1984 playoff drive by asking fierce-looking reliever Lee Smith (actually a mild-mannered man): "Hey, Lee, why bother washing your car? Just glare at it and the dirt will fall off."

BAD GUY MAKES GOOD

In his first stay with the Cubs, 1982 to 1984, pitcher Dickie Noles had other priorities besides pitching. Mainly, they were drinking, brawling, and alienating teammates and sportswriters.

Along with a big-league fastball, Noles had a big-time attitude problem. He seemed bent on self-destruction, drowning his talent in an ocean of beer. Suddenly, after turning off most of the Chicago media with profane clubhouse tirades, the burly right-hander insisted he'd seen the light.

"I want to be a pitcher, not a drunk," Noles told one of his few friends, *Philadelphia Inquirer* sports editor Frank Dolson. What he didn't tell Dolson was that on bus trips to spring training games, Noles would hide in the bathroom, downing cans of beer slipped to him by a teammate.

Soon after the 1983 season started, Noles spent 15 days in jail for his role in a Cincinnati bar fight. Both his career and his life seemed to be heading straight down the drain. He was fortunate to find a savior in the Cubs' front office.

It was general manager Dallas Green, a gruff, no-nonsense type, not noted for sympathizing with troublemakers. Underneath that tough hide, though, Green had a soft spot for struggling young pitchers, perhaps because he had been one himself. A highly touted bonus rookie when he signed with the Phillies, Green got booed out of town by those ferocious Philadelphia fans. The lowlight of Green's career was serving up the 100th career home to Jimmy Piersall—whereupon Piersall celebrated by running around the bases backwards.

Green gave Noles two choices—go to an alcohol treatment program or get out. Noles made the right decision, pulling himself out of the gutter via a miraculous transformation. He changed, seemingly overnight, into a family man, a pleasant, soft-spoken, and above all, sober ballplayer. When Noles came back to the Cubs for a brief stint in 1987, he admitted that Green had saved his life.

"At first, the combination of booze and pitching in the majors was too much for me," Noles said. "Now if I drank, I'd be cheating myself. When I talk to kids, I tell them what I went through. It helps them understand they can choose the right direction for themselves."

KINGMAN GETS CROWNED

Cubs fans can't say they weren't warned about Dave Kingman.

The strapping slugger was high on their villains list a year before he came to Chicago in 1978. He soon became the toast of the town, but adulation apparently was too hard to handle for him. A series of run-ins with the media, along with some depressingly dumb opinions in his ghostwritten newspaper columns, and King Kong was back on the fans' Get Lost list. That took some doing, because Kingman lit up Wrigley Field in 1979, leading both leagues with 48 homers, 25 of them in the Friendly Confines.

But there was no love lost on the North Side on August 8, 1977, when the Cubs and Kingman's San Diego Padres got involved in a beanball brawl. Kingman picked the wrong target after taking a retaliatory plunk from Cub pitcher Steve Renko. Glaring, King Kong trudged to first base instead of charging the mound, a choice he soon regretted.

Sure enough, the next Padres hitter, George Hendrick, bounced a double-play grounder to short and when second baseman Mick Kelleher took the throw, Kingman barreled into him with the best takeout block since the Packers' Jerry Kramer leveled the Cowboys' Jethro Pugh, opening the door for Bart Starr's legendary 1967 touchdown sneak on Green Bay's frozen tundra.

That got Kelleher's Irish up, so the five-foot-nine mighty mite leaped up and climbed Mt. Kingman, taking him down with a flying tackle. The ensuing melee was a dandy, wounding three Cubs—Kelleher, Jose Cardenal, and Steve Ontiveros.

"It was a cheap shot," said Kelleher, nursing a sore neck and bruised ribs.

Kingman talked freely after that ambush, unlike the way he clammed up soon after joining his former antagonists a season later. In his version, the little guy was the aggressor.

"I didn't throw a punch," he lamented. "If I'd known the umpires were going to throw me out of the game, I would have gone right after Renko."

Despite his power at the plate, Kingman's chief legacy in Chicago consisted of opening an ice-cream parlor, dumping a bucket of water on a sportswriter, and tossing a female TV producer from his boat into Lake Michigan. When he demanded a hefty raise in 1980, the Cubs gladly shipped him to the New York Mets, presumably as revenge for 1969.

MR. CLUBHOUSE CUB

One of my favorite Cubs people never wore a uniform but handled thousands of them. He's equipment manager Yosh Kawano, beginning his 61st year with the club. The Cubs dress in the Yosh Kawano Clubhouse, though he now handles a lighter load in the Wrigley Field visitors' bathhouse, upstairs on the first base side.

Kawano, a Wrigley fixture since 1943, has his name on the Cubs Walk of Fame as well as the clubhouse. In the tradition of Wrigley family loyalty, the 1981 sales contract to the Tribune Company assured his job for life. Yosh and I used to talk about golf, because he's a friend of touring pro Raymond Floyd, but he politely declined any sort of personal publicity.

"I never won or lost a game for the Cubs, so why would anybody be interested in me?" he said.

PEPI PEPS UP CUBS

For a few shining moments, Joe Pepitone sang a hit tune for the Cubs. Sadly, Pepi's Wrigley Field rhapsody in 1970 did not turn out to be a long-playing record. His emotional temperament soon struck a sour note with maestro Leo Durocher, leader of the discordant Cubs band. Pepitone was the featured soloist, at least temporarily, but the whole Cubs orchestra sat on folding chairs.

It was a sad ending to the Durocher era, which had showed steady improvement since 1966, built up to a crashing 1969 crescendo and slowly disintegrated in the wake of that crushing defeat. At the end, Durocher and Pepitone, a pair of hot-tempered New York types, switched from Chicago buddies to exiled enemies.

By then, even the most rabid true believers in the Wrigley bleachers had to admit that Leo the Lip and Pepi the Hipster had outstayed both their welcome and their usefulness. It was the stuff of musical comedy, with an unhappy final act. Carmen Fanzone, a first-rate trumpet player and a second-rate third baseman, joined the Cubs just in time to blow taps over this sad affair.

Pepi arrived on August 11, 1970, triggering an orgy of optimism for the struggling Cubs. His antics turned the clubhouse into Comedy Central, notably a side-splitting imitation of Marlon Brando's "I coulda been a contendah" scene from On the Waterfront. On the field, Pepi stirred up renewed pennant fever with fancy fielding and clutch hitting. Fans were entranced by his showbiz glamor, and he was quick to cash in with "Joe Pepitone's Thing," a swinging cabaret in the Rush Street night-life hub, plus a hair salon.

"This really is my kind of town," Pepi proclaimed, starring at his club nightly after doing so daily at the Friendly Confines.

Unfortunately, the fun and games failed to translate into winning games. The Cubs trailed NL East Division winner Pittsburgh at the end in 1970 and again in '71 and '72. By then, the Durocher-Pepitone love fest was deader than the short-lived hula hoop fad. Finger-pointing, blame-dodging, and buck-passing replaced peace, harmony, and other remnants of Pepi's hippie image.

So nobody was surprised when Pepitone announced that he was quitting, barely a month into the 1972 season. He came back briefly, but Durocher was gone soon after, leaving behind a trail of might-have-beens. Pepi hung around a bit longer, although when he left town for good in 1973, few fans bothered to notice or lament.

"Joe just had to do things his own way," said Ron Santo, Pepi's nightclub partner.

CHAW? NAW, THANKS

For old-time fans, the sight of Mark McGwire chomping a wad of gum and blowing a big bubble before stepping into the batter's box marked the end of an era. For me, too.

I recall going to Kansas City in 1980 to track George Brett's quest to become the first .400 hitter since Ted Williams. One more face in the media mob surrounding him nightly in the Royals' dugout did nothing to ease the pressure on Brett, who finished that year agonizingly short of his goal at .390. He had a quaint way of displaying his displeasure—spraying the writers' shoes with tobacco juice in an ever-widening circle.

It didn't bother me.

I can be numbered among the vanishing breed of diamond scribes who often left the park with tobacco-stained shoes. So I'm glad I wandered down to the Cubs' bullpen before a game in 1972 for a chat with reliever Steve Hamilton. The lanky left-hander was an authority on the theory and practice of The Chaw.

"My grandfather used to make the real stuff, so strong it would turn your hair gray," Hamilton said. "I've been chewing since I was 12. Now we have chewers like [fellow relief pitcher] Jack Aker, with finesse but no power. He spits straight down. Ralph Houk [Yankee manager] is a power chewer. It's not smart to get too close to him on a windy day. Rocky Bridges could do it all, but Les Peden would wrap his chaw in a napkin and take it out after lunch. He usually ate alone."

Hamilton was a Yankee teammate of Joe Pepitone. They both still chuckle about the day Hamilton blended his chaw and a big orange soda, with catastrophic results.

"I went out to the mound and couldn't stop barfing, in front of 30,000 people and a TV audience," Hamilton recalled. "Pepitone was laughing so hard, he fell off the dugout bench."

JOSE, CAN YOU FLEE?

Jose Cardenal was one of my favorite Cubs. I wasn't alone, because Jose was always entertaining, even at his most exasperating. Either way, the colorful outfielder's niche in Cubs lore is secure, although he still denies two tales most often cited to illustrate Jose's unique style. One, repeated gleefully by Chicago media icon Mike Royko in his occasional columns about the joyfully hopeless lot of Cubs fans, had him sitting out an exhibition game because his eyelid got stuck shut. The other had Cardenal talking his way out of the lineup due to sleeplessness.

It seems a cricket chirped under his bed all night, keeping him awake.

"None of that stuff ever happened," Cardenal told me once, angered by my factual report that he had run through a stop sign at third base, quashing a promising Cubs rally. "You writers think all Latin players are dumb."

Dumb, no. Crazy like a fox, yes. Cardenal knew how to play games with the media, and he enjoyed doing so. Mostly, the wiry little guy, just five foot ten and 160 pounds stripped, was a capable fielder, with surprising power at the plate and base-stealing speed. He also knew how to keep his name in print.

My personal tell-all—no, make that show-all—Cardenal escapade was in 1976. I was seated in manager Jim Marshall's clubhouse office, seeking nuggets to write about after a 2-0, two-hit Cubs loss. Cardenal's seventh-inning single broke up a budding no-hitter for the Giants' Ed Halicki, and he wanted to make sure we saw something to remember him by during the upcoming All-Star break.

So into the office strolled Jose, wearing only an oversized Mexican sombrero, to wish the writers a jolly holiday. Unfortunately, the photographers for all four Chicago papers already had departed, but how could anyone stay mad at a good-natured guy like that, especially au naturel?

Well, nobody except Herman Franks. When Marshall spun out of the Cubs' revolving managerial chair a year later, and the roly-poly Herman spun in, Cardenal's antics no longer got guffaws. Exiled to Philadelphia in a trade, Jose delighted in re-kindling the feud, tormenting his ex-skipper by driving home seven runs in only 19 at-bats against the Cubs. When Franks gave the Phils' burly Bull Luzinski (later a flop for the White Sox in their 1984 playoff loss to Baltimore) an intentional pass to load the bases, Cardenal promptly emptied them, rifling a game-breaking double.

"All that hot dog knows how to do is cause trouble," Franks lamented.

Whatever he did, Jose got it done with crowd-pleasing flair.

NOT-SO-WILD THING

The wildest thing about Mitch Williams was his control, not his velocity. Try as they might to turn this fireballing Cubs relief pitcher into a superflake, straight out of Ring Lardner's classic baseball satire *You Know Me Al*, it didn't work. Williams was a left-hander, adding more spice to the fictional web spun by some writers, anxious to turn Williams into the Cubs' counterpart to William "The Refrigerator" Perry of the Bears. That might not have been all bad, because Perry, an amiable young man, turned into an overnight millionaire, thanks to coach Mike Ditka's decision to let the hulking defensive tackle score a touchdown on national TV.

But Williams was neither a flake nor a southpaw version of Dizzy Dean, the loquacious Cardinals pitcher who cheerfully gave each interviewer several likely spots for his birthplace, along with a smorgasbord of conflicting, confusing anecdotes about his rise to stardom. Mainly, Mitch was a pleasant young guy, trapped on the media treadmill because he came along at a time when the Cubs were contenders.

I can still see him, slouching in a corner of the dugout, trying to say what he thought the pursuing array of pens, pencils, tape reorders and microphones wanted from him. Later, when the media crowd thinned, the Wild Thing could relax and gab about stuff he really enjoyed, such as bowling and riding motorcycles.

Williams racked up 36 saves while manager Don Zimmer steered the Cubs into the 1989 NL playoffs. The fireballing southpaw did it the hard way in his Wrigley Field debut on Opening Day, entering in the ninth inning to yield three singles. Then, with the bases full of Phillies and no outs, he did the wild thing, driving Cubs fans wild by striking out the side, including longtime Cub-killer Mike Schmidt, to preserve a 5-4 victory.

Control problems turned many of Williams's save situations into Perils-of-Pauline horsehide operas, with the hero surviving lots of self-inflicted peril, at least in 1989. Unfortunately, as so often happens in baseball, he soon self-destructed, plummeting from atop the heap to the bottom of the pile.

"I'm trying not to overthrow," said Williams, who threw over the heads of quaking hitters more often than over the plate throughout a 1990 season he wanted to throw out.

No wonder. Hobbled by a knee injury, the suddenly Mild Thing walked 50 in only 66 1/3 innings, getting raked for 60 hits in the process. His record was a dismal 1-8 that year, with his save total sliced in half to 18. Williams never did bounce all the way back, eventually drifting to Philadelphia, where his career imploded with a cataclysm that gave renewed credence to the Big Bang theory. Ex-Cub Joe Carter set off a wild explosion in Toronto by nuking Williams's last pitch of the 1993 World Series over the fence in Game 6, giving the Blue Jays the second walk-off, Series-winning homer in Fall Classic annals. The other one? Bill Mazeroski's 1960 ninth-inning, seventh-game blast to stun the Yankees.

As always, Williams refused to alibi or hide from the media after that game. He admitted his confidence was shot and that his control probably deserved the same fate.

MUCH TOO FRANK

Stormy sojourns are nothing new for the Cubs. Neither is political incorrectness. Going all the way back to ancient history, the 19th century, their Hall of Fame player-manager, Cap Anson, refused to take the field against teams with black players in their lineup. No storms of protest greeted his stand, because that's the way it was then in baseball and most of American society.

But when temperamental Cubs pitcher Julian Taverez opened his mouth and inserted his foot, he picked both the wrong time and the wrong place. Enraged by heckling from fans at San Francisco's Pac Bell Park on April 28, 2001, the right-hander erupted after a tough 2-1 loss to the Giants. Angrily shrugging off the booing he got throughout the game, he went totally off his John Rocker.

"These fans are *bleeps* and *bleeps*," Tavarez fumed, refusing to retract his derogatory terms for gay men and women, even though onlookers warned him such language would stir up a storm in San Francisco, a haven for alternative lifestyles.

Not since Cubs manager Lee Elia roasted Wrigley Field fans ("They can kiss my *bleep*") 18 years earlier, on April 29, 1983, had a postgame tantrum backfired so badly. The reaction to Tavarez's childish fit of pique was so harsh that Cubs manager Don Baylor had to kick off damage-control efforts almost immediately. Baylor sat down with the native of the Dominican Republic and put his freedom of speech on a short leash, something totally at odds with Tavarez's tendency to shoot from the lip.

So phase one of the spin solution began when Tavarez held court the next day with Chicago and San Francisco writers. Basically, the baffled pitcher used the same defense Dizzy Dean employed when Cards manager Frankie Frisch jumped him after the colorful pitcher got picked off first base.

"Frankie, I musta gone into a transom," Dean said.

Because there was no way to deny his words, especially after they became the lead story, even on network news broadcasts, all Tavarez could do was backpedal.

"I didn't mean it," he said. "My emotions got in the way, and I'm totally sorry. I want to apologize to San Francisco and the Cubs and everybody who was offended by what I said."

Anxious to avoid another John Rocker-style uproar, commissioner Bud Selig's office issued a tut-tut, tsk-tsk statement, along with the obligatory suspension for Tavarez, plus a fine, donated to organizations serving the groups he had slurred. As soon as they could, the Cubs unloaded Tavarez, the same fate that had befallen Elia soon after his 1983 outburst.

HARD-LUCK BUCKNER

Nobody could question Bill Buckner's work ethic. His judgment? That's another matter. An intense, competitive guy, Buckner hustled, scrapped, and clawed for everything, sometimes too hard.

He was a big-league hitter for eight eventful Cub seasons (1977-84), but his ego got him into frequent hot water. His image got pummeled by a series of strange escapades, notably a deserved mauling in 1982 from Cubs manager Lee Elia after Buckner called pitcher Dan Larson "a gutless so-and-so." It happened on the bench during a game in—where else?—San Diego, with TV cameras relaying the blow by blow to Chicago for a late, late show.

Buckner and Herman Franks also got into a remarkably silly name-calling contest when the Cubs manager stepped down in 1979. Mainly, they served to reinforce the notion that some ballplayers are overgrown, as well as overpaid, kids, exchanging taunts on the playground.

"Buckner goes nuts if he doesn't get a hit every game, regardless if the Cubs won or lost," Franks snorted. "Herman's a fat clown," Buckner retorted.

Hitless or not, handsome Buckner was a hit with female fans. Even hard-core bleacherites admired the way he played through the pain of ankle operations and assorted injuries. They all would have turned on him, though, if Buckner had told them what he really thought of Wrigley Field before leaving town.

"I hate this place," he confessed. "Wrigley Field plays with your mind, especially when the wind blows in day games. That's practically all the time. It's the worst place in baseball, but the fans are great."

HILL OF A BLAST

Did Glenallen Hill propel the longest ever Wrigley Field home run? And did it really soar 451.2 feet, as the Chicago Sun-Times claimed after hiring surveyors to track Hill's titanic clout on May 11, 2000?

That was a little less than the 490-foot distance estimated by the Cubs at the time Hill unloaded on a delivery from Steve Woodard of the Milwaukee Brewers. And a lot less than Hill figured.

"Hey, I hit that ball 700 feet," the muscular outfielder said.

One glance at Hill's bulging biceps could have convinced some of us overweight, out-of-shape diamond scribes that he was capable of propelling a pitch into nearby Lake Michigan, if the fickle Wrigley winds happened to be blowing toward the fences. Whatever the distance, it was a formidable poke, clearing the screen in back of the left-field bleachers, soaring majestically across Waveland Avenue and bouncing on the roof of a brick apartment building across the street.

How far it went, or would have gone if it had landed unimpeded, is anyone's guess. That's just fine with the trio of Cubs employees who list homer distances on the scoreboard. Wayne Messmer, the golden-throated vocalist who turns his rendition of the Nation Anthem into an instant July 4th celebration, huddles with his co-PA announcer, Paul Friedman, and Gary Pressy, the Wrigley Field organist. On homers hit into the stands, they add three feet of distance for each row deeper. But Hill's homer, Messmer cheerfully agrees, will remain a Cubs trivia topic and a matter of conjecture for the bleacher creatures and all Cub fans. It should give Hill a convincing argument whenever ex-Cubs gather to rehash all those strange goings-on in the Friendly Confines. Every year, as Cubs Hall of Famer Billy Williams pointed out, "All our homers get 100 feet longer."

With or without the extra distance, Hill qualifies as a Cubs character, even though he wasn't around all that long in two separate stints during the '90s. He liked to hold court in the clubhouse, pontificating on a potpourri of subjects, always with his short-sleeved T-shirt rolled up to display those Mike Tyson-sized arm muscles. When Hill slammed a 3-0 pitch from Mets closer John Franco for a game-winning pinch homer on July 26, 1988, he was ready for the postgame media invasion.

"I don't think I can hit a ball harder than that one," he said of the payoff shot into the center field bleachers. "Just like a snake layin' in the weeds, I was ready."

But Hill's defensive liabilities made him expendable, so a week after Cubs president Andy MacPhail tapped himself to replace embattled general manager Ed Lynch, Hill got dealt to the Yankees on July 21, 2000, for a couple of minor-leaguers.

"If I start reflecting on my Chicago memories, you'll see a 235-pound man cry," was Hill's farewell salute.

Chapter 4

CUBBY BLUE, WE LOVE YOU

Cubs fans come in all shapes, sizes, ages, sexes, nationalities, races and occupations, regardless of social class, high school class or total lack of class. It's a wholly democratic (Republicans allowed, too) equal-opportunity fraternity, dedicated to the proposition that all Cubs fans are created equal, with the same virtually limitless capacity for frustration. Regardless of where they come from, this band of brothers and sisters comes together every year on Opening Day, united in the belief that the unbeaten Cubs will stay that way— at least until later that afternoon.

Wealth and status can't inoculate anyone with an antidote to Cub Fever, a rampaging virus that's been known to bring Chicago (except for stubborn pockets of South Side immunity) to its knees. Fan clubs run the same eclectic gamut, from the snobby Emil Verban Society, mostly a bunch of power-lunch-ingWashington, D.C. dilettantes, to the Wild Bunch, a band of beer-guzzling diehards hanging out at Bernie's saloon, right across Clark Street from the ballpark. The most famous group of all was the Left Field Bleacher Bums, emerging in the late '60s to swear allegiance to Cubs manager Leo Durocher and swear at anyone fearless or foolish enough to trample on Wrigley's sacred turf while wearing the uniform of a visiting team. Standards have changed in America since the 1960s—unhappily, not for the better—so the verbal, and perhaps actual, bile dumped on opponents by the Bums was not nearly as vile as the language hurled at them nowadays, even from some box-seat bellowers.

Still, the Bleacher Bums' exploits became the stuff of Wrigleyville legend, and some of the outrageous stunts attributed to them actually did happen. Just like the lengths of players' homers after they retire, stories of malicious mischief in the bleachers tend to escalate with the passing years. Through it all, though, the constant element has been the unswerving, undying loyalty of Cubs fans. Together or singly, in packs or slacks or cutoff jeans or bare-chested (this brand of ultimate fan is all male, at least so far), the Wrigley royal rooters keep coming, keep hoping and keep soaking up the magnificent mixture of suds and sunshine that annually adds new chapters to the lore—and lure—of Wrigley Field.

MOODY MOVEMENT

If the Cubs win, the mood is lighter and so is the exit traffic. Cubs fans linger longer in their seats, savoring the sunshine and what Jack Brickhouse used to call the "happy totals" on the center field scoreboard. A totally different karma fills the air, as noticeable as the fog that sometimes shrouds the place in spring or fall, if the Cubs lose. In that event, the exodus tends to be quicker and gloomier. Instead of departing with loud, surly second-guesses of their team's misfortune, Cubs fans seem to exhale a collective sigh of regret, trudging out in resigned silence.

Soon after, their irrepressible optimism triggers the bounce-back process, sometimes within minutes. Before they reach home, the friendly confines of the Cubby Bear Lounge, Bernie's Saloon or some other Wrigleyville oasis, the real diehards are already regenerating the optimism that seems to be the native state and lifelong fate of Cubs fans. Over the years, I've heard them say basically the same thing again and again, in slightly different terms, on the way out of Wrigley Field:

"I wish the Cubs had better [hitting, pitching, fielding, or whatever combination was lacking that day], but this is a great place to see a game."

ONE BIG HOPEFUL FAMILY

Cubs fans agree their affliction is a terminal disease. Highly contagious, too. It's passed along from grandfathers and grandmothers to moms and dads to sons and daughters and on and on, with no discernable generation gap. Whenever I hear bunches of them talking among themselves, the dialogue is strikingly similar to the same stuff emerging from the mouths of 1969 survivors. Those fans didn't blame the players then. Now, more than three decades later, the voices of former Bleacher Bums still ooze nostalgia when they recall that smooth-as-silk infield—Ernie Banks, Glenn Beckert, Don Kessinger, Ron Santo—Sweet Swinger Billy Williams, fiery catcher Randy "Rebel" Hundley, or pitchers Fergie Jenkins, Ken Holtzman, and bullpen cutup Dick Selma.

GABBY ABOUT BABE

A longtime Cubs fan named Bob Callahan was one of the fortunate few to be connected personally with the two most famous home runs in Wrigley Field's storied history. Younger Cubs fans will talk about Sammy Sosa's historic 60th and 61st homers, both at the Friendly Confines on the same day, September 13, 1998. They also savor Slammin' Sammy's September 18, 1999, blast off teammate-to-be Jason Bere, making him the first big-leaguer ever to swat 60 home runs in two seasons.

Others can't forget the hysteria triggered by Gary Gaetti's clutch two-run homer on September 28, 1998, sending the Cubs to a 5-3 victory over San Francisco. The Cubs and Giants met in a Wrigley Field first that night—a one-game playoff for the NL wild-card berth. Cubs fans celebrated the victory as though their team had just won a World Series game, though any chance of that got snuffed out in a three-game Atlanta Braves sweep in the first round of the playoffs.

Or how about Ryne Sandberg's back-to-back home runs in the ninth and 10th innings on June 23, 1984? Ryno's heroics earned the ultimate tribute from Cards manager Whitey Herzog: "Here comes Baby Ruth." Throw in Willie Smith's two-run pinch homer in the 11th inning on Opening Day, 1969—Jack Brickhouse's personal favorite—to beat the Phillies, 7-6. And the three straight round-trippers by Karl "Tuffy" Rhodes of the Cubs on Opening Day, 1994.

But the real Babe Ruth stands tallest on the list for his "called shot" World Series homer. In Game 3, on October 1, 1932, Ruth swaggered to the plate in the fifth inning, pointed to the center field bleachers and parked Cubs pitcher Charlie Root's next serve in that spot, sending the Yankees toward a 4-0 sweep. Of course, diehard Cubs fans insist that catcher-manager Gabby Hartnett's celebrated Homer in the Gloaming, as darkness shrouded Wrigley Field on September 28, 1938, was more important. It beat Pittsburgh, 6-5, and put the Cubs in first place, enabling them to edge the Pirates in a tight NL pennant race.

That's where Bob Callahan comes in. He was a Wrigley Field spectator for Ruth's called shot, insisting that's exactly what the Bambino did.

"I saw Babe point to the stands and hit the ball where he said he would," Callahan related.

Years later, Callahan told me of the day he played golf with Hartnett, who was behind the plate for the Cubs in that '32 World Series. Both men agreed it was too dark to play ball in Wrigley Field when Gabby connected for his all-time clutch Cub homer in 1938. When asked if Ruth really pointed with his bat toward the bleachers, as Callahan and some Wrigley Field spectators swore he did—while others, including Root, swore he didn't—Hartnett merely smiled.

"We're talking about Babe Ruth here," the Hall of Fame catcher said. "Some people like to tear down legends, but I'm not one of them."

RAISING THE ROOF

Short of hitting the Illinois Lottery jackpot, one of the best investments in the last quarter-century has been Wrigleyville real estate. This little slice of turf, about one square mile, nestled inside a Chicago neighborhood called Lake View, became a gold mine for some speculators along with individual investors. The mother lode of this bonanza sits on one block of Waveland Avenue and another on Sheffield Avenue. These fortunate three-flats offer a view of Cubs games from their rooftops—Waveland behind the left field bleachers and Sheffield in center and right. Who knew, back when economic times were tough in the mid-'70s and the Cubs' self-imposed postseason boycott stretched on year after year that those aging apartments would become cash-cow centers of controversy?

Buildings that sold for just over $80,000 in that era now are worth millions, embroiled in legal warfare with the Tribune Company over their right to sell rooftop seats for Cubs games. It's trendy to roost up there, so the in crowd snaps up those

Rooftop fans across the street from Wrigley Field watch an enemy homer soar toward them. They're used to dodging brickbats in the legal battle with the Cubs over the big bucks people pay to see games from those perches.

outside perches, the ultimate in viewer chic, paying more than they would to get inside Wrigley Field. Responding to a lawsuit filed by the Cubs, alleging that rooftop owners "unjustly enrich themselves," 13 of the landlords pointed out that they've been licensed by the city of Chicago since 1998, paying taxes on the big bucks they rake in. The ongoing court battle finally got settled.

Rooftop owners kept renting out their lucrative game-day glimpses of Wrigley action, with 12 houses—a half-dozen each on Waveland Avenue (left field) and Sheffield Avenue (right field)—designated as "rooftop partners" of the Tribune Company's ivy-covered money tree. In return, the Cubs got approval for 1,790 more bleacher seats, the most prestigious place of all for fanatical fans to park their fannies. Along with other improvements, the spiffed-up, beefed-up 2006 version of Wrigley Field was scheduled to debut on Opening Day.

"Roof rights" to some buildings with a view are owned by a company that rents to groups throwing upscale—and upstairs—tailgate parties for as much as $10,000 per game. That includes catering service and an open bar. Single rooftop tickets can go for more than $100, higher on weekends.

VERBAN TO REAGAN TO WHITE HOUSE

Emil Verban played in one World Series during his undistinguished big-league career. It was in 1944, a year before the Cubs made their final 20th-century appearance in the Fall Classic. Verban made the most of his one shot, batting a hefty .417 on seven singles in 17 trips—better than Stan Musial's .304—in pacing the Cards to a six-game victory over the Browns, the only all-St. Louis World Series. By the time the second baseman got to the Cubs in 1948, the postseason was only a fond memory for him and them.

Verban did stroke his only homer in the majors as a Cub, ending his career with one for 2,911 in the round-tripper column.

So it seemed fitting for an exclusive band of Cubs fans, including former President Ronald Reagan, to label themselves the Emil Verban Society. Reagan, who recreated Cubs games via Western Union ticker for radio station WHO in Des Moines during the 1930s, hosted Verban at a White House meeting of his fan club. Cubs fans really do come in all shapes, sizes, social strata, and political persuasions.

DR. ERNIE PRESCRIBES...

When Ernie Banks visited the 2003 Cubs fan convention, he got the same riotous reception they give him whenever and wherever the Hall of Fame shortstop/first baseman appears. In between signing autographs on caps, his familiar No. 14 jersey and just about anything thrust at him by older fans, who remember him well, and younger ones, who never saw him play, Mr. Cub reflected on today's changing expectations.

"Even Cubs fans can't live only on love any more," Banks told me. "They need to be rewarded by watching a winning team. In my career, just playing in front of those Wrigley Field rooters every day was like being in the World Series. Their loyalty to the Cubs made me feel the same way toward them and Mr. [Phil] Wrigley, who did everything he could to bring Chicago a winner.

"So the way they stuck with us, win or lose, mattered more than anything else. But times have changed. The fans today want success."

AND SOME WANT EXCESS

Banks was right on both counts. New Age Cubs fans might not totally share the win-or-else fervor sweeping through all sports at all levels, but they're much less willing to accept mediocrity. And Wrigley Field, for decades an oasis of tranquility in a tidal wave of fan upheaval, now has to deal with occasional outbursts from rowdies in the stands. The ugliest incident in recent years erupted on May 17, 2000, in the ninth inning of a 6-5 Cubs loss to the Dodgers.

In a nutshell, heckling directed at the visitors' bullpen escalated into throwing hot dog buns, not-entirely-empty beer cups and eventually punches at the Dodgers sitting there, with their backs to the stands. One of the victims, ex-White Sox catcher Chad Kreuter, got punched in the head while his cap was being stolen. Kreuter made an unwise decision, chasing the capnapper into the stands, followed by truculent teammates, to trigger a fist-swinging brawl. Fortunately, no skulls got fractured, although the inevitable aftermath was another battle royale of conflicting finger-pointing and blame-dodging. It was followed by hefty fines and suspensions for Los Angeles players and coaches involved in the melee, plus cash settlements for alleged injuries to other participants.

The major victim was Wrigley Field's time-honored tradition of harmless fun at the old ballpark. With heightened security and more restrictions on fan access to the players, the Friendly Confines began to look a little like Fort Wrigley—an outcome deplored by the vast majority of real Cubs fans.

"It's hard to put a happy face on things like this," admitted Cubs president Andy MacPhail. "I hope this is not the new reality, but whatever it is, we have to deal with it."

ROCKER AND ROLLING

Actually, not much fan unrest in this new era of victory celebrations often marked by overturned, burning cars and shattered store windows was first seen in or around Wrigley Field. The genteel family and fan-friendly tradition of the Wrigley family, especially P. K.'s insistence on having 15,000 or more seats for sale on game days, had something to do with that. So did the obvious charm of their ballpark, a place that blended the relaxed atmosphere of a summer picnic with baseball.

In my first 20 years of Cubs coverage, it's hard to recall much violence, aside from the sort perpetrated by visiting hitters on Cubs pitchers when the wind blew out. Before then, even with the winds of change blowing across America, sparking upheaval and unrest during the Vietnam war, Cubs fans were too busy celebrating the excitement of self-proclaimed managerial genius Leo Durocher's bid to win pennants.

Leo the Lip made a lot of noise but couldn't steer a star-studded team into the playoffs. The late fade of 1969 shaped the attitudes of many young Cubs fans, tempering their diehard loyalty with a blend of resigned reality.

But Wrigley Field's idyllic image could not hold out forever. Jack Brickhouse's mellow voice got replaced by Harry Caray's rallying cry—"You can't beat fun at the old ballpark!" Harry certainly was not a member of the MTV generation, and his passion was baseball, not the Woodstock lifestyle. Regardless, the gap between older and younger fans on the definition of "fun" widened considerably, resulting in a few escapades that raised eyebrows in and out of Wrigleyville. Unruly conduct sometimes went beyond the innocent fun of Yuppie-style streakers dashing harmlessly, if revealingly, through the outfield.

THE BEEF GOES ON

Cubs fans weren't whistling "Dixie" when John Rocker slouched into Wrigley Field on May 29, 2000. It was Memorial Day, but what everybody remembered on this visit was the way the loose-lipped pitcher had opened his mouth and inserted his foot, displaying monumental stupidity.

The closer for the Atlanta Braves almost closed his own career by unleashing a tirade against various minorities and even one of his own teammates. It appeared in Sports Illustrated, earning Rocker a hefty fine and suspension and baseball some unwelcome publicity. Understandably, beefed-up security forces were on full alert wherever the Braves went after Rocker returned to their bullpen. That was especially true in Wrigley Field, still reeling from the charge of the Dodger Blue brigade into the stands less than two weeks earlier.

That altercation had broken out in the same right field bullpen area where Rocker took a seat with the Braves' relief crew. In the interim, beer sales were cut off earlier, chug-a-lugs per customer limited and area vendors reduced, so thirsty would-be hecklers at least would have to walk off some of their alcohol-induced ire. Kevin Hallinan, baseball's boss cop, was in Wrigley Field for Rocker's appearance, an indication that commissioner Bud Selig believed both the game and the rowdy fans got a black eye in the Dodger rumble.

"The commissioner could end all that by ruling any player who goes into the stands for any reason automatically gets suspended for one year," prescribed Atlanta manager Bobby Cox.

The Braves' skipper had no way of knowing he'd be thrown off the field, while Rocker sat it out peacefully, for harassing the umps. Neither man was needed, because ex-Cub Greg Maddux tormented his old team, 1-0. Pitching in typical tough luck, Cubs starter Jon Lieber spun a perfect game until Andres Galarraga's two-out homer in the seventh inning.

THE ROAR OF '84

The Cubs' collapse in San Diego, where they struck out three straight times to end that agonizing NL Championship Series right where they started—one game short of the World Series—was the true test of their fans' mettle. Of all the painful episodes in baseball history, that weekend has to rank up there with the worst.

Before the crash, the Cubs and their fans were flying high. Just like the Super Bowl-bound Bears did a year later, the players recorded their version of the "Super Bowl Shuffle." The baseball rendition was a country-western foot-stomper called "Men in Blue," with Rick Sutcliffe, Jody Davis, Leon Durham, Keith Moreland, and Gary Woods vocalizing. A few lines from the lyrics:

"It's been a long time since 1945, but the Wrigley Field faithful always kept the spirit alive,

"And now's the time and here's the place we even up the score,

"The hopes are high, the pennant will fly over Wrigley in '84,

"And as sure as there's ivy on the center field wall, the men in blue are going to win it all."

That prediction by those Tribune Company employees proved just as accurate as the *Chicago Tribune*'s banner headline—"Dewey Defeats Truman"—about the outcome of the 1948 presidential election. The Cubs led in the standings, just like Thomas E. Dewey led in the polls, but victory predictions for both turned out to be monumental goofs. At least, the losing 1984 Cubs evoked an outpouring of sympathy in Chicago and all over America. Harry Caray's flamboyant style made him a household word—and the Cubs household faces—all over the country.

"People have adopted the Cubs," Caray told me during that upbeat season. "The ones living far away can't get to Chicago, so they show up in Atlanta, Houston, Cincinnati, or wherever we play, holding up bedsheets and banners with the Cub logo, wearing Cub hats and waving Cub pennants. If I read all the Go-Cubs notes they send to the TV booth, I wouldn't have time to broadcast the game."

FANS FAN THE FLAME

In the end, just about the only people not waving a 1984 pennant were the Cubs themselves. Regardless, Cubs fans refused to give up on them after that playoff disaster. Ditto for the playoff setbacks of 1989 and 1998. Adversity seems only to toughen their battered hides and renew their weary spirits. One of the most remarkable things about Cubs loyalists, to me at least, is the way they seem frozen in time.

The rest of the country and the whole world, for that matter, changes by the minute in rapid-fire sequences. Yet the way these people feel about their baseball team, and the pleasure they derive from sticking with it, win, lose or tie, remains the same. I honestly don't know why, but any objective observer would have to conclude Cubs fans are the blue-ribbon champions of undying, although not always unquestioning, loyalty.

THEY LOVE IVY AND SAMMY

Maybe the most remarkable thing about Cubs fans is the way they express their emotional attachment. Almost universally, it's evenly divided between Wrigley Field and the players. That equation never seems to change. Every time I start to write a book about the Cubs, I dig out notebooks, scraps of paper, and dog-eared scorecards with quotes from fans, going all the way back to 1970. Other files, newspaper clips, and similar sources, some as far back as the World Series of 1908—their last 20th-

century postseason victory—contain remarkably similar sentiments about the players of that era.

But almost as soon as the Cubs moved into Weeghman Park
in 1916, the place that's been home to them ever since, the players had a rival for the affection of their supporters. It was the
ballpark, where fans have remained so close to the action that
they can relate to it more than anywhere else. I went to the 2003
Cubs Convention to see if a new generation of fans had emerged
to salute the dawn of the Dusty Baker era. Here's what I found:

One of my all-time favorite Cubs fans was there early, waiting patiently for encouraging words from new manager Baker,
anxious for some autographs and ever-hopeful that the breakthrough year is at hand, at last. He's Casey Knapp, a wheelchair-
bound youngster from Lake Geneva, Wisconsin, who qualifies
as a Cubs fanatic in all categories, especially optimism. And like
most of the conventioneers, his affection is equally divided between Wrigley Field, Sammy Sosa, and any other bodies draped
in Cubbie Blue.

"It's such a fan-friendly ballpark," Casey said of Wrigley.
"Going to a game there is more fun."

Wayne Wysocki grew up on the South Side, but now lives in
Munster, Indiana, closer to Chicago's Loop than some Northwest suburbs. He's living proof that geography is no impedi-
ment to Cubmania.

"White Sox fans were all around us when I was a kid,"
Wysocki said. "But my Dad was a Cub fan and he made sure I
turned into one. I guess there's no way you can stop rooting for
the team that Ernie Banks played for."

Charlotte Santore and Carol Berg live in far-apart suburbs,
but shared affection for the Cubs lures these longtime friends to
the ballpark. So does a chance for close-up looks at their favorite
players in skin-tight double-knit pants.

"I love the park and I miss Mark Grace," Berg said. "The way
he dug throws out of the dirt at first base saved Shawon Dunston a lot of errors, and he's a good-looking guy."

"Going to Wrigley Field is always exciting," Santore chimed in. "It's a great way to spend an afternoon, even when the Cubs don't win."

Individual touches on Cubs attire enable fans to add some style to their rooting. Heads swivel in the stands whenever the guys from Kenosha, Wisconsin, show up wearing their snappy Cubs caps adorned with moose ears. They claim it's a tribute to Moose Moryn, the outfielder who saved Don Cardwell's Wrigley Field no-hitter on May 15, 1960, with a diving, two-out catch in the ninth inning. Whatever, Bill Chase, Greg Picazo, Bob Rubeck, Jeff Galligan and all that gang are certified Cubs maniacs. So are Phil Ertel and his three sons, posing for pictures in their Cubs shirts after driving from Cary, North Carolina, to soak up more Cubs lore.

CUB ONE, CUB ALL

They come in all shapes and sizes, from everywhere under the sun. The old Die-Hard Fan Club and yesteryear's hangout, Ray's Bleachers, have been replaced by today's Wild Bunch, which hangs out at Bernie's bar. The names and faces change, but Cubs loyalty exists, persists, and refuses to desist. The way it is gets summed up for all of them by Deborah Martinez, a true blue North Sider.

"Take the Cubbies out of Wrigley Field, and it wouldn't be the same," she said. "If they played in a new stadium, I'd have to go see them, but it wouldn't be as much fun."

Yes, you can't beat fun and sun or moon, day or night, in this old ballpark.

Chapter 5

TOWERS OF CUBS POWER

The Cubs have enough Hall of Fame performers, past, present, and future, to keep them busy polishing plaques. Their own Walk of Fame, moved inside Wrigley Field to make space for all those tributes to the growing list of memorable Cubs, adds a pleasant pregame trip to the tradition that bonds generations of fans.

So far, 42 Hall of Famers with at least some Cub connections adorn the walls of the baseball museum in picturesque Cooperstown, New York, a sleepy village that seems frozen in the era when James Fenimore Cooper wrote his legendary Leatherstocking Tales about this upstate area. That group grew in 2005, with second baseman Ryne Sandberg taking his deserved place among baseball's immortals. I was surprised, although not shocked, when Ryno didn't make it on the first ballot.

Members of the Baseball Writers Association of America are eligible to vote after covering the big leagues for 10 years, a chore I take seriously. It seems likely Sammy Sosa's entry to the Hall will be delayed when the ex-Cub slugger's career ends. Although rumors of steroid use by Sosa have not been proven, that cloud of suspicion, plus the corked bat episode that speeded his departure from Chicago, ended Sammy's long honeymoon with Wrigley's right-field bleacher creatures. Eventually, Sosa should get there.

Ron Santo belongs, as well, because he passed the major test of consistently outstanding performance at third base and at bat for the Cubs. I'm surprised the Old Timers committee didn't let him join Cubs buddies Ernie Banks, Billy Williams, and Fergie Jenkins in 2003. Pitchers Lee Smith and Bruce Sutter, along with outfielder Andre Dawson, spent significant parts of their careers with the Cubs, and all three are good bets to get there sooner or later. Among the serious candidates now eligible for the Hall of Fame, pitcher Rich "Goose" Gossage had more success with the White Sox and other teams, so Cubs fans don't consider him one of their own.

LONG ROAD AHEAD

It's too early to tell whether the potential of Cubs right-handers Kerry Wood and Mark Prior will translate into enough victories to make them viable candidates, especially with the arm trouble that seems to plague all hard-throwing pitchers. But Cubs fans have their own Hall of Fame. Such longtime favorites as Santo, "Hawk" Dawson, catcher Randy "The Rebel" Hundley, pitchers Rick Sutcliffe and Rick Reuschel, and shortstop Don Kessinger might not make it to Cooperstown, but their fame is secure in Wrigleyville. Real Cubs fans tend to go for players fitting the tradition and lifestyle of Wrigley Field—gamers who enjoy the ivy on the walls and the electricity of this unique ballpark.

Two classy right-handers, Greg Maddux and Jon Lieber, would have qualified. Sadly, Maddux fled to Atlanta when the Cubs wouldn't pay him what he was worth—a Chicago sports blunder rivaled only by the Blackhawks letting Bobby Hull get away in 1972—and arm woes cut short Lieber's stay. Still, superstars are much more plentiful than pennants for the Cubs, especially since 1945. For instance:

SAMMY SLAMMED

Sosa's reign as Chicago's most popular sports figure since Michael Jordan ended abruptly on February 2, 2005, when he got shipped to the Baltimore Orioles for versatile Jerry Hairston and a couple of guys named Joe—a sad ending for a Chicago career that took fans to the heights during Slamming Sammy's tenure.

"Sammy was kind of a wild kid in his younger days," said Gene Lamont, who had just been named White Sox manager in 1992 when Sosa got traded to the Cubs. "I could see he'd be good eventually, but nobody thought he could hit 60 homers or become the superstar he is now."

Sosa's first Sox manager, Jeff Torborg, got a glimpse of that raw, untapped potential. In his 1989 Sox debut against the Twins, Sosa lashed a two-run homer, a pair of singles, and even walked twice.

"Sammy swung at a lot of ball-four pitches and dropped some catchable fly balls, but you could see all that ability, just waiting to come out," Torborg said.

What made the difference for Sosa was his willingness to work on his weaknesses. He made himself into an adequate, if not spectacular, guardian of Wrigley Field's tricky patch of right-field turf, learning how to cope with glaring sun and treacherous winds. It was as a hitter, though, that Sosa made giant strides, electrifying the entire country with his titanic 1998 home run duel that the Cards' Mark McGwire eventually won, 70-66.

His incredible June of 1998, a 20-homer rampage that smashed all long-distance records for a single month, propelled Sosa to international celebrity status, and he rode that multimedia horse until the corked bat caper.

Sammy Sosa adds another homer to the career bag that should reward him with a Hall of Fame plaque.

Some breathless pundits actually tapped Sosa and McGwire as baseball's twin saviors because they bashed a combined 136 homers in their fence-busting derby. That was more than a slight exaggeration, although both sluggers spun a merry turnstile tune everywhere they went, diminishing some leftover fan enmity from the bitter strike-walkout that erased the 1994 World Series.

WOOD HE KERRY THE CUBS?

Yes, he Wood—if he could. Cubs fans can't help wondering what might have been if Kerry Wood's right arm, perhaps the deadliest weapon in Chicago sports since Bobby Hull's slap shot, had stayed sound.

It didn't, of course. Wood missed all of 1999 to recover from Tommy John surgery on a torn ligament in his right elbow. Many Cubs fans feel that if only Wood was a trifle less competitive and more willing just to pick up a paycheck, instead of playing hurt, things could have been different. That's not Wood. His insistence on starting Game 3 of the 1998 NL playoff with Atlanta, despite that ailing elbow, was a bad decision, but the one he wanted to make. For the Cubs and Wood, that raw, windy night was another Wrigley Field reenactment of Custer's last stand.

Obviously toiling, Wood somehow pitched a gritty five innings, yielding just one run on three hits—and still lost, completing a three-game sweep for the Braves. Could it be that Wood's most magnificent moment, a 20-strikeout Wrigley whitewash of the Houston Astros on May 6, 1998, triggered the damage that forced the right-hander to undergo career-threatening surgery the following spring?

A chart of Wood's 122 pitches (84 for strikes) in that awesome effort clocked more than 30 of his fastballs at 95-plus miles per hour, with a couple of them at or above 100 MPH. For a 20-year-old kid in his first big-league season, even this muscular phenom, elbow-wrenching curves and sliders take more of a toll than than unhittable heat.

Wood doesn't want to talk about such stuff. Mainly, he wants to pitch—and win—for the Cubs.

"I don't want to make excuses," he said. "The Cubs haven't been winning, and I take my share of responsibility. Our fans won't stop hoping, no matter how much we let them down."

Wood's struggles, especially with control, since he came back to the starting rotation in 1999 have been frustrating. Mixed with flashes of true greatness, he's had wild spells, walking too many batters and falling behind in the count to others. Even pitchers with Wood's smoke get burned when they have to throw fastballs over the plate.

NO PRIOR RESTRAINT

Kerry Wood might have thought he was watching a Wrigley Field videotape on May 22, 2002. At times, this looked like a rerun of K-K-K-Kerry's demolition job on Houston four seasons earlier. Well, not quite.

Cubs rookie Mark Prior struck out a mere 10 Pittsburgh Pirates in six innings, only half of Wood's total against the Astros. And this game was at night, unlike the sunlit afternoon that seemed to be lighting up Wood's can't-miss Hall of Fame prospects. Regardless, Prior showed the same sort of unlimited potential on this eye-opening spring evening that had been displayed by Wood on his 20-K day.

Bleacher fans got just as excited, too, pinning those paper Ks up on the back screen as Prior's total swelled. At last, the Cubs boasted No. 1 and No. 1-A starters to trot out for Dusty Baker's 2003 managerial debut. They're both right-handers with level heads and crackling fastballs. All the Cubs can do is hope Prior doesn't keep facing the run of misfortune that's pared more than a year off Wood's career, to mend from elbow and shoulder surgery.

For his part, Prior didn't bring the typical rookie's "Gulp, gee whiz" demeanor up to the majors with him. Even a cool customer like Wood confessed that his knees were shaking when he took the Wrigley Field mound for the first time in 1998. Not Prior.

"I've pitched under pressure," said the 2001 national college Player of the Year after beating the Pirates 7-4 in his Cub debut. "I didn't feel pressure tonight. Pitchers should concentrate on winning every inning, because that's the way to win every start. If you keep your mind on that, there's no time to get distracted."

Pretty blasé stuff for a 21-year-old who only a year earlier was pitching for USC, where baseball ranks far behind football, surfing, tanning, bikini-watching, and numerous other sunny California pastimes.

Impressed, Wood welcomed his new rival for ace status on the Cubs by remarking, "He's a lot more prepared than I was to step right in."

MEDIA SANDBAGS SANDBERG

Ryne Sandberg's brilliance got plenty of appreciation from Cubs fans. It was well deserved. For 15 years, from 1982 through 1997, he was as consistent at bat and in the field as the Cubs were in the NL standings. He was mostly up; they were mostly down.

For me, at least, Ryno's success story provided one of the major puzzles in all my years of Chicago hoop, grid, and diamond scribing. It seemed the longer he did his job with such understated efficiency, the less media appreciation he got. When another No. 23, a fellow by the name of Jordan, showed early every night before games in Chicago Stadium and later in the United Center to perfect his laser jumpers from every angle, his work ethic rated raves from writers, radio, and TV.

Yet hours before every Cubs game, their No. 23 would be out there around his second base turf, taking grounder after grounder. His brilliant fielding was no accident—or error—though few seemed to notice.

"I have a routine before every game," Sandberg told me. "Grounders to my left and right, some double-play pivots. Wrigley Field has high grass, so the ball gets through a lot faster in other parks, but you have to practice every day on cutting down the angle. I know what pitch is coming [because he can see the catcher's signs] and I know the hitters. I still have to work at it all the time."

This from a man who fielded his position better than anybody I've ever seen, with a major-league record of 123 straight errorless games, from June 21, 1989 to May 17, 1990, to prove it. Sandberg's range was astonishing, especially on shots up the middle. Old-time fans still talk about the play Jackie Robinson made against the Phillies to delay the Whiz Kids' 1950 pennant-clinching, but Sandberg turned in such semi-miraculous stops so often that they seemed routine.

"Whatever Ryne hit was a bonus," said Harry Caray. "Everything a second baseman has to do, he was near the top in all of them. And he was the Cubs' leader by setting an example of coming to work every day, instead of the showboating and arm-waving you see now."

Yet when Sandberg signed a five-year contract worth over $30 million in 1992, the uproar drowned out the daily exploits of this latter-day Quiet Man. The wails of some Chicago columnists and electronic shouters was so loud, it sounded like they had to pay his salary. Above and beyond that, with the emergence of charismatic Sammy Sosa and the presence of quotable Mark Grace, Sandberg's reluctance to hold court at his locker actually seemed to be resented by some of the media.

"He has no personality," was the most frequent grumble, even though Sandberg answered all questions and never stalked away from the postgame grilling in a huff, like some of his temperamental teammates (Danny Jackson, Scott Servais, and Delino DeShields, to name a few) did when they had bad games.

When Sandberg retired abruptly in midseason, 1994, sat out a year, then came back to play two more seasons, he got bashed for both decisions. I still can't understand why, any more than the reasoning that led less than half of the eligible voters (he got only 49.2 percent) to agree this obvious Hall of Famer should make it in 2003, his first year of eligibility. Regardless, his 1996-1997 swan song produced 37 more homers, enough to become the all-time leader at second base with 277 (plus five more as a third baseman). That, along with 2,386 hits—all except one as a Cub—nine straight Gold Glove awards and a 1984 NL Most Valuable Player Award bought Ryno a Hall of Fame ticket to ride.

GRACE SELDOM OFF BASE

Mark Grace always knew the score and how to play the game, on and off the field. That's what made him a Chicago favorite for a dozen years as the Cubs' first-base fixture. When he opted for free agency, to finally get a 2001 World Series ring from the Arizona Diamondbacks, it marked a turn-of-the-century farewell to all that.

Grace's Cubs lost more than they won, but he knew how to make it more Graceful. Besides banging out more base hits (1,754) than any other big-leaguer during the 1990s, he probably was the biggest clubhouse hit. Sammy Sosa was the emerging superstar, but Grace was the one who put things in perspective for the media.

The numbers he piled up with glove and bat earned Ryne Sandberg his Hall of Fame berth. Still, Cubs fans wonder why Ryno didn't make it on the first ballot.

Instead of those can-of-corn quotes ("That was a big win for us"—any manager, or "We're busting our butts out there"—any player), Grace almost always had something interesting, and above all, quotable to fill notebook scribblings and tape recorders in postgame postmortems. Sosa got much better at it as his homer total mounted, but was not quite as glib and facile as Grace.

"I only hit one like that every couple of years, so I enjoyed watching it go," Grace said after launching a rare tape-measure Wrigley Field homer in 1993.

That was typical of Grace's knack for snappy repartee. The fancy-fielding first baseman knew when to play it straight, when to go in depth for earnest, young would-be Red Smiths, when to kid around, and when to be diplomatic about the Cubs' habit of coming up short, year after year. It was natural, almost inevitable, for friction to develop between him and Sosa, though both men were canny enough to keep it under wraps.

"It was probably a little misunderstanding," Sosa said of the growing gap between his and Grace's lockers, which were at opposite ends of the clubhouse, both geographically and emotionally. "If Sammy's taking shots at me, I won't shoot back," Grace responded. "I thought we had a good relationship on the field."

Off the field? That's another story, although singles and doubles hitter Grace's career should not be defined by a spell of the petty jealousy almost all ballplayers get embroiled in. He was an outstanding first baseman, especially adept at scooping up shortstop Shawon Dunston's errant throws from the dirt, turning potential errors into outs and rescuing legions of grateful Cubs pitchers. Gracie won't get enough votes when he appears on the Hall of Fame ballot five years after retirement, but for Cubs fans, there is a highly unofficial, totally emotional Hall of Fame. It lives on in the Wrigley Field bleachers, and Grace belongs.

THE RED BARON'S A REAL GAMER

Maybe the main reason for Cubs fans' love affair with Rick Sut-cliffe was his abnormally high tolerance for pain. That's something they can relate to in the bleachers, the box seats and every other nook and Wrigley Field cranny, crammed with rooters smiling through their own wait-till-next-year misery.

A pitcher like Sutcliffe, going out to do battle inning after inning with a sore arm and little left on the ball except the cover, is their kind of guy. With all the teeth gnashing, weeping, and wailing when the Cubs blew that horrific 1984 NL playoff to the San Diego Padres, virtually nobody blamed the Red Baron. Sure, he went down in flames, letting a 3-0 lead evaporate in the fateful fifth game, but it was with all guns blazing. Sutcliffe's ailing shoulder throbbed by the time Cubs manager Jim Frey (too late) took him out during the Padres' game-winning rally.

What endeared the Red Baron to Cubs fans, besides his flaming beard, was the way he refused to blame anyone, other than himself, for the 1984 playoff calamity. He was not a finger-pointer or clubhouse lawyer, unlike some of his teammates. The search for scapegoats centered on Frey and first baseman Leon Durham, who committed a critical error in Game 5 at San Diego, shattering the dream of one more Wrigley Field World Series in the 20th century. Sutcliffe refused to take part in that witch hunt.

"Everybody else on the Cubs was as heartsick as I was when that series got away from us," the towering (six-foot, seven-inch) right-hander told me. "It was nobody's fault. Baseball can be a strange, humbling game."

Sutcliffe never stood taller than he did in the wake of that traumatic loss. His never-give-up attitude was to undergo even tougher tests in the years ahead. He took home a unanimous 1984 Cy Young Award for going 16-1 to spark the Cubs to their first-ever NL division crown, but arm trouble plagued him from then on. Despite pitching in pain, Rick barely missed a second

Cy Young trophy in 1987, then became the first Cubs pitcher since Grover Cleveland Alexander (1925-26) to win consecutive home Opening Day starts in 1988-89.

Through it all, family man Sutcliffe kept his perspective and his sense of humor. Like most pitchers, he was superstitious. When arm woes multiplied during the '80s, he took to throwing away his spiked shoes after every game, wearing a new pair for the next start.

"I got to figuring they were bad luck," Sutcliffe said. "I finally figured out the problem was not in my feet. It's tough to win games when your shoulder hurts, your leg hurts, and you can't throw hard."

THE HAWK FLIES HIGH

In a narrow sense, Andre Dawson was a one-shot deal for the Cubs. The intense veteran, already hobbling on two sore knees, had to beg them to let him climb aboard their sinking ship in 1987.

The Cubs did so grudgingly, though only after a spring training circus that was highly entertaining for the fans, but demeaning to Dawson, a 10-year veteran, who offered a badly needed package of class, ability, and results. Signing Dawson for $500,000, far below his market value, required a series of daily insult-trading screaming matches between Cubs general manager Dallas Green and agent Dick Moss.

Before long, The Hawk was whipping right field bleacherites into a frenzy that set the stage for Sammy Sosa's decade-plus of dominance on that same patch of Wrigley Field turf.

Dawson didn't own the North Side for nearly that long, but he certainly did in 1987. The right-handed slugger had the kind of year Robert Redford never did in The Natural, slamming 27 of his 49 homers at home. He shared the home run crown with

Oakland's Mark McGwire, but topped Sosa's future NL rival in other categories, especially fielding, to run away with National League MVP honors.

The list of Dawson's feats that year reads like a Babe Ruth biography. In a stretch that started with a game-winning grand slam on April 22, he piled up 131 RBI in 140 games. Eight days later, he hit for the cycle against San Francisco and threw out the Giants' Roger Mason at first base after the startled batter thought he had singled to right. Twice, Hawk tomahawked five homers in a three-game stretch and drove Andre's Army into total delirium by whacking three out of Wrigley Field in consecutive turns at bat against the Phillies on August 1.

No wonder the right field bleachers rose en masse to salute Dawson with bow-from-the-waist salaams when he hobbled out to his position. After a decade of virtual anonymity in Montreal, the taciturn outfielder, weary of the constant pain from a high-school football injury, was riding a wave of adulation.

"I never knew there were fans like that, anywhere," Dawson marveled.

Not one to wear emotion on his sleeve, Dawson let it all hang out on occasion, especially after Padres pitcher Eric Show, a notorious flake, bloodied the Hawk's lip with a high, hard fastball. Enraged, Dawson got up with fire in his eye and charged, chasing Show off the mound and into the visitors' dugout, while Wrigley fans roared gleefully. He showed a more compassionate side to me when I got a letter from a fan whose mother was terminally ill with cancer. She listened to games on a bedside radio, and Dawson was her hero. I took the letter to Hawk, who copied the lady's name on a baseball he autographed with a personal inscription.

A few months later, another letter asked me to convey the family's gratitude to Dawson.

"That baseball brightened my mother's last days," it said. "She died with it right next to the radio."

Dawson stuck around long enough to help the Cubs get into the 1989 NL playoffs. They lost, but he departed in 1993, still a winner.

ERNIE'S PLACE

He's still Mr. Cub, all these years later. The legend of Ernie Banks is the one thing that won't change as long as Wrigley Field stands where it is. I suppose that Clark and Addison will have to become a mega-mall or a 200-story condo or a home for aged and indigent aldermen one of these years, but I hope not in Ernie's lifetime—or mine.

I first met Ernie Banks around the Wrigley batting cage in 1970. Jack Brickhouse introduced me as a new guy on the Cubs beat. I don't recall the handshake banter that ensued, but I remember the smile that went with it. As long as he played there, Wrigley Field didn't need lights, because that smile lit up the park.

Banks was based in Los Angeles 15 years later, when I wrote my second book about the Cubs—*So You Think You're a Die-Hard Cub Fan,* but that cheerful smile came right through the phone when he agreed to do the foreword. Very few people have his ability to see the best in everything and everybody, without sounding like a used car salesman. What he sells is sunshine, fun, and Wrigley Field, all wrapped up in the title he gave to his ballpark—the Friendly Confines.

That's not all Ernie contributed, through good times and bad for the Cubs. He never got to the World Series everybody thought was coming in 1969 to cap his magnificent career. Definitely unfair, but so is baseball at times, because it's so much like life. The good guys don't always win, and Banks is exhibit A in that category.

Still, 512 homers, a Hall of Fame berth, 19 years as the Cubs' shortstop, first baseman, and chief cheerleader, plus his personal No.14 flag, flapping in the breeze above Wrigley Field's left field foul pole, compensate for that one missing link to complete the chain of a wonderful life in baseball. In truth, *It's a Wonderful Life* should be the title of a movie starring Ernie, not Jimmy Stewart. Although Banks endured his share of the shabby treatment routinely meted out to black players in his younger days with the Kansas City Monarchs, it couldn't dent his spirit. Neither did scrawled death threats from hateful morons to Banks, Hank Aaron, and other black stars following the trail blazed by Jackie Robinson.

That's why it was fun to be around Ernie. He enjoyed life, people, baseball, and good times. I really enjoyed writing about the Wrigley Field festivities on May 30, 1970, honoring Banks and Billy Williams between games of a doubleheader. Colleague Dick Dozer of the *Tribune* gave Ernie a bronzed sports page trumpeting his 500th homer on May 12. My dressing room story was on that page, and one of my most prized souvenirs is a T-shirt reproduction of it. Before or since, I never wore one of my bylines on my chest, but in this case, I'm happy to make an exception.

Even more than his feats on the field, though, Banks's memory endures because he's a rallying point for Cubs fans. When Harry Caray lauded fun at the old ballpark, he agreed that Ernie's legacy was the source.

"Opening Day [at Wrigley Field, of course] should be a national holiday," Banks trumpeted.

None of the 2,793 Wrigley Field customers thought a legend was in the making when the skinny shortstop started his first Cubs game on September 17, 1953, at the tail end of another losing (65-89) season. The Cubs got edged out by the Phillies, 16-4, and Banks went hitless, but that didn't last long. It seemed like the blink of an eye—and 499 home runs—later that 39-year-old Mr. Cub disappointed a 1970 Mother's Day

Ernie Banks salutes Wrigley Field fans, waving the ball he just drove into the bleachers for career home run No. 500. It's a new century now, but Ernie's still the people's choice.

throng of 32,255 by just missing that historic 500th. It came two days later, but that sunny afternoon would have been the perfect time in the Friendly Confines.

It might have been, it could have been, but it wasn't. Banks lined a vicious shot into the left field vines off Reds fireballer Wayne Simpson (who had vowed "Banks won't hit No. 500 off me"). He was right, only because Ol' Ern's sore knees made him stop at third, while the ball ricocheted wildly.

"I need more speed," he chuckled. "I thought about going for an inside-the-park homer, but between second and third, I felt like I had a piano on my back."

Anyway, Ernie carried the Cubs on his back for almost two decades.

SWEET SWINGER'S REWARD

There's always one mope who can't help raining on a sunny parade. In this case, it was a journeyman player named Wally Moon, whose specialty was lofting pop-fly homers over the screen the Dodgers erected in their makeshift Coliseum ballpark when they first moved to Los Angeles in 1958. He'd have to buy a ticket to get into the Hall of Fame, but got miffed when Billy Williams was voted in.

"They've watered down some of the criteria," Moon moaned. "Williams hit .290, but others hit .330. The Hall should be a very exclusive club."

He was a very small minority, drowned out by the tidal wave of congratulations when the Sweet Swinger took his rightful place among baseball's immortals, class of 1987. Williams was among the classiest of big-leaguers for all of his 18 seasons, 16 with the Cubs. He proved it again with an emotional speech when his plaque went up in Cooperstown.

"I wouldn't be here without Shirley," he said of his wife, who sobbed through the ceremony, with their four daughters. Billy also took quiet pride in his then-NL record streak of 1,117 consecutive games. I covered the streak-breaking game on September 3, 1970, watching Billy handle it with his innate dignity.

When Williams was swinging a hot bat, pitchers quaked. Line drives seemed to explode off his bat in those stretches, like July 11, 1972, with eight for eight in a doubleheader against Houston and April 9, 1969, when he became only the 28th player in history to collect four doubles in a game.

"Doubles for Abner Doubleday," Williams cracked.

FERGIE'S FINE

Ferguson Jenkins played baseball the same way fellow Canadian Gordie Howe played hockey. No nonsense, all business, eye on the ball—or the puck. If anybody got in the way of either man, he was likely to be knocked down, with a brushback pitch or a cross-check.

Jenkins was a fan favorite because he was the Cubs' ace for most of his eight Chicago seasons, the stopper they depended on to snap losing streaks. The strapping right-hander seldom got the headlines he deserved, despite six straight 20-victory seasons, from 1967 through 1972, a feat matched by just one other Cubs pitcher, Mordecai "Three-Finger" Brown (1906-11). I dubbed him the "Unknown Winner," and Fergie agreed.

"I don't know why I don't get the same national publicity as Tom Seaver and Vida Blue," he told me. "The first time I won 20, they said I was lucky. I kept doing it, and they didn't say anything."

A 1980 drug bust cast a shadow over Jenkins's Hall of Fame prospects, but his 284-236 career record, along with 49 shutouts and 3,192 strikeouts provided his passport. He joined Banks and Williams from the 1969 Cubs, adding a known winner to the talented team that couldn't win, for unknown reasons.

"Fergie made it look easy," said his Cub catcher, Randy Hundley. "He just went out there, took the ball and threw it past the hitters."

Chapter 6

GOING OUT OF THEIR MASTERMINDS

A lot of ex-Cubs managers probably would agree with the chicken thief who got tarred and feathered and ridden out of town on a rail. When asked for his reaction to the ordeal, the miscreant replied, "If it wasn't for the honor of the thing, I'd just as soon walk."

Well, manager after manager has taken that one-way walk, a treadmill to oblivion from the Cubs' dugout to the unemployment compensation office, since I wandered onto the baseball beat a year after the colossal calamity of 1969. Leo Durocher was the dugout dictator then, alternately charming, haranguing and finally infuriating the Cubs into contending status. But he couldn't get them over the hump and into the playoffs, so Leo had to go, opening the floodgates for a tidal wave of managerial impersonators.

Dusty Baker, one of the few who looked like the genuine article, became the 20th Cubs manager since Durocher. Sometimes as many as three in the same season spun in and out of that revolving door with dizzying, dismaying rapidity. That wasn't quite as ridiculous as owner P. K. Wrigley's brainstorm, the College of Coaches, featuring a hilarious five-way backstabbing tournament in 1961-62, although just as futile. Jim Riggleman (1995-99) was the only field boss who lasted for five years in the odd Cubs odyssey from Durocher to Dusty.

If I ranked Cubs managers by listing the characters at the top, Durocher would be the leadoff bench brainstormer, followed by Herman Franks, Lee Elia, and Jim Essian. I have too much respect for Don Zimmer to call him a character, except in the most affectionate sense, because he has real character, besides being a walking baseball museum and treasure chest of diamond lore. So, starting with the new kid on the block, here's a look at all those would-be Casey Stengels.

DUSTY ROAD TO WRIGLEY

Mike Remlinger tried to be a prophet while profiting from the Cubs. When he signed a three-year, $11 million contract to switch bullpens, from Atlanta to Chicago, the lefty reliever predicted, "Dusty Baker will give the Cubs the credibility they needed. Spend a few minutes with him, and you feel at ease."

What the Cubs really needed from their new manager, of course, was an incredible leap to the top of the NL Central Division standings. Before leaving the Golden Gate Bridge behind to work for a team that's had fans jumping off the Michigan Avenue Bridge for a half-century, Baker got assurances that the Tribune Company's deep pockets would cough up cold cash to lure new talent for 2003.

Sure enough, Dusty hadn't even dusted off his clubhouse desk when Cubs general manager Jim Hendry plunged into a frantic flurry of roster roulette. With all those new faces to plug in around superstar Sammy Sosa and a promising array of starting pitchers, expectations were high for the former San Francisco skipper. Perhaps for the first time since Durocher departed in 1972, Cubs fans felt that Baker could take them to where he couldn't quite get the Giants—a World Series victory.

"Why not us?" Baker asked when he took the reins soon after the Cubs concluded their 2002 orgy of self-flagellation under fired Don Baylor and the interim innocent bystander, Bruce Kimm.

Naturally, the Cubs pounced on that as their new marketing tool. It worked for the White Sox (remember "The Kids Can Play"?), but Cubs fans won't really be happy unless their next T-shirt reads "Knock their Sox off in '06". That puts added pressure on Baker to make it happen overnight. If he does, Chicago will erupt like Mt. Vesuvius, erasing a bear market of frustration.

Baker roamed the outfield for 19 years with the Braves, Dodgers, Giants and Oakland A's, hitting a solid .278 with 242 homers and a growing reputation as a manager on the field. Understandably, the California native needed only a short apprenticeship as a Giants coach before starting a decade as their manager in 1993. Like the rest of the Giants, he was mentally measuring himself for a World Series ring before the Anaheim Angels rallied to win Game 6 and snatch the prize away in the winner-take-all finale.

"We got to the doorstep, but they [the Angels] slammed it in our faces," Baker said with a resigned shrug.

Undeterred, the Cubs blew the dust off their purse strings to enrich Dusty by $15 million over four years. If he wins, it could be a lot longer. If not, the 53-year-old Baker won't age gracefully in the Friendly Confines.

LEO, YOU AIN'T LION

In 1966, Leo Durocher came to Chicago, touted as the savior of the sagging Cubs franchise. Fans with long memories saw some irony when the same role was thrust on Dusty Baker more than three decades later. Actually, comparing these two Cubs managers is an exercise in apples-and-oranges futility.

It's more than just that Baker is a California guy, bringing his laid-back image to Chicago, or that Durocher was a New York guy, wrapping up every abrasive Big Apple stereotype in his stylishly dressed, flamboyant lifestyle. After all, Leo ended up in Palm Springs, hanging out with such transplanted Easterners as Frank Sinatra.

And Baker, in almost three decades of baseball travel, along with playing for ultra-competitive Dodgers manager Tommy Lasorda, quickly learned that the meek do not inherit first place.

Still, Durocher was unique, in or out of baseball. Maybe the most self-centered man I ever met, he knew how to play the role, changing personalities in the blink of an eye to deal with any situation. I've seen him charm the pants off banquet audiences, lowering that rasping voice to make even the drunks at the back tables believe they were being taken into his confidence.

"Why, gentlemen," Durocher would purr. "You wouldn't believe these umpires nowadays. There's nobody like Jocko Conlan today. The way Jocko and I got into it, chest to chest..."

And Leo was off and running, reinventing for the 1,000th time his famous shin-kicking duel with Conlan. Each version was different, but they all ended up with the same punch (or rather, kick) line: "I got hurt a lot worse, because Jocko was wearing shinguards and steel toe plates, kicking my ankles. I only had baseball socks on."

It always brought down the house. Leo knew they were waiting for his most famous line, "Nice guys finish last," so he saved it for last, denying he ever said it without actually denying it. This man was much too smart to disown the misquote that

Leo Durocher (2, back to camera) greets his up-and-coming Cubs in Wrigley Field. Leo the Lip had them on the verge of the 1969 play-offs, but it was all downhill for him after the late-season fadeout.

earned him immortality of sorts in *Bartlett's Quotations*. What Leo actually did in his Brooklyn Dodger managing days was point to the New York Giants' dugout and say, "Lot of nice guys over there, but they're in last place."

But that was Durocher all over, adapting whatever happened to suit his purposes. He reveled in the labels hung on him by sportswriters ("Lippy Leo" or "Leo the Lion" or "The Little Shepherd of Coogan's Bluff" or whatever), rewarding them with choice quotes from his bottomless pit of baseball savvy. Yes, he was a great manager for 24 years, with an overall 2,008-1,731 record (535-526 as Cubs skipper), and I stand by the column I wrote years ago, outlining the reasons why Durocher belonged in the Hall of Fame.

He finally got there in 1994, years later than he should have.

Why? Because there was a dark side to this complex man. Leo made so many enemies and piled up so much emotional baggage over the years that it's a wonder he got in at all. Some purists still point to Durocher's shady connections and backroom dealings with gamblers, hoodlums and assorted lowlifes that got him suspended from baseball for the 1947 season "for activities detrimental to baseball."

In his stormy six-plus years on the Chicago scene (1966-72), Durocher's penchant for alienating people played a major part in his downfall. Case in point: Cubs broadcaster Jack Brickhouse, eventually turning from a Leo booster to a Leo basher. When I sat down with Brickhouse to tape some memories for a previous book, he fed me lots of insight on the unraveling of Durocher's Cubs.

"Getting his facts straight never was a priority for Leo," Jack told me. "He gradually lost that razor-sharp instinct for managing and took the team down with him."

The ball was still very much in Leo's court when I arrived on the Cubs scene in 1970. I believe that team was even better than the failed Cubs of '69, but it again finished in second place. Durocher gave me the once-over when I first walked into his clubhouse office. He had a knack for gravitating to the most important people in any crowd. I wasn't important, but the *Chicago Tribune* was, so he knew he had to deal with me.

I couldn't figure out why Leo once raised his voice, to make sure I overheard him, while ostentatiously phoning to order roses for his wife, Lynn Walker Goldblatt, a Chicago TV personality. After a while, I began to understand that impressing the peasants was just part of his lifelong ego trip. Anyway, two and a half years of covering Leo, the increasingly toothless Lion, was a fascinating, spicy bowl of my Chicago sports stew.

NICE GUY FINISHES FIRST—ONCE

The poster boy for all the nice guys in baseball was—and doubtless still is—Jim Riggleman. In his five seasons of struggling to nudge the Cubs into the postseason picture, I don't recall Rigs raising his voice in anger more than once or twice, despite unlimited opportunities to do so. Maybe that was his fatal flaw.

Or perhaps not. It's entirely possible that a reincarnation of Connie Mack, John McGraw and Casey Stengel couldn't have manged the Cubs of 1995-99 into the playoffs more than once. The one time they got there—in 1998—was a quintessential Cubs moment. They trudged off the field in Houston on Sept. 27, believing a last-game loss to the Astros had ended their season. Instead, the Cubs backed into a wild-card tie with the Giants, then beat them in a one-game playoff for the right to get swept out, 3-0, of their playoff with the Atlanta Braves.

'Twas ever thus for the Cubs, at least since 1945. Riggleman, liked and respected by his players and the media, was a good manager for the Cubs, but like a lot of bad managers who preceded him, he was unable to break their cycle of one good season, three or four or more bad seasons. His frustration couldn't be contained in 1999, when Cubs contenders became pretenders with startling swiftness.

Sitting pretty at 32-23 on June 8, they folded like wet Kleenex, plummeting to 30 games under .500 at the end, on the wings of an 8-24 August record.

Naturally, Riggleman had to take the fall for his players' shoddy performance. He saw it coming midway through the season and tried, too late, to stop the bleeding.

"The rats are the first ones to jump off a sinking ship," Rigs said. "We'll find out who the rats are."

The other major Riggleman meltdown was a dugout shouting match with Sammy Sosa in 1997, when the slugger ignored a sign, ran on his own and got cut down trying to steal second base. Tempers already were frayed by a horrendous 0-14 start that season, the worst losing streak in Cubs history.

"Sammy wasn't supposed to run, but he did anyway," the miffed manager said. "I had to talk to him in front of the club or the other players would have lost respect for me. I want everybody, not just Sammy, to play for the team."

Predictably, soon after the 1999 debacle, the rats were still cashing paychecks, but Riggleman wasn't.

Seasoned in the ups and downs of the game, he took it in stride. The Cubs had a fatal hole in their rotation during his final season at the helm, because Kerry Wood, '98 NL Rookie of the Year, missed it all to recover from elbow surgery. So Jon Lieber, at 10-11, was their only double-digit winner. Rather than get Riggleman fresh talent, his bosses elected to make him walk the plank. Characteristically, he took it in stride.

"Maybe I should have agreed about some [players'] shortcomings, instead of defending them over and over," Rigs reflected.

BAYLOR'S JAIL

Perhaps pondering Riggleman's fate before he came aboard as manager in 2000, Don Baylor decided that the Cubs needed two things—one: discipline, and two: a different attitude. Before Baylor got fired, midway through his third season, there was an attitude change—from bad to worse.

As for discipline, most of that got inflicted on the media covering the Cubs. Sammy Sosa's terrific home run duels with the Cards' Mark McGwire, on top of the Cubs' rare playoff appearance in 1998, intensified the pre- and postgame crush of writers, radio, and TV people, clamoring to shower free publicity on the team owned by a mammoth communications empire.

For Riggleman, it was no problem, because that gabby guy gladly would talk your ear off, one on one or the whole media mob on him. It soon became clear that access to Baylor would be much more severely limited. Only the media biggies were allowed in the manager's office, upstairs in the new home clubhouse under the left-field stands. That cozy hideaway, where I'd spent hours yakking about this and that, sometimes even baseball, with Don Zimmer, Jim Lefebvre, Riggleman, and other Cubs managers, now was off limits.

But the move that stuck in almost everybody's craw was cramming the postgame media sessions into a tiny cubicle next to the umpires' dressing room. Baylor and requested players took turns squeezing behind a roped-off desk, often encircled by a ring of TV cameras that made it difficult for the ink-stained wretches in the rear to see or hear what was going on. My old *Chicago Tribune* sports editor, Cooper Rollow, used to caution us beat guys, "Don't expect sympathy from the fans when you gripe about your working conditions. Lots of them would kill to have your job."

Coop was right. Kiddingly, I dubbed the Cubs' cramped postgame penalty box "Stalag 25," a pointed reference to Baylor's uniform number, but other media people beefed less good-humoredly, including visiting writers. Regardless, the real focus on the Baylor regime was, as it should have been, on the Cubs' performance. With occasional exceptions, the new manager's honeymoon with Chicago's media and fans lasted through his mostly dismal 65-97 inaugural in 2000, because they wanted both him and the Cubs to succeed.

"Our fans expect us to lose," he told me early in that season, taking a look at Wrigley Field's rapidly filling seats, although gametime was hours away. "They come out here to enjoy this ballpark. I want them to start enjoying watching the Cubs win."

In 2001, they did, albeit briefly. The Cubs ripped off a 12-game victory streak (May 19-June 2), their longest run of total success in 66 years, only to become the Cubs again—and as usual—down the stretch.

Injuries added to the frustration, so Baylor couldn't even make it past the 2002 All-Star break. Both he and the Cubs were out of it by then, so the axe fell on July 5, with ex-Cub and White Sox catcher Bruce Kimm coming in from Iowa to rearrange the deck chairs on the sinking S.S. Cubtanic.

"The talent on the field does not equal the victory total," was Cubs president Andy MacPhail's terse see-you-later message, resigned to paying Baylor another $1.3 million for not managing the Cubs in 2003.

TREBELHORN'S IN TROUBLE

King Louis XVI accurately predicted the bloodshed of the coming French Revolution when he proclaimed: "After me, the deluge." Emperor Leo the First might well have foreseen the same gory future for the Cubs when Durocher went to the guillotine (figuratively speaking, of course) in 1972.

With few exceptions, the parade of fruitless, and mostly clueless, pretenders to the Cubs' managerial throne has continued in an unbroken shuffle since then. Tom Trebelhorn was one of them in the strike-shortened 1994 season, his lone turn at the helm, with few noticing his arrival or departure. This could have been one of the most forgettable Wrigley Field campaigns of all time, and that's saying a lot.

In fairness to the former Milwaukee Braves pilot, his opening-day pitcher was lonesome traveler Mike Morgan, making the first of two brief sojourns on the Cubs' roster during his lucrative 12-team tour of both leagues. Perhaps arm-weary from toting suitcases from town to town, the right-hander spent much of that season on the disabled list, in between compiling a 2-10 record and a 6.69 ERA. Rookie Steve Trachsel was the staff ace, so to speak, with a 9-7 record, but Willie—no, not Ernie—Banks made 23 starts, more than any other Cubs pitcher. No wonder Trebelhorn was reduced to responses like this when asked, during another of the '94 Cubs' frequent tailspins, if losing bothered his players:

"Of course," he sputtered. "They're human, just like anybody else."

NO PENNANT FEVER FOR LEFEBVRE

Jim Lefebvre was bitterly disappointed when he didn't get re-hired after managing the Cubs to a rare glimpse of break-even territory at 162-162 overall in 1992-93. The longtime Dodger second baseman was a fierce competitor and a solid baseball man. He just couldn't get on the same page with Cubs (and ex-White Sox) general manager Larry Himes, who ruffled feathers wherever he went.

So Lefebvre lost that power struggle, although Himes got handed his own bus ticket after the Trebelhorn debacle of 1994. The cycle of inept Cubs management, continually hiring managers who couldn't get the job done because their teams were not stocked with multimillionaire free agents, continued right up to 2003, when Dusty Baker made signing some high-priced talent a condition of his leaving the Giants to manage the Cubs.

GRADE A FOR Z-BALL

The Cubs should have kept Don Zimmer, moved him into the front office, paid for titanium replacements of his chronically sore knees and given him enough money to stock the roster with guys who would run through ivy-covered brick walls to catch fly balls. In the end, all Zim got was the gate.

He left behind a legacy of one NL Eastern Division crown in 1989, followed by an excruciating NL pennant playoff loss to the Giants, when the Cubs unaccountably left their hearts in San Francisco, along with an awful lot of high-energy, high-risk, highly entertaining baseball.

Zim was a riverboat gambler at heart. He had the Cubs doing things they haven't done before or since, especially on the bases. The 1989 bunch did things under Zimmer's fiery prodding that almost all teams did back in the dead-ball era—bunt, squeeze, steal, hit-and-run, run-and-hit, even the lost art of hitting behind the runner. Listening to Zimmer talk about how baseball should be played was even more fun than watching the Cubs try to play it his way.

"A lot of these kids get rushed up to the majors now before they've seen a lot of fundamentals," Zimmer told me during one of those relaxed bull sessions in his clubhouse office. "Let's be realistic. If you got a million-dollar bonus just to sign a contract right out of high school, would you want to go down to the minors and listen to some bald-headed old coach tell you how to play the game?"

If that bald guy happened to be Zimmer, young players willing to listen could get a priceless free education. Zimmer had seen and done it all through his eventful half-century as a player, manager, and coach in the minors and majors. The scrappy infielder paid his dues along the way, as evidenced by a silver plate in his head to mark the spot of a near-fatal beaning.

When Zim was in an expansive mood, he'd talk about the most bitter defeat of them all. That was the 1978 American League pennant playoff in Fenway Park, when he managed the Boston Red Sox. They lost it to the Yankees on ex-White Sox shortstop Bucky Dent's three-run homer, lofted over the left field Green Monster.

"When Bucky hit the ball, I thought it was a pop fly," Zimmer related, with a sad shake of his head. "It just kept carrying."

The Red Sox and White Sox were the only other big-league team capable of matching Cubs fans' tales of woe at a might-have-been meeting on Heartbreak Hill. Until 2004, the Beantown Brigade hadn't won a World Series since 1918, a decade after the Cubs captured their last one. So Zimmer knew what he was up against in Wrigley Field, where he played for manager Lou Boudreau in 1960 and for the infamous Cubs' revolving College of Coaches in 1961.

Despite his hobbled knees, advancing age, and assorted ailments, Zimmer's zest for battle never dimmed.

As Cubs manager (1988-91) or on their coaching staff (1984-86), whenever tempers flared and benches emptied for brawls, Zim led the charge and leaped into the fray. He wrenched his neck in a 1984 battle royale with the archrival Mets, but earned respect from the players, bringing them together for a drive that ended the Cubs' 39-year absence from the postseason picture. A Met pitcher named Ed Lynch touched off the fisticuffs by throwing at Cubs batter Keith "Zonk" Moreland.

Ironically, a decade later, it was that same Lynch who began a six-year stint with the Cubs as their general manager. In sharp contrast with Zimmer's bottomless reservoir of how-to-do-it-right baseball in their employ, his Tribune Co. bosses chose to get rid of him. He's still bitter about that, especially the final kiss-off.

"Guys in Italian silk suits who knew nothing about baseball were telling me I wasn't doing the job," he said.

For Zimmer, at least, things turned out right. Yankees manager Joe Torre, a league leader in class and savvy, brought Zim in to be his bench coach. The results of firing Zimmer in Chicago and hiring him in New York can be gauged simply by comparing the Yankees' yearly spot atop the AL standings against the Cubs' customary lease on the NL basement.

THE ESSIAN EXPERIMENT

When Don Zimmer departed after the Cubs got off to an 18-20 start in 1991, the Cubs went to the other extreme, bringing in a man with no big-league managing experience. He was former White Sox catcher Jim Essian, summoned from the Cubs' Iowa farm team on May 22.

Even Cubs fans, accustomed to seeing unlikely suspects posing as their team's manager, were perplexed by this move. Essian, the 40-year-old freshman, astonished them even more by winning his first three games.

"That man is a genius," gushed Cubs outfielder Dwight Smith, whose objectivity might have been slightly tarnished by the fact that Essian started him in left field, replacing George Bell, who got traded a year later to the White Sox for Sammy Sosa.

Essian, a yoga devotee, brought in former Sox teammate Richie Zisk as the hitting instructor. They'd been together on the fondly remembered 1977 South Side Hit Men, who packed Comiskey Park that summer for Bill Veeck's rent-a-player 198-homer derby, featuring Zisk ("Pitch at Risk to Richie Zisk") and ex-Cub Oscar Gamble. Unfortunately, Zisk couldn't get either team into the playoffs, sealing Essian's fate as a one-shot pilot for the Cubs.

"STICK" THE WRONG PICK

The Cubs' managerial circus hit a new high, or perhaps low, in 1986, when Dallas Green thumbed through a directory of big-league executives, searching for a successor to manager Jim Frey. Green's self-styled "New Tradition" for the Cubs crumbled when he came up with the wrong name.

It was Gene "Stick" Michael, an ex-Yankee shortstop who stuck around in their front office to cope as best he could with volcanic eruptions from the powerful ego of "The Boss," George Steinbrenner, a force to be reckoned with, both in baseball and New York cafe society. Michael managed the Cubs through the last half of 1986 and yet another losing season in '87, then went back to New York, leaving no noticeable trace of his short stay.

"It was hard to tell whether Stick or John Vukovich [Cubs bench coach] really ran the team," a baffled player opined.

Another entry in the It Figures department quickly followed for the rudderless Cubs organization.

Green quit abruptly—or was he pushed?—right after the 1987 debacle, heading back East for (surprise) a couple of contentious, unproductive managerial tours with both the Yankees and Mets. In his place, the Cubs installed—who else?—Jim Frey, the Cubs manager Green had hired and fired.

FREY NOT?

Jim Frey's tenure in the Cub dugout was a smashing success in 1984. The Cubs turned on this toddlin' town by barging to the doorstep of their first World Series since 1945, but got no closer. The trauma of losing three straight playoff games in San Diego, when all the Cubs needed to wrap up the NL pennant was to play at their customary .333 road pace, hung over the team like an epidemic of swine flu.

True, the constant arm and shoulder miseries of Cubs ace Rick Sutcliffe played a major role in their downfall. Nothing much else worked, either, so the bottom dropped out in 1985, and another managerial troika of Frey, John Vukovich, and Gene Michael couldn't stop the bleeding a year later. Oh, well, the Roar of '84 sure was fun while it lasted.

WE FEEL FOR YA, ELIA

Lee Elia was one of the finest all-around athletes ever to come out of the Philadelphia area. When I was a young cub (reporter, not player) at the *Philadelphia Inquirer*, his feats in football, basketball, baseball, and track made the paper almost daily. Elia chose to become a baseball lifer, playing briefly for the 1966 White Sox (80 games, .206 batting average) and the 1968 Cubs (15 games, .176 average) before turning to managing in the minors.

Eddie Stanky [Sox manager] was about to cut me in spring training," Elia recalled. "Then I hit a pinch-hit grand slam off Bob Gibson, so they let me go north with the team."

When Elia came back to Chicago 14 years later with some impressive coaching and managing credentials, Cubs fans were willing to take a wait-and-see-attitude on the newcomer. After all, he had been manager Dallas Green's third base coach with the Phillies, the team that knocked off the favored Kansas City Royals in the 1980 World Series. Elia looked, walked, and talked like a young man (only 44) with leadership skills, ready to grow as a manager. It didn't take long for that rosy scenario—and Elia himself—to go down in flames.

"Dallas and I look at things the same way," Elia said before taking the reins in 1982. "He's tough, and if he's losing the argument, he just yells louder."

Those words proved prophetic on April 29, 1983, just after reliever Lee Smith's wild pitch cost the Cubs a 4-3 loss to the Dodgers. Enraged because his players got heckled by the sparse Wrigley Field crowd, Elia blew up like a runaway rocket, spewing profane venom over Cubs fans.

"If they're the real Cub fans, they can kiss my ass," Elia said in one of his milder references to Wrigley customers during a lengthy, emotional tirade. It almost got him fired on the spot when general manager Green heard the tape made by veteran Chicago sportscaster Les Grobstein.

As things turned out, Elia's quick, profuse apology earned him only a stay of execution. He was gone before the 1983

Manager Lee Elia can't believe what he's hearing from umpire John McSherry in this 1983 debate. Box-seat fans tune in eagerly, but pitching coach Billy Connors (right) feigns disinterest.

season ground to a merciful 71-91 halt, with interim manager Charlie Fox at the helm. Basically a nice guy, Elia coached elsewhere and mended fences on every trip to Chicago.

FROM HOT DOGS TO FRANKS

If they ever want to make a TV sitcom about baseball, blending humor with reality, the Chicago Cubs would be the role-model team, with a manager who looks and acts a lot like Herman Franks.

Herman was definitely not your stereotype skipper, the crusty old coot with the heart of gold, like the ones in *Damn Yankees* or the Bob Uecker movies. Not that he was mean and dumb; far from it. Franks had a mean streak, but he knew a lot about baseball and business, enjoying far more success in the latter field. A millionaire investor, he struck out as Cubs manager (1977-79) and later as their general manager (1981).

On a 1978 Cubs trip to San Diego, Franks took some writers, including myself, for a stroll near the world-famous Del Coronado Hotel. Pointing to a row of luxury apartment houses farther down the beach, he said, "Those are mine."

The Cubs did make a pretty good run at the top in 1977, Herman's dugout debut. The familiar late-fade scenario removed the rosy glow of optimism, and Franks had to settle for entertaining the fans during the rest of his tenure by staging running feuds with Jose Cardenal, Bill Buckner, and assorted media critics. It was a fun time to be on the Cubs beat, with every day providing new grist for the comedy mill. Through it all, the rotund manager held court every day in the dugout or his office, spraying tobacco juice with equal-opportunity zest on his shoes and those of bystanders.

Herman didn't need the money or the job, and he certainly didn't need the media. Sometimes he just liked to have us around while he alternately talked and munched his postgame beef sandwich, dripping gravy on his undershirt. Any conclusions we drew about the Cubs' performance, he made it clear, were strictly up to us.

"You saw it—you write it," was the customary response when asked for his insights. This was not a man who dwelt on history, tradition or Sparky Anderson-style diamond lore. I knew Franks had broken into the majors as a catcher with the Philadelphia A's, so I asked him what it was like to play for legendary manager Connie Mack, also a catcher back in the 19th century.

"How would I know?" he replied. "Who gives a damn about that?"

That was Herman all over—a big barrel of laughs.

MOTLEY CUB CREW

Lots of other managers came and went during my three-plus decades of trying to figure out, mostly in vain, what the heck the Cubs were up to now. Some were mere blips on the radar screen, like Preston Gomez (1980), Frank Lucchesi (1987), Joe Altobelli (1991) and Bruce Kimm (2002). Even such a respected baseball figure as Whitey Lockman (1972-74), who picked up the baton dropped by Leo Durocher, couldn't turn the Cubs around.

For my money, the runners-up to Don Zimmer and Jim Riggleman in the good guy category were Jim Marshall (1974-76) and Joe Amalfitano (1979-81). Marshall tried to stretch a thin staff by yanking his pitchers quicker than most managers, so I dubbed him "Captain Hook."

That winter, I got a Christmas card from Marshall. It was signed, "Captain Hook." Anyone capable of managing the Cubs and keeping his sense of humor gets my vote.

Chapter 7

THE WALLS OF IVY

Wrigley Field belongs to a lot more people than just Tribune Company stockholders. This one-and-only baseball park, seemingly frozen in time, is more than just a slice of Chicago history, too. It's a symbol of what James Earl Jones described in that famous movie as "What baseball should be, and could be . . ." In short, it's America's field of dreams.

Only one other ballpark can rival Wrigley, both in longevity and loveability. That's Boston's Fenway Park, which opened for business in 1912, two years after the original Comiskey Park, on Chicago's South Side. But in 1914, another park went up at Clark and Addison Streets on the North Side at a cost of $250,000, heavy money for those days.

It was Weeghman Park, built to house the Chicago Whales of the short-lived Federal League. Not much of a team, as things turned out, but a whale of a baseball shrine. Soon known as Cubs Park, when that charter NL franchise moved there in 1916, it became Wrigley Field in 1926, because the gum company's family had bought out owner "Lucky Charlie" Weegh-man in 1919.

Before long, everybody knew the name and fame of a place where new chapters of diamond lore were added yearly. The incredible double no-hit duel between Jim "Hippo" Vaughn of the Cubs and Cincinnati's Fred Toney on May 2, 1917, served as a warning that the home team was fated to suffer many such heartbreaking moments in decades to come. Vaughn lost his no-no and the game, 1-0, in the 10th inning.

Even Wrigley Field's all-time moment piled more misery on Cubs fans. It was Babe Ruth's called-shot home run off the Cubs' Charlie Root in Game 3 of the World Series, on October 1, 1932. The Bambino allegedly pointed to the center field bleachers before depositing Root's next delivery there, setting up a Series sweep for the Yankees, along with one of baseball's most durable controversies. Root denied to his dying day that Ruth had called his shot, but I don't believe him.

Why? Because Pat Pieper, the Wrigley Field public address announcer, had been moved upstairs, over his loud protest, from the field to the press box when I started covering the Cubs in 1970. Pieper was a living witness to Wrigley history from the day the Cubs moved in until he retired in 1974. For years, he walked around the field, from first base to third, shouting that day's batteries through a megaphone. Later, generations of Cubs fans grew up savoring Pieper's stentorian tones on the field mike: "Tenshun! Tenshun, please! Have your pencils and scorecards ready and I'll give you the correct lineups for today's game . . ."

If Pat Pieper said something happened at Wrigley Field, I'm convinced that it did happen. So one day I asked him about it in the lull between batting practice and the game's start. He'd been grilled about the Ruth-Root dispute many times, but the grand old man of Wrigley Field never tired of talking about it.

"Absolutely, the Babe pointed to the center field bleachers," Pieper told me. "I was sitting a few feet away from him [on his familiar three-legged stool, perched against the low grandstand wall to the right of home plate], and there was no mistaking where he pointed. He was telling Root where his next pitch would go, and that's exactly where it went. Ruth called his shot."

That majestic gesture overshadowed the most famous Wrigley home run by a Cub. Gabby Hartnett's "Homer in the Gloaming," off Pittsburgh's Mace Brown on September 28, 1938, wrapped up the NL pennant for the Cubs, boring through the gathering darkness to land in the left field bleachers. Ernie Banks launched his 500th career home run into those same seats 32 years later. In between, Stan Musial got his 3,000th hit and Pete Rose tied Ty Cobb's big-league record with his 4,191st hit, both in Wrigley Field.

Sammy Sosa's prodigious home runs provided plenty of thrills in the 1990s, but a new generation of Cubs fans doubles its pleasure with four-baggers by the 1-2 punch of Derrek Lee and Aramis Ramirez. And the pitching performances keep piling up. Kerry Wood's 20-strikeout magnificence against Houston on May 6, 1998, might not be matched in the remainder of Wrigley's legendary lifetime—but don't bet on it. Despite the frigid temperatures of April, the fickle winds and blinding sun of every part of every season and the constant uproar about proposed alterations, the Friendly Confines endure, just too beloved to die. While Fenway Park belongs to all of New England, Wrigley Field belongs to all of America.

No ballpark generates the kind of emotion I've been hearing about Wrigley Field for over three decades. Overwhelmingly, it's favorable, much more so from the fans than the players. Some of the notes and quotes I've gathered over the years follow.

ASK THE MAN WHO KNOWS

Mention Bill Veeck's name in Chicago and fans automatically think "White Sox." That's natural, because Barnum Bill, one of the game's truly great showmen, produced two hit shows on the

Back in the 1930s, the Great Depression gripped America, but things were more cheerful around Wrigley Field. Cubs fans flocked for tickets to the 1935 World Series, though the Detroit Tigers beat their team in six games.

South Side—the Go-Go Sox of 1959, and the 1977 Hit Men, who provided lots of thrills, but no postseason payoff.

But Veeck literally grew up in Wrigley Field. His dad, William Veeck, Sr., was president of the Cubs, so young Bill got to pal around with legendary slugger Hack Wilson, go to spring training on Catalina Island, off the coast of Southern California, with fun-loving manager Jolly Cholly Grimm and his band of free-spirited players, and most of all, soak up his lifelong love of baseball.

It was Veeck, borrowing the idea from a minor-league ballpark in Indianapolis, who planted the ivy on Wrigley Field's outfield walls in 1937.

"We did the job of stringing the wires and hanging bittersweet with ivy on them basically overnight, because the Cubs were coming back from a road trip," Veeck told me. "Bob Dorr [veteran Wrigley groundskeeper] and his crew worked with me until the sun came up to get it done."

Veeck's most-remembered stunt was thumbing his nose at pompous fellow owners in 1951 by sending midget Eddie Gaedel, wearing No. 1/8, up to pinch hit for the St. Louis Browns. When I see the ivy, though, I figure that should stand as his permanent bequest to all baseball fans. No wonder Veeck never lost his interest in the Cubs and his nostalgia for their—and his—ballpark.

"Wrigley Field is a living thing, adapting to its environment," Bill told me once, while we were watching a high school game there. "For the sake of an extra buck, too many owners would willingly destroy traditions like this. My father and I always thought we were custodians for the real owners, the fans. This location was selected for the ballpark because streetcar lines converged here, so people hopped off the trolley and walked to the park."

WRIGLEYVILLE, USA

Now, fans come in a steady stream from all over the Midwest, elsewhere around the country and even from overseas. Japan's prime minister threw out a ceremonial first pitch a few years ago, just like a former Eureka College football player and Cubs broadcaster named Dutch Reagan once did. For many of today's visitors, piling off rows and rows of buses, Wrigley Field is more of an attraction than the game itself.

Harry Caray had much to do with that. He created Cubs fans everywhere with his rousing, off-key, seventh-inning rendition of "Take Me Out to the Ball Game," a tradition wisely continued by John McDonough, the marketing director who thinks like a fan. McDonough's Beanie Baby promotions have become a huge lure, adding even non-fans to Wrigley's ticket-window crush.

"We have a situation here unlike anything I know of," McDonough said. "Putting a winning team on the field has to be our first priority, but when it's Wrigley Field, lots of people come just to enjoy the surroundings. They love this place as much as they live and die with the Cubs."

CONTINUITY COUNTS

The loyalty of Cubs fans has not changed since the 20th century vanished into the mist of time. They still see Wrigley Field as the lone constant among the ever-changing faces on the Cubs' roster, while the front office unveils the latest in an interminable array of rebuilding plans. Although he spoke these words almost 30 years ago, Chicagoan Dick Karlov sounds like he's saying them in 2003—and probably 3003, if their hallowed playpen is still here then.

"Wrigley Field is about the only thing that hasn't changed since I was a boy," Karlov said. "The ballpark is the main attraction, because it's such a good memory for all of us. There's no nicer place to spend an afternoon in the sun."

SOME PLAYERS LOVE IT

"Ivy on the walls, crazy fans in the bleachers, not much room outside the foul lines," longtime first baseman Mark Grace said of his affection for Wrigley, despite just two playoffs for the Cubs in his 13 seasons (1989, 1998). "The fans are right on top of you. The pitcher can hear them yelling at him. The Cubs get used to that, just like the crummy weather in April."

One of those Cubs pitchers, Mike Bielecki (1988-1991), enjoyed the Wrigleyville ambience so much that he perched during the season in a high-rise apartment near the park. That way, he could check which way the wind was blowing on days he was due to start.

"Wrigley Field is more fun, because it's not one of those cookie-cutter places," Bielecki said. "The fans are the 10th man for us. Every game is an event, like a Michael Jackson concert."

For perennial Gold Glover Ryne Sandberg, the Wrigley mystique was easy to define. "Tradition," Ryno said. "Year after year, it goes on. Fans react to us and we react to them. In a small park like this, it keeps building."

Lots of Cubs managers also realized the fans' fervor gave them an edge. Leo Durocher had ways of whipping them into a frenzy, but Don Zimmer and Jim Frey were content to watch and admire the pandemonium in the stands.

"Day ball, night ball, it doesn't matter," Zimmer said. "There's no place that can match Wrigley Field. It's just one of the few old shrines that still belongs to the fans."

Frey, a real traditionalist, couldn't conceal his disdain for the plague of round stadiums with artificial turf that sprang up like weeds in both leagues.

"Baseball as we knew it is not played in those parks," Frey said. "On a field with a carpet, it's a different game. Instead of swinging at the ball, batters slap at it, trying to bounce one 30 feet in the air and beat it out. If I had to watch games like that, I wouldn't be a baseball fan."

THE VOICES OF EXPERIENCE

Jack Brickhouse found out early that Wrigley Field was special, long before he knew most of his working life would be spent there.

"I first came to the park on a train with a couple of hundred people when I was a young man-on-the-street radio interviewer in Peoria," Brickhouse recalled. "My introduction to Wrigley was watching Zeke Bonura [later a White Sox first baseman] beat the Cubs with a home run for the New York Giants. It never occurred to me that I'd be a witness to so many wonderful things in this place.

"Even then, it was so intimate that you felt right at home. I once told [Cubs owner] P. K. Wrigley that I didn't enjoy games nearly as much in other parks. He stopped me in my tracks by saying, 'Jack, other cities have baseball stadiums. We have a real ballpark.'"

Because he stepped into the TV booth when he came over from the White Sox in 1982, Harry Caray became the pied piper for new generations of Cubs fans from every nook and cranny of America.

Brickhouse's radio and TV voice lured them to Chicago ballparks from surrounding states, but both men agreed that Wrigley Field was the end of the rainbow.

"Day baseball and the compact size set Wrigley Field apart," Harry pointed out. "Fans can see the expressions on the players' faces and hear what they're saying."

The last word in the Wrigley accolades that overflowed my notebooks belongs to Ernie Harwell. The legendary Detroit Tigers broadcaster had seen them all, old and new, come and go for almost 60 years, so his vote for Wrigley Field carries more weight.

"When this place is gone, there will never be another to replace it," Harwell said.

CUBS WIND! CUBS WIND! (FANS FREEZE!)

The wind always blows around Wrigley Field. Even if cold air is not coming from the skies, there's plenty of hot air on that topic in home and visitors' clubhouses and dugouts. Pitchers insist the Wrigley gale blows in, especially when it's their turn to take the mound. Hitters beg to differ, although I can stand at the batting cage any day when there's a breeze, however slight, out toward the fences and watch them uppercut their pregame swings, sometimes without even realizing it.

Wind-trend statistics kept by the Cubs indicate in recent years that it has blown in, toward the plate, almost twice as much as out, toward those inviting bleachers. Either way, it can turn everything hit in the air into a guessing game for the defense and an out-of-control game on the scoreboard. The famous 23-22 Phillies victory over the Cubs on May 1, 1979, is the modern-era horror show on the dangers of pitching in Wrigley when the wind blows out. They combined for 50 hits, 11 of them homers—three by the Cubs' Dave Kingman and a pair, including the 10th-inning winner, from Cub-killer Mike Schmidt.

"I saw the flags blowing straight out, so I pointed to [Cub infielder] Mick Kelleher's No. 20 and told him 'Get ready—it's a 20-20 day,'" Schmidt said after this dual slaughter.

Every spring, northwest winds off Lake Michigan bring biting chill to the ballpark. It's the same Arctic blast, called "The Hawk," that cuts wintertime Michigan Avenue pedestrians almost in half. Andre "Hawk" Dawson learned to cope with it, as all outfielders must, but he didn't like it.

"It affects you at bat, too," Dawson said. "You can get into a bad habit of trying to jerk the ball. I figure, whether the wind blows out or in, it's important to hit for average, not for homers."

Fans love it when the breeze—or gale—is in their faces, of course, because they know the basket of baseballs batting practice pitchers lug to the mound will end up in their laps. Since the game hasn't started yet, they don't have to throw enemy drives back.

WINDY OPINIONS

Everybody talks about the weather, particularly at Wrigley Field. Unlike elsewhere, fans and players can do something about it. Fans bundle up on chilly afternoons, while players pray for the ball to be hit elsewhere. No matter what, it plays on their minds, like this:

Keith Moreland: "Some days, you couldn't shoot a bullet out of Wrigley Field. Other days, my little daughter could hit a wiffle ball out of here."

Don Baylor (early in 2000, his first season as Cubs manager): "I talked to people about how to deal with this before I came here, but there's not much you can do. The wind blew out for the first few innings today, and then it turned around, making this a pitcher's park. By the end of the day [with fog creeping in], you couldn't even see the buildings across the street."

Billy Williams (veteran Cubs left fielder and coach): "You need two teams to play at Wrigley Field. Your power team has to outslug the other guys when the wind blows out. Other days, you have to do whatever you can for runs and take some chances on the bases. If you play in Chicago, you know it'll be warm one day and cold the next, so it's important to stay loose as you can."

Pitcher **Rick Sutcliffe** (after a windblown 3-1 loss to the Cards in 1994): "More than any other place, this becomes a pitcher's park when the wind blows in. There are no big innings on days like this. If you don't walk anybody and keep the ball in the park, you'll win."

Cubs center fielder **Doug Dascenzo** (after battling the wind in 1990): "They're hitting everything to me, to my left, to my right, sinking liners. Playing in that wind is like catching a Frisbee. I might be a better Frisbee player before long."

First baseman **Matt Stairs** (after opening his brief Cubs career by batting .186 in 20 Wrigley Field games and .315 for 20 road games): "When I get out of Wrigley, I get into a good hitter mode."

*   *   *   *

Stairs is far from the only player who didn't hit in what's supposed to be a hitter's park. And the moans and groans about Wrigley Field didn't stop there. For instance:

Don Kessinger, dependable Cubs shortstop for a dozen years, still believes Wrigley Field's sun burned out the Cubs in their quest for the 1969 NL pennant: "That heat, day after day, drains your energy," said Kessinger, who had his career day two years later, going six for six in Wrigley Field on June 17, 1971. "By August, the regulars were tired, but [manager Leo] Durocher kept us in the lineup every day. When the Mets made their move, we had nothing left."

Jay Johnstone, Cubs outfielder and clubhouse cut-up: "Wrigley Field is the toughest—windy, sunny, rainy. When there's so much glare, you can't see the ball."

Tommy Helms, Reds infielder: "I've seen pitchers discover they had a sore back or a headache when they came out of the dugout and looked at those Wrigley Field flags."

Pete Rose: "Even if you take care of your body, playing day games makes you more tired."

Bill Buckner, Cubs first baseman: "When the Cubs leave Wrigley Field to go on a trip, it takes three games for the hitters to start seeing pitches again."

Hall of Fame Cubs pitcher **Fetguson Jenkins**: "[Catcher] Randy Hundley lost so much weight in that sun, he needed suspenders to keep his pants from falling down. The players sweated like pigs, but the fans were in the bleachers with their shirts off, getting a tan. It looked more like Oak Street beach."

Cubs pitcher **Burt Hooton**: "Playing in Wrigley Field, the Cubs will never win a pennant."

WRIGLEY REBUTTAL

Former Cubs general manager Bob Kennedy and ex-Cubs coach and manager Joe Amalfitano were ballplayers in their younger days. Both of these up-front, honest guys knew that players, like the rest of us, look for excuses when they don't perform well. They didn't mind that, but making Wrigley Field the scapegoat for underachievement offended them.

"The problem for the Cubs in 1969 was not too much sun on the field," Kennedy said. "It was all the agents and hangers-on in the clubhouse, trying to make a buck by signing the players up for commercials, endorsements, personal appearances, radio spots, and all kinds of time-consuming things. These guys were just too popular."

Amalfitano, a Durocher disciple, managed the Cubs from 1979-81. He felt the same way Ron Santo did about Wrigley Field, defending it from critics. A longtime Dodgers coach after he left Chicago, Pal Joey savored a pregame stroll around his old park when he came to town.

"I enjoy seeing the place come to life," Amalfitano said. "The players say hello, some of the ushers remember me, and when the gates open, those Cubs fans let me know I'm no longer on the right side. They don't care that I love Wrigley Field as much as they do."

THE SHOW MUST GO ON

Unless it snows—a lot—or the rain turns the outfield into a swimming pool or the wind-chill reading dips to the teens—so frigid that even Ernie Banks would say "Let's play one today!"—the Cubs try to play ball.

Often, the resemblance to actual baseball, the summer game, is purely coincidental. I've sat through many of those icicle tour-

Wrigley Field was home to the Bears for many years, until their 1971 shift to Soldier Field. They're practicing in 1963, preparing to beat the New York Giants, 14–10, for their final NFL championship under coach George Halas, while workers try to thaw out the frozen turf.

naments, still chilly despite closed press box windows, wondering why anybody would (a) play or (b) watch a game under such conditions. And I still miss Jack Brickhouse, who never closed the windows in his booth, flinging open the press box door to yell at the writers, "Open those windows, you hothouse flowers!"

Hard as it was to type or take notes with frozen fingers, I managed to do both while the Cubs battled the elements and the opposition, frequently losing that doubleheader. I was there on a chilly day in June, 1972, when the Pirates completed a three-game sweep that signaled the beginning of the end of that season's Cub playoff hopes. The wind played tricks on them, turning Billy Williams's blast to center into a just-missed homer and transforming Willie Stargell's slice to left into a double.

"The wind just brought it back across the line, from foul to fair," left fielder Williams said of Stargell's bloop hit.

"Then it took one bounce and spun foul again, right in the clubhouse door."

That wasn't a typical Wrigley Field day, mainly because there seems to be no such thing. The wind blows in, out, crossways, sideways, or sometimes all of the above, changing with the weather and temperature from inning to inning. I recall a drop of 20 degrees in 10 minutes, with fog swirling over the scoreboard to blot out the bleachers and turn a sunny afternoon into the British moor scenario for a Sherlock Holmes mystery. The wind wasn't the problem on July 4, 1988, when the Cubs built a quick 12-4 lead over the Pirates, only to stagger the rest of the way through a windblown 12-9 victory. The Cubs launched four homers into the wind, then committed four errors, three in a bizarre ninth inning.

"Losing this one would have been hard to handle," said Cubs manager Jim Riggleman, between clenched teeth.

Generations of Cubs fans, players and managers have echoed the same sentiments. Take the snow bowl on April 27, 1973. The Bears had fled Wrigley Field for Soldier Field three years earlier, but this seemed like a replay of them vs. the San Francisco 49ers, right down to the final score—Niners 7, Bears 3.

Actually, it was Giants 7, Cubs 3, but at least the shivering fans didn't have to stick around to the bitter—very bitter—end.

"You expect Chicago to be cold in the spring, but not this cold," grumbled the Giants' Willie McCovey.

Some years, the chilblains hang around all spring and into the summer. Such was the case in 1990, frustrating the Cubs' efforts to start fast in defense of the division title they had won a year earlier. Instead, the '90s got off to a dull thud, and the Cubs made the playoffs just once in the decade, although it took a one-game wild-card playoff victory over the Giants in 1998 to get them there.

It hurt at the box office, as well. A downpour washed out the May 25, 1990, weekend series opener with Houston, dampening an advance sale of 33,000. Sunshine would have lured a full house to the Friendly Confines, but the drenched Cubs had to huddle in their clubhouse, brooding about the gloomy skies.

"This is the worst spring I can remember in Chicago," said second baseman Ryne Sandberg. "Normally, things get better in May. Not necessarily hot, but at least you get some playable conditions. When the temperature got up to the 80s in April, we were on the road."

LET THERE BE LIGHTS

With all the problems during Wrigley Field's unpredictable and sometimes unendurable daytimes, you might think that the 1988 installation of lights would have been met with unanimous approval. Think again.

Before it finally happened, in 1988, a Civil War of sorts convulsed Chicago, spreading from the North Side throughout this toddlin' town—even into White Sox territory—thence to the suburbs and downstate Illinois. Before long, a couple of Chicago mayors, the city council, the state legislature and the courts got involved in a modern-day opera, pitting the mammoth Tribune Company, owner of the Cubs, against a small but determined band of urban guerillas, who cleverly dubbed themselves C.U.B.S. The acronym translated into Citizens United for Baseball in Sunshine—get it?

This battle royale raged in every street, every alley, every lamppost, every saloon, and every patch of turf in Wrigleyville, the square mile of teeming, turbulent neighborhood surrounding Wrigley Field. It was an all-out struggle, featuring lots of nose-to-nose combat between adamant Tribune executives and vehement residents. Naturally, enough legal briefs got filed to provide plentiful yacht payments for flotillas of lawyers.

The whole affair should have become a musical comedy, if not a hilarious sketch by the Second City troupe, with John Belushi portraying Cubs general manager Dallas Green. The death knell for C.U.B.S deserved a score by Verdi—Giuseppi, not Bob. The little guys probably knew from the start that they couldn't prevail against the Tribune's bottomless barrel of clout, but they went down fighting.

Unwittingly, I got the ball rolling on this drama. Soon after William Wrigley, Jr., ended more than 60 years of the gum family's domain by selling the Cubs in 1981 for a mere $21 million, I was assigned to probe the burning question: Would the *Tribune* defy tradition by installing lights in Wrigley Field, the last big-league park without them?

My quest led to Andy McKenna, a Chicago executive with unlimited connections, in and out of the sports world. I soon discovered that the dictionary definition of the word "clout" should have been accompanied by McKenna's picture. We sat down for a lengthy Q-and-A session, and the result was a banner headline atop the front page—the lead story in the news section, not sports—in the next morning's *Chicago Tribune*. It said: NO LIGHTS IN WRIGLEY FIELD: MCKENNA.

Seven years later, the Cubs played their first night game in Wrigley Field. The intrigue, arm-twisting, backroom wheeling and dealing and political power plays that transformed "NO LIGHTS" to "LIGHTS" is indescribable, so I won't try to describe it. Personally, I knew the no-lights game was over when the *Tribune* started playing hardball on its editorial page. All it took on February 10, 1988, was a reference to "political bums" and a blunt threat to move the Cubs out of Chicago. A few months later, the first bank of light towers was being lowered into place on Wrigley's roof.

SAME BATTLEFIELD, NEW WAR

The crusade to control what will happen in and around Wrigley Field goes on unabated. With the park selling out, day and night, the demand for tickets finds almost all of its 39,111 seats filled with fannies almost all the time. Despite their disastrous 67-96 record in 2002, a finish 30 games behind division-winning St. Louis, the Cubs drew an amazing 2,693,096 for only 78 dates, an average of 34,527.

The Cubs want to play more than the 18 night games per season permitted under the original "let there be lights" agreement. Predictably, neighborhood groups were up in arms about both projects, this time with a powerful ally on their side. Richard M. Daley, who wields his mayoral mallet more erratically, although not as effectively, as his father, Richard J. Daley, Chicago's original "Da Mare," balked at giving carte blanche to the *Tribune.*

The mayor also insisted that community groups get input, somewhere short of veto power, into all Wrigley renovations. The simmering controversy over rooftop seats across the street, enabling apartment owners to charge fancy prices for status seekers to upstage the peasants in the bleachers, escalated when the Cubs installed what they called "windscreens," although everybody knew they were view blockers.

Adding the hot potato of pending landmark status for Wrigley Field made alterations and/or expansion more difficult, although not impossible. Despite almost as many quandaries for the North Side showplace than its tenants constantly face on the field, deals finally were cut. As Harry Caray might have summed it up, "You Can Get It Done at the Old Ballpark." The *Tribune*'s limitless clout won the war over rooftop seating rights and enlargement of Wrigley Field's bleachers.

IT ALL HAPPENS HERE

Comedian Red Buttons said it best years ago, starting his TV show by chanting "Strange Things Are Happening." Long before Buttons, the Cubs were flipping their lids in Wrigley Field, a place where unfathomable goings-on go on so often that Cubs fans are surprised when something strange does not happen daily, or nightly.

Maybe a lot of trouble would have been avoided if everybody felt like Philip K. Wrigley, the Cubs owner who paid for a full-page newspaper ad to defend his embattled manager, Leo Durocher. Wrigley always had qualms about lights in the park named for his father.

"If a louse like me put in lights, it would wreck the neighborhood," P. K. predicted.

Actually, what night games did for Wrigleyville was to accelerate the boom that began with general manager Dallas Green's "New Tradition" in the 1980s. The Cubs didn't get much better in the standings, except for 1984 and 1989, but the spruced-up ballpark lured more and more cash customers, triggering bonanzas for neighboring bars, restaurants, stores, and shops. Housing prices went through the roof, as well, especially for dwellings and apartments with rooftop views of Cubs games.

Despite the boom, what Cubs fans inside or outside Wrigley Field saw ranged from bad baseball to bizarre antics to magic moments. Such tales are legendary, like these:

*   *   *   *

Cubs rookie Burt Hooton's no-hitter against Philadelphia on April 16, 1972, almost was gone with the wind, but the frigid gale deflated Bull Luzinski's blast, enabling Rick Monday to nab it at the wall.

*   *   *   *

The fickle Wrigley breeze also saved Ken Holtzman's no-hitter against Atlanta on August 19, 1969. When Braves slugger Hank Aaron unloaded in the seventh inning, Billy Williams sprinted to the fence, expecting to watch The Hammer's sure homer soar high over his head. Instead, the ball curved back into the park, just enough for the Cubs' left fielder's frantic leap to pluck it out of the ivy.

*   *   *   *

Fortunately, the wind was no deterrent to Gary Gaetti's two-run homer on the night of September 28, 1998, clinching the Cubs' only postseason berth in that decade.

*   *   *   *

Stan Musial's 3,000th hit on May 13, 1958; Pete Rose's 4,191st hit, on September 10, 1985, tying Ty Cobb's supposedly un-matchable all-time record. Both the Cards and Reds wanted their superheroes to reach those pinnacles at home, but it happened in Wrigley Field.

*   *   *   *

So did Sammy Sosa's historic 60th and 61st home runs in three separate years (1998-99 and 2001), creating a six-pack of ecstasy for Cubs fans everywhere. Tradition is so much a part of this game that even though Mark McGwire already had surpassed Babe Ruth's 1927 record of 60 homers (and Barry Bonds far eclipsed it with 73 in 2001) there was special significance in Slammin' Sammy's three-peat besting of the Babe.

*   *   *   *

For Cubs fans everywhere, whether they've lived the pregame excitement at Clark and Addison or merely shared it vicariously on TV, this park is baseball's answer to Disneyland.

Chapter 8

"Hey! Hey!" and "Holy Cow!"

In the beginning, the written word was much more important to baseball than the spoken word. Not any more, though the change was gradual.

For most of the 20th century, the Baseball Writers Association of America ruled press boxes in big-league parks, with veto power over who got in and who didn't. Tape recorder-toting radio people were unwelcome, and shoulder-mounted TV cameras hadn't been invented when I first encountered Elmer, the burly Andy Frain usher who served for years as guardian of the narrow, cramped old Wrigley Field press box, next to the third base catwalk.

Even then, Jack Brickhouse on TV and Vince Lloyd, paired with Lou Boudreau, on radio were closing the gap rapidly. With the explosion of interest in the Cubs during and after that 1969 season in the sun, notwithstanding their September in the tank, the media crush in the clubhouse and on the field mushroomed

A pair of Chicago aces, Jack Brickhouse and Ernie Banks, man the WGN microphones. They became lifelong friends as soon as Ernie joined the Cubs in 1953.

to Lake Shore Drive traffic-jam proportions. It was merely the opening pitch for what happened when Harry Caray jumped ship from the White Sox, taking over the Cubs' TV booth in 1982.

And that wasn't all the Holy Cow! man took over. Already a cult figure in decrepit Comiskey Park, Harry had the South Side in his hip pocket and was anxious to prove that there was room for the rest of Chicago. In the next 15 years, he did much better than that. Before long, the Cubs were one of America's favorite acts, with him as the ringmaster and the headliner, all rolled into one charismatic package.

But Jack Brickhouse got the ball rolling much earlier, opening an era by describing WGN's first Wrigley Field telecast on April 16, 1948, when the White Sox beat the Cubs 4-1 in a City

Series matchup. For five decades, his voice probably was one of the most-recognized ones within reach of WGN's powerful radio and TV signals. In the summertime during the 1950s, '60s, '70s and on into the '80s, it was impossible to walk down any street in Chicago or its booming boondocks without hearing Brickhouse's voice, resonating loud and clear from open windows in house after house: "Back she goes! Back, back . . .Hey! Hey! Attaboy, Ernie! Whee!"

Cornball? Maybe. But it was vintage Chicago, an echo that hangs on in memory vaults inside the heads of just about everybody who grew up around these parts after World War II. Caray's signature routine, warbling "Take Me Out to the Ball Game" in his rasping voice during the seventh-inning stretch, was derided as a vaudeville show by some media sophisticates, as well. But the people who professed to be too hip to enjoy such Wrigley Field window dressing made up a tiny minority.

The vast and far-from-silent majority loved Harry even more outside his TV booth. They still do, even though he's been gone since February 18, 1998.

WE'RE STILL WILD ABOUT HARRY

In Chicago sports history, there have been lots of superstars. Only two of them in my time became megastars: Michael Jordan and Harry Caray.

An unlikely pairing, the pudgy announcer and the magnificent athlete. About the only thing they had in common was that both of them came from elsewhere to become the two biggest names in Chicago. And not just in sports. Caray and Jordan, Jordan and Caray. The biggest names—period. Yet if it came to a one-on-one showdown between them, I could pick a clear winner.

Author Bob Logan, left, with Harry Caray in Wrigley Field.

Harry Carabina. That was his real name, but nobody remembers Cary Grant's real name was Archibald Leach, either. Accept no substitutes. Harry was the one and only.

I first met him in 1971, the night he came to town to take a bow at the annual Chicago baseball writers' dinner. Instead, he took the spotlight and held it until the day he died. Nonnative Harry was Chicago, in the same wonderful, inexplicable way that Mayor Richard J. Daley, a Chicagoan by birth, was Chicago.

"There were only two big names in St. Louis—Stan Musial and me," Harry told me that night in '71, after wowing the baseball banquet with the new routines that never got old for the next 28 years. Caray went on and on, telling me more and more and still more than I thought fans might want to know about him. Boy, was I wrong. Harry then embarked on the first of hundreds of what would become his legendary Rush Street bar-hopping tours, greeting cabbies, waitresses, bartenders, fellow night owls, and just plain fans with equal-opportunity gusto. His modus operandi never varied: waving, signing autographs, shaking hands, and buying a round at every stop. Later, I went on a few of those journeys with Harry, and I never saw him let anyone else pick up a bar tab.

Around dawn on that first night, the time he got to his permanent Chicago home base, the Ambassador East hotel, Harry had picked up the paper with the story I'd written about him hours earlier. He promptly sat down and wrote me a note, now one of my most prized sports souvenirs, ending with the words, "We will have a tall one soon."

Well, Harry and I had lots of tall ones, along with more than a few short ones, over the next couple of decades. Some of the charges leveled by Caray's critics, mainly that he was a shameless self-promoter, might have been true. For me, it came down to the undeniable fact that Harry promoted baseball, first, last, and always. He was a tonic for the game, a goodwill ambassador for Chicago and a morale booster for White Sox and Cubs fans, who certainly needed that after watching their teams play. When Caray switched to the Wrigley Field TV booth in 1982, his powerful personality soon made Cubs fans out of people who had never been near Chicago. Because of him, thousands of them made the trek to the Wrigley throne of St. Harry, oftentimes more to sing along with him at the seventh-inning stretch than to see the game.

HEY, HAR-EEE!

That was the battle cry of Harry's adoring legions. South Side, North Side, it made no difference. He was the fans' guy, wooing them on the air, charming them in person, and above all, luring them to the place where he really believed, "You can't beat fun at the old ballpark!" Without a doubt, Caray saved the White Sox from bankruptcy and/or getting sold out of town—probably both—in his eventful Comiskey Park decade.

That would have been a hard act for anybody to follow, except him. Then Harry topped himself by almost single-handedly transforming the lowly Cubs into one of America's most beloved sports franchises. How did he do it? Here are some clues:

*   *   *   *

In 1981, the year before Caray became their TV voice, Cubs cablecasts reached one million households. By 1984, that total had rocketed to over 20 million. Some of that boost could be credited to the Cubs' drive to end their depressing streak of 39 years without a postseason berth. Most of it was pure Harry and the way he re-energized Wrigley Field, whipping increasingly bigger crowds into daily—and since 1988, nightly—frenzies.

Not surprisingly, one of Caray's best friends in Chicago was Butch McGuire, a saloon keeper and proprieter of a wildly popular Division Street singles meet market. He summed up Harry's brand of salesmanship by saying, "If this man sold elephants, I'd have them on my shelves. He's the world's greatest salesman."

*   *   *   *

Harry's fisherman's net, a broadcast booth staple, allegedly was intended to snare foul balls. Actually, it was another aspect of his genius at showmanship. All Caray had to do was wave the net out the window to trigger a "Hey, Hareee!" roar from the stands.

"When I lower the net, I'm amazed at some of the things people put in it," he told me. "Most of them just send blank pieces of paper for autographs, but I've found keys, phone numbers and even dollar bills. I'd never charge any fan to sign my name for them."

MILD ABOUT HARRY

Caray's outspoken style ruffled feathers, of course. Many ball-players complained bitterly about the way he pinpointed blame on the spot when things went wrong. Most of them suffered in silence, although White Sox third baseman Bill Melton once confronted his tormentor in a Milwaukee hotel lobby, and punches nearly were thrown. Harry stood his ground, as he always did, eventually earning grudging respect by never hesitating to face the people he had zinged.

Even Melton joined that chorus after getting a game-winning hit against the Sox, who had traded him to California in 1976.

"That was to win a game for the Angels, not me saying 'Take that, Harry,'" Melton confided to me. "He has a lot of power, and we [the players] get mad at him sometimes, but there's no doubt the fans love him."

That was the key, pure and simple, of Harry's enormous popularity. He loved the way the fans loved him, and he loved them back. Those who dared to attack Harry in Chicago soon discovered they had made a multitude of instant enemies. When he switched to the Cubs in 1982, the whole country tuned in on his wavelength. Caray could say things other broadcasters would have been pilloried for, like, "How could a guy born in Mexico lose a pop fly in the sun?" He got away with slips of the tongue, bloopers, malaprops, mangled pronunciations, and just plain mistakes, especially after suffering a stroke on February 17, 1987.

WHEN HARRY MET RONNIE

Harry might have lost a foot off his fastball, as the pitchers say, in his final years with the Cubs. He didn't lose an inch off his grip on the fans. When he came back to work, just three months after the 1987 stroke, his longtime producer, Arne Harris, switched a phone call to the Wrigley Field TV booth.

"Harry, this is Ronald Reagan," said the president of the United States. "A lot of celebrities filled in during your recovery, but there's no substitute for the real thing."

"What a pleasant surprise," responded Caray in one of the few moments he was at a loss for words.

"Last time we were on the air together, you were playing Grover Cleveland Alexander in a movie."

HOW OLD HARRY AND CARY?

Caray was as nimble as another fan of his, actor Cary Grant, in declining to get pinned down about his real age. A vintage Hollywood story had some brash Eastern magazine writer sending a telegram to the star, demanding: "How old Cary Grant?" He got a quick reply via Western Union: "Old Cary Grant fine. How you?"

Caray's method was the same one used by Dizzy Dean, a colorful Cardinals pitcher in the 1930s. He gave different interviewers a variety of birth dates, ranging from 1914 to 1920. Shaving a few years off is a common practice among ballplayers, and it worked just as well for the ageless broadcaster.

THE DAY THE MUSIC DIED

Those of us who were around Caray in the middle '90s could see his strength diminishing. He never lost his zest for the game until his death. A showman to the end, Harry would have been pleased by the statue of him that was dedicated with full fanfare on Opening Day, April 4, 1998. It was the location that doubt-less would have pleased him most—outside the bleachers at the corner of Clark and Sheffield.

RIGHT TOWN, WRONG SIDE

"I'm glad I'm here to broadcast White Sox games, instead of the Cubs," Caray quipped in 1971, when he came to Chicago. "By the time I get back from Rush Street, it would be too late to get to Wrigley Field for those day games."

Day or night, he helped us have a lot more fun at any old ballpark. Harry's signature "Holy Cow!", originally a defense mechanism for a young broadcaster to avoid slipping back into the profanity he learned on the streets of St. Louis, became the battle cry for new generations of Chicago fans.

BRICK'S HOUSE A MANSION

Jack Brickhouse was the voice of Chicago sports long before Harry Caray showed up to usher in a new style and a new era of micsmanship. Harry was brash, breezy, and bold. Jack was soothing, subtle, and serene. Trying to draw comparisons be-tween these two giants of the broadcast business would be as futile as preferring balmy breezes over summer sunshine.

Caray was a man mostly for one season—baseball—although he did other sports, as well. When the game was dull, he suf-fered along with his listeners. And when things got exciting, he could bring the fans bolt upright in their chairs at home—"Here it is! Heee had a cut! It's in there, a curve, a beauty! There's danger here, Cherie..." And on and on, into the night. Harry's charisma came right through your radio and/or TV set.

Jack Brickhouse? A different story entirely. Even if I could, I wouldn't try to draw parallels between him and Caray. Both were friends, fellow travelers in the sports world, even though they traveled in much loftier circles than I did. Everybody wanted a piece of their fame—and them—because sports, despite all the ways it gets weighted down with the drug, sex, and violence baggage that now afflicts our society, still makes grownups feel like kids again. Harry was aware of the power he wielded, and he used it.

So did Jack. But their styles were different, which explains the totally diverse way they called a ballgame. Brickhouse's Cubs reflected his personality—easy-going, ever-hopeful. He was the right man to start announcing Cubs games on WBKB-TV in 1947 for the princely sum of $35 a game. Listeners quickly got the impression he'd gladly do it for free.

Brickhouse was still the right man in 1981, 34 years and more than 5,000 games later, when he described the Cubs' daily doings for the last time on WGN-TV. And he still talked, felt, and sounded like someone who would gladly have done all of them for free.

"Bob, the only thing I would change is getting to call the seventh game of a Cubs-White Sox World Series in Wrigley Field," Jack told me when we sat down to tape some of his stories for one of my earlier books. "From a young guy doing 'man on the street' radio interviews in Peoria to sitting down for chats with presidents, kings, and even the pope, my career keeps convincing me I'm the luckiest stiff in the world."

He might have sounded like a politician, but he wasn't. The difference between Brickhouse and many politicians was that he was not trying to get elected to anything. His enthusiasm was genuine, just like he was. That's one major reason why a couple of generations in Chicago grew up liking baseball in general and the Cubs in particular. Day baseball had a lot to do with it, too, along with the elevated trains and buses that stopped at Wrigley Field's front door. The fan-friendly ballpark was another drawing card for young people, hooking kids into lifelong espousal of Jack's wait-till-next-year optimism.

So most Cubs fans now in their 50s or even older came to associate baseball with Brickhouse's voice, drifting out of windows on a summer day, from car radios or portables on the beach. He was their Pied Piper—not Pat Pieper—assuring them that the Cubs would get better someday, and that things would get better for them immediately if they came to Wrigley Field.

ERNIE BANKS ON BRICK

No wonder there was such a bond between Ernie Banks and Jack Brickhouse. They were two of a kind, peas in a pod. On my all-time, all-cheerful list, they've always been a Top 10 entry. Brickhouse took the 22-year-old rookie under his wing in 1953, as soon as the Cubs bought the kid shortstop from the Kansas City Monarchs. Their friendship was still going strong, right up to August 6, 1998, the day Brickhouse died. Ernie still has a fund of stories about his pal Jack.

"We always knew how lucky we were to be doing what we wanted more than anything else," Banks told me while we were talking about what he wanted to say in his foreword for my book, *So You Think You're a Die-hard Cub Fan.* "Next to Mr. Wrigley [Philip K., the Cubs' owner, who took a chance on signing the slender youngster and always called that move his smartest decision in baseball], Jack was my biggest supporter in Chicago. I always tried to help him out whenever I could, because he did so much for me.

"When I hit a homer in the first inning of the 1960 All-Star Game, it was for him. He was broadcasting the first few innings, so I wanted to give him something to talk about."

THAT'S GRATITUDE

Brickhouse never came up short in the words department. One of the few times he regretted that was when P. K. Wrigley asked him in 1966 if the Cubs should gamble on hiring Leo Durocher, a man with a rough-and-ready past and a shady reputation.

"I told P. K. to take a chance on Leo," Brickhouse said. "After a while, I could see it wasn't going to work out."

Brickhouse admitted to me privately what he seldom said publicly: Durocher tripped over his own massive ego, eventually getting more caught up in Chicago's social whirl than the fortunes of the struggling Cubs. When the tired club faltered in 1969, on the doorstep of a division title, Leo's bubble burst, even though he hung around for a few more fruitless years.

MAN FOR ALL GAMES

Workaholic Brickhouse always needed a mic to talk into, a game to describe, and an audience to listen to him. I first met him in 1966, when my 16-year merry-go-round on the Bulls' beat began the day they got an NBA franchise. Naturally, Jack jumped in feet first to help a team few others figured would last long in Chicago. He negotiated a WGN-TV contract with Dick Klein, the colorful pitchman who concocted the Bulls out of thin air, and went on the road with them to do play-by-play. When the Bulls won their first game, pulling an upset in St. Louis, Jack was there to give the newcomers his traditional "Hey! Hey!" salute.

Then there was the trip to Cincinnati (temporary home of the Royals, formerly based in Rochester, N.Y., later the Kansas City-Omaha Kings and now the Sacramento Kings) to do a Bulls game. In the hotel that afternoon, Bulls coach Johnny Kerr maneuvered Brickhouse and me around strategically placed floor lamps to show us his version of that basketball standby, the pick-and-roll play. He did all that and lots more while working a full schedule of Cubs and/or White Sox telecasts and teaming with Chicago columnist Irv Kupcinet for 24 years (1953-76) on Bears play-by-play.

Brickhouse switched gears and seasons with the same unflappable, affable ease. John McDonough, marketing director of the Cubs, has no doubt about his place in broadcasting history.

"Jack was the best ever in Chicago," McDonough asserted. "Not just sports, but in everything, from on-the-spot breaking news to major events like political conventions, interviews with world figures and just plain people. With all of that, he found time to make more charity and fundraising appearances for worthy causes than anybody else. He took everything in stride and he laid the foundation for the Cubs' popularity. Harry Caray spread it all over the country, building on what Brickhouse did."

JACK OF ALL NATIONS

The first words heard live on an intercontinental telecast were spoken by Brickhouse: "No score in this ballgame." It happened on July 23, 1962, when the Telstar satellite beamed a 90-second glimpse of Wrigley Field, during a Cubs-Phillies game, to Rome, Vienna, and Stockholm.

THE TRUE TEST

Many temperamental celebrities show a phony facade to the public. The people propping them up behind the scenes bear the brunt of preserving the image. That never was the case with Brickhouse.

His crews and cameramen conspired to make Jack's "Hey! Hey!" home run call a household word by flashing the words on the screen while the Cubs hitter circled the bases. And his two closest associates for decades, TV director Arne Harris and WGN sports editor Jack Rosenberg, were unabashed Brickhouse boosters.

"Jack always looked for something in the stands to brighten up the game when things weren't going well on the field," Harris said. "He knew when the Cubs were bad, just like the fans did, but he found something good to talk about."

Rosenberg underscored that was the real reason why Brickhouse lasted so long and wore so well with his vast audience.

"Jack Brickhouse was the man you wanted as a friend, a brother, a father or a co-worker," he said.

LOU CAN DO

Lou Boudreau did not look like a great athlete, even in his playing days. He had bad ankles, tightly wrapped before every game to ease the constant pain. The shortstop and player-manager did not look like a great competitor, either. In his case, those looks were extremely deceiving.

Long after his career was over, Boudreau's inner fire still burned brightly in the WGN radio booth. He refused to give up on the Cubs, no matter how inept the team or how hopeless that day's deficit. His usual even tones went up a couple of octaves while he told broadcast partner Vince Lloyd what the Cubs should have done in any situation, often the exact reverse of what they actually did. He never lost that zest for the game or that burning desire to win.

Not that he asked other players to do things he couldn't do. In the clutch, with a game or a pennant on the line, few athletes in any sport could come through like Lou Boudreau did.

His WGN tenure was interrupted in 1960, when he switched places briefly with Cubs manager Charlie Grimm. Ed Alsene, my sports editor in Springfield, Illinois, summed up that strange move with a brilliant headline: "GRIMM GETS AIR (WGN); BOUDREAU TO MANAGE CUBS." But there were few Boudreaus left for Lou to manage, because he was one of a kind. When he went back to the radio booth for good in 1961, it was a break for him and a boon for thousands of fans, who listened and learned the right way to play this game.

Lou was pleased when I told him the best entertainment on a Cubs broadcast in those days happened when there was a rain delay. Boudreau would talk baseball with Vince Lloyd and Jack Brickhouse, who were smart enough to toss a question at him, so that he could swat it out of the park. Tapes of those interludes should have been preserved for generations of young players to learn how to hit the cutoff man; how to detect pitchers tipping off pitches by failing to conceal their grip with the glove and a multitude of other subtle skills that keep vanishing in this swing-from-the-heels era.

When Lloyd came to Chicago for the debut of Brickhouse's Broadcast Museum exhibit in 2001, we sat down and talked about those days. Vinny and Lou, a matched set of soft-spoken gentlemen, called each other "Good Kid," a totally accurate sobriquet for them.

"I was constantly amazed by Lou's encyclopedic knowledge of baseball," Lloyd told me. "He taught me a lot. We used to go to the race track on off days. Maybe he couldn't pick the horses too well, but he sure had a handle on what might happen in every situation or any pitch."

A HOME RON HITTER

Just like he was for the Cubs, Ron Santo is a heavy hitter in the WGN radio booth. His banter with play-by-play announcer Pat Hughes probably kept some frustrated Cubs fans from taking a leap off the Michigan Avenue Bridge into the Chicago River during Don Baylor's depressing two-and-a-half-year managerial tenure. Even eternal optimist Santo might have been tempted to join them at times.

"Yes, it's hard to talk about the Cubs coming up short on the radio, just like it was when I played for them," Santo told me while he was recovering from surgery to remove his right leg, below the knee. "But I learned a lesson in 1969, and it still sticks with me."

Santo was at third base that wonderful, woeful summer, when the Cubs got to third base in their seeming cakewalk to the World Series, only to get hung up there while the New York Mets roared past.

It was a bitter blow to Santo, an emotional Italian, although he knew the Cubs did not blow it, contrary to what many Cubs fans felt then, and still do, more than three decades later. The Mets were simply unbeatable down the stretch, a runaway train that crushed Chicago's hopes like tinfoil on the tracks.

"I was very unhappy until Glenn Beckert [second baseman on that team] convinced me that some things can't be changed, no matter how hard you try," Santo said, "Beck was right. It was just the Mets' year."

That philosophy came in handy when a small sore on his right foot suddenly triggered a life-and-death crisis in June 2002. A lifelong diabetic, Santo had been battling the disease and leading a fight against it, especially to help kids, even before 1974, when his baseball career ended. His courage in that effort

Pat Hughes (left) and Ron Santo provide a one-two punch on Cubs radio broadcasts. Hughes's easy-going style blends well with the former Cubs third baseman's emotional approach.

surpassed anything he did on the field, where the fiery third baseman never backed away from any opponent.

After electing to lose his left leg, also below the knee, in 2002, Santo felt he would finally earn that long-delayed Hall of Fame welcome. "Devastated" by another rejection, he went to spring training with the same unbeatable optimism.

That's why I've been a Santo fan for a long time, even though writers are not supposed to root. Still, we're human, despite what some ballplayers, many readers, and even a few editors might think, and we all have our favorites. My yearly Hall of Fame vote went to Santo as long as he was on the ballot, and I do not believe it was a homer decision on my part. Anyone looking objectively at Santo's stats—344 homers, 1,331 RBI, and a .954 fielding average—has to conclude that he compares favorably with George Kell, Pie Traynor, and even the great Brooks Robinson, all of them in the Hall.

I'll let fans and old-timers stage that debate. The way Santo came back from every ordeal, even his heart stopping during one of numerous operations, convinces me he belongs. When he came back to resume the good-natured razzing of his friend, Pat Hughes, and walk daily to the Wrigley Field stands to sign pregame autographs, a Chicago winner was back in action.

STONE ROCKS

Steve Stone's gentle kidding and easy repartee with Harry Caray was a real touch of class, especially after the Chicago icon suffered a stroke in 1987 and came back to work, despite losing a little more of his cutting-edge sharpness with each succeeding year. He had a valuable ally in Wrigley Field's TV booth, because Stone was always ready to pick up the ball with a low-key correction or a timely pun.

"Harry was always No. 1," Steve said. "My job was to back him up, any way I could."

He could—and did.

Chapter 9

ALL ARE CUBS—SOME ARE FLUBS

"You can't tell the players without a scorecard." That's been the battle cry of countless program peddlers in and around thousands of ballparks for 150 years, give or take a strike-shortened season or two.

Such a sales pitch seldom is necessary for Cubs fans. They know their players, all right. And they take a proprietary interest in any body draped in Cubbie blue, from superstars of the Kerry Wood-Sammy Sosa stripe to such cup-of-coffee trivia questions as Joe Strain (batted .189 in 1981) or Bryan Hickerson (6.82 ERA in 1995). Partly, that's the legacy of Ernie Banks, the most beloved Cub of them all, and still "Mr. Cub" more than 30 years after his 512th—and last—homer for them.

Partly, it's the lure of Wrigley Field, the place where kids get hooked for life on the Cubs, while their parents relive their own youth. Before, during, and after games, fans are so close to the field that they can see the players' faces and even hear what they're saying. When the outcome of games no longer is in

Catcher Jody Davis, a Cubs fan favorite, shakes off the punishment that comes with his demanding position. Umpire Bruce Froemming, whose borderline call deprived Milt Pappas of a 1972 perfect game, lends a hand, while trainer John Fierro (right) comes in to assist.

doubt, my habit for years has been to leave the press box and sit where I can watch the fans' reactions, as well as the final outs.

No need to look at the scoreboard to tell who's ahead. A glance at the faces around me does the trick. Cubs fans have learned to tolerate losing, but unlike their counterparts in New York, Boston or Philadelphia, they seldom vent their frustration on the players. No wonder most Cubs, from cult figures like Sosa, Andre "Hawk" Dawson and Gary "Sarge" Matthews Sr. to raw rookies, get psychic income from performing for such faithful fanatics.

Unfortunately, even that unflagging loyalty has not translated into enough Cubs victories, Cubs playoff berths, and the ultimate fan fantasy—a Cubs return to the World Series. Despite the paucity of postseason glory, Cubs fans greeted the dawn of the Dusty Baker era with a renewed burst of optimism. They saw new faces on the roster and bought into Baker's promise to weld their team into a pennant contender.

In my years on the Cubs scene, I've seen such rosy expectations run smack into a reality roundhouse and get counted out in the '70s, '80s (with two exceptions), '90s (one breakthrough) and the same script early in the 21st century.

Even if the drought never ends, Cubs fans and I will share good memories of sunny days and fogless nights in the Friendly Confines. Plenty of rain, wind, and chill, too. For me, watching hundreds of guys in Cub suits, from Hall of Famers to barely famous, has been more fun than work. With some notable exceptions (see chapter 2), they were easy to talk to, deal with, and write about. I tried using tape recorders to gather quotes on occasion, but that method didn't work well for me, especially on deadline. Wading through the 90 percent of meaningless postgame cliches ("That was a big win for us," or "I know my teammates are busting their butts for me") to get to one punchy quote is too time-consuming.

Writing 900 to 1,000 words under relentless time pressure, struggling to make it an entertaining, relevant, complete, and above all accurate portrayal of the game you're covering, is no easy task. I learned long ago that scribbling gibberish-free words, sentences, and sometimes even paragraphs of good quotes in a notebook enabled me to fit them into the story's framework much more efficiently.

Those scribblings are my reward for many years of sportswriting, including this book. One thing I'm proud of is that I have seldom been accused of misquoting a player or manager or taking what they meant to say out of context. Another reason why I enjoy doing this is my belief that these slices of sports history should be preserved and passed along to new generations of readers and fans. Out of all those notebooks, for all those years, here's a glimpse at some of the players I can't forget.

WRITTEN IN STONE

Steve Stone is one of the most interesting, certainly among the brightest, people I've met in sports. That covers a lot of territory. Ever since the 26-year-old right-hander came to the White Sox in 1973, moving to the Cubs a year later, he brought along an impressive blend of poise and savvy. Unlike most young players, Steve really understood baseball, and he knew how to interpret the game's nuances. So fans applauded when he came back to the WGN-TV booth in 2003, teaming with Harry Caray's grandson Chip. They liked it lots less when Stone and Caray left for greener pastures, frustrated by the whining 2004 Cubs.

It was clear from the outset that this man was going places. While winning the American League Cy Young Award with a 25-7 dream season for Baltimore in 1980, Stone was already a successful restaurateur, with a piece of Chicago's legendary Pump Room and successful operations in Arizona. WGN was smart enough to summon him back to the Cubs in 1983 as the TV interpreter for Harry Caray's entertaining jumble of malaprops, mispronouncements, name mangling, and occasional glaring errors.

Stone fielded them all with a smooth blend of humor and insight, playing enough defense in the TV booth to deserve a Gold Glove. I've always wondered why some team (the Cubs, for instance) didn't snap him up as general manager. Maybe it's because his tough-minded analysis of every team's strengths and weaknesses did not paint the unrealistic picture many egotistical owners prefer to hear. Anyway, Stoney's quotes were way ahead of his contemporaries as a player, and they got better as the years went by. A couple of my personal favorites, set in Stone:

"The writers, in their infinite wisdom, were crying for me to be buried in the bullpen," Steve told me in 1979, when his rediscovered forkball turned him almost overnight into one of baseball's best pitchers.

"I've had my differences with Earl Weaver [the Orioles' feisty manager], but he keeps telling me, 'Here's the ball. You're a starting pitcher.' Something had to be done, because I gave up about 15 homers on hanging curveballs. So I thought back to the forkball Fred Martin [former Cubs pitching coach] taught me in 1974."

The results were magical. Struggling with a 6-7 record at the '79 All-Star break, Stone racked up a 30-7 mark over the next one and a half seasons, baffling hitters with his new out pitch. He stopped losing games, although he kept the quick wit that set him apart from the herd.

"I don't hang around the clubhouse much after games," he said. "Being surrounded by a bunch of hairy-legged guys in their underwear never was my idea of fun."

DREAM SEQUENCE

When Don Zimmer was their manager (1988-91), the punchless Cubs scored even less than Rodney Dangerfield. Zim had to try almost everything except stealing first base to generate some offense, so imagine his elation on June 8, 1990, when the Cubs poured across 11 runs in the third inning to pulverize the Phillies, 15-2. His reaction?

"I slapped myself to make sure I was awake," Zimmer said.

An even bigger surprise during that rout was shortstop Shawon Dunston's long-awaited 100th career base on balls. Dunston usually started swinging in the on-deck circle and didn't stop, even if the pitch was in the dirt or over his head. He went into the game with only 98 walks in 2,420 at-bats—an astronomical ratio of one for every 25.2 trips—but strolled twice to reach the century mark.

"I took a lot of razzing," the grinning Dunston confessed. "After the second walk, they tried to give me the ball."

PERFECTLY TRUE

If anybody knows anything about all-around pitching, it's 43-year-old Mike Morgan, who's been all around both circuits, into his fourth big-league decade. There's no truth to the rumor the ex-Cub was the starting pitcher in the 1839 game of town ball in Cooperstown, New York, when Abner Doubleday allegedly invented baseball, but he's performed for almost everybody else, from coast to coast. The durable right-hander kept on going into the 21st century with the attitude that served him well during his two stints with the Cubs (1992-95 and 1998).

"I got a pitch up and he hurt me," Morgan said after yielding a homer to the Phillies' Dave Hollins in Wrigley Field. "We're not perfect. If pitchers were perfect, there wouldn't be any hitters."

TRADE FADE

Cubs fans can't help wondering what might have happened in the '90s—and beyond—if the Cubs hadn't made a bad trade on December 5, 1988. They shipped first baseman-outfielder Rafael Palmiero, along with pitchers Jamie Moyer and sore-armed lefty Drew Hall, to the Texas Rangers. Tough-luck Hall opened some eyes in his Cubs debut when he fanned 10 White Sox batters in seven innings on May 19, 1986, but never lived up to his promise.

Palmiero and Moyer sure did—unfortunately, elsewhere. In between making semi-raffish Viagra commercials, Raffy became one of baseball's most consistent power hitters. Until the 2005 steroid scandal blighted the end of his career, Palmiero seemed a cinch for the Hall of Fame, with more than 500 homers and 3,000 hits.

Just suppose, drooling Cubs fans, that your team had kept Palmiero and Moyer and stopped nursing nickels long enough to re-sign Greg Maddux in 1992. That was the same year they stole a young outfielder named Sammy Sosa from the White Sox. Dream on.

While Palmiero and Moyer were doing just fine in the American League, Maddux had to build an extra mantelpiece for his Atlanta collection of Cy Young trophies. The Cubs, even with Sosa's budding superstardom, got sentenced to another might-have-been decade. Singles (and doubles) hitter Mark Grace was a fancy-fielding first baseman, but the Cubs got to first base in the pennant race just once with him, backing into a 1998 wild card spot, only to back out of the playoffs even faster.

Meanwhile, Palmiero was wearing out AL basepaths with his home run trot, Moyer's dipsy-do soft stuff kept baffling hitters, and Maddux joined Tom Glavine and John Smoltz to pitch a dynasty teepee for the Braves.

CUBS GET TAPPED OUT

Pitchers seldom finish what they start nowadays. Still, Cubs fans couldn't blame Kevin Tapani for wanting to change Leo Durocher's famous quote to "Nice guys finish best." One of the best people I encountered on the Cubs beat, the veteran right-hander deserved lots more help than he got from the bullpen in his five North Side years.

Tapani kept the Cubs in the game for most of his 128 starts. Relievers frequently provided little or no relief, especially in 2000, when he started 30 games, left with the lead six times and the score tied four times, only to get a no-decision in all 10 of those. Pitchers with 20-victory seasons usually can look back on a couple of starts when they trailed,

Without recurring ailments, hard-luck Kerry Wood's right arm might have become the deadliest weapon in Chiago sports since Bobby Hull's slap shot. **Photo courtesy of the Chicago Cubs.**

got the hook and still ended up as the winner because their team rallied. Not Tapani.

So, especially for a man with ample reason for clubhouse tantrums, the former White Sox hurler showed remarkable restraint by not hurling gloves, bats, the postgame food spread, or even epithets at a handy target—the media converging around his locker. No matter how tough the loss, Tapani never ducked us, dealing with all questions and inquisitors in the same even-tempered tone.

"Getting mad at you guys won't make me feel better," Tap told me in the middle of his personal 12-game losing streak that stretched for 15 starts, from June 24, 1999, until April 28 of the following season.

"Besides, it can't change what happened. Everybody in this clubhouse shared the credit when we made the playoffs [in 1998]. You can't put the blame for losing on one guy, either."

Nobody blamed Tapani when the Cubs sneaked into that one-game wild-card playoff with the Giants in '98. He stepped up to become the ace of the staff after Kerry Wood missed the final month with the elbow misery and eventual surgery that kept him out of action until May 2, 2000. Tapani (19-9), Steve Trachsel (15-8) and Wood (13-6) combined for 47 victories—more than half of the Cubs' total of 90.

Sadly, they got no more in an 0-3 first-round playoff wipeout by the Braves and old pal Greg Maddux.

Far above and beyond his 48-48 record with the Cubs, Tapani's ability to put things in perspective made him a quiet clubhouse leader and a teacher for Wood and other young pitchers. He was at his best after one of the worst losses of them all. That was in Cincinnati on May 7, 1999, when Tapani worked a gritty eight innings, turning a 2-1 lead over to Cubs closer Rod "Shooter" Beck. The Shooter shot only the Cubs, blowing the save and the game to the Reds on Barry Larkin's two-out, two-run double. Tapani's response should have been taped to become mandatory listening for every rookie pitcher.

"I was driving on an empty tank in the eighth inning, so I can't second-guess Jim [Cubs manager Riggleman]," he said. "We did everything by the book, the way a winning team should all the time. The starter [himself] got the ball to Rod with the lead in the ninth. That's how we made it to the postseason last year, and I don't see why it can't work again."

A major reason why it didn't was the string of injuries plaguing Tapani near the end of his career. He was far from through when the White Sox mistakenly gave up on him, despite a 13-10 record in 1996, but the new Cub's debut was delayed by finger surgery in 1997. Afterwards, shoulder, back, and knee problems put Tap on the disabled list at various times, curtailing his Cub starts. None of those ailments hurt worse than Game 2 of the 1998 NL playoff in Atlanta, where he had a 1-0 lead until Javier Lopez homered to tie it in the ninth inning, and the Braves won, 2-1, in the 10th.

"No regrets about that game or anything that happened in Chicago," Tapani said after the Cubs declined to pick up his $4 million salary option for 2002. "I'll never forget how the guys stuck with me through the [12-game] losing streak. They were beginning to press, because everybody was aware of the streak and nobody wanted to make a mistake when I pitched."

ZONK SNIFFS AT CUBS

Keith "Zonk" Moreland could be counted on for two things when he played for the Cubs from 1982-87. The former Texas defensive back, nicknamed for Zonker Harris of "Doonesbury" fame, never stopped hustling—or telling the truth. That's why he was a fan favorite in 1984, while the Cubs had them dancing in the streets by coming within one game of a 1945 World Series rematch with the Detroit Tigers.

Moreland refused to alibi during a nightmarish 0-3 playoff weekend in San Diego that turned the dream into a nightmare. He was still telling it like it was two years later, with the self-destructing Cubs already 20 1/2 games behind the Mets, before the end of June.

"Right now, we stink," Moreland confessed, lamenting a 7-4 loss on June 29, 1986, to the Mets and Cub-killer Dwight Gooden. "I can't say one person's not getting the job done. It's all of us, including me, I'm right down there with the rest of the team.

"Fortunately, every season has a second half. If we want to stay in Chicago, we better make the most of it."

Moreland's premonition proved accurate. The staggering Cubs, already out of the race, were laboring under their third manager before the season's midpoint. Jim Frey, the toast of the town only two years earlier—at least until that traumatic play-off collapse in San Diego—stepped down early in 1986, with coach John Vukovich taking the reins for two games. For the record, Vukovich split his pair of decisions, joining an exclusive Cubs managerial club.

He became just one of three pilots in the franchise's first 128 years to finish with an even .500 record, joining Jim Lefebvre (162-162 in 1992-93) and Bob Ferguson (30-30 in 1878). A few notable exceptions who barely made it to the plus side were Leo Durocher (535-526 in 1966-72) and Don Zimmer (265-258 in 1988-91).

General manager Dallas Green, a self-styled baseball genius, made sure the Cubs wouldn't repeat their 1984 heroics, replacing the Frey-Vukovich regime by thumbing through a big-league executives' directory to come up with Gene Michael, a Yankees lifer. Michael knew little about the National League and less about Chicago, so he was doomed from the start, fleeing town before the next losing season ended.

SUTTER SPLITS FOES' BATS

Bruce Sutter's split-fingered out pitch got the Cubs out of numerous jams in his 1976-80 reign as bullpen king. He racked up 133 saves, with a season-high 37 in 1979. Yet Cubs fans got on him when he didn't close the deal every time out. The jeers were loudest in '78, with Sutter suffering through a slump while the Cubs fizzled at the end, an all-too-familiar scenario.

"Hey, Herman—go kick Sutter in the ass!" a frustrated Wrigley Field spectator bellowed at rotund Cubs manager Herman Franks, himself nearing the end of his final season at the helm.

The same sort of unrest broke out in the Cubs' clubhouse, as well. Ken Holtzman, author of two no-hitters for them in 1969 and again in 1971, was finding it hard to keep his cool in the lefty's second term on the pitching staff.

"We haven't had a clubhouse fight since Ron Santo tried to choke that despicable Leo Durocher," Holtzman recalled of that memorable blowup on August 23, 1971, with Durocher barking, "I didn't realize you guys hated me so much," then ripping off his uniform before general manager John Holland had to talk him out of quitting on the spot.

"Leo wanted respect, so he asked the players to speak up, and Santo, Milt Pappas and other guys told him what they really thought about him," said the quiet man, Billy Williams.

Holtzman, no fan of Durocher, held his tongue in that uprising, but blew up when he heard Cubs players talking of sharing third-place money with Montreal at the tail end of 1979.

"I almost went crazy," Holtzman said. "With a month left, some of these guys were quitting."

Sutter refused to give up on himself or the team. He added 32 victories to those 133 saves, but the Cubs refused to yield when an arbitrator decided their closer was worth $900,000, so they dealt him to St. Louis after the 1980 season for Leon Durham, Ken Reitz, and Ty Waller. Shrugging off shoulder problems, Sutter helped the Cards win the 1982 World Series, then signed a whopping $25 million contract with Atlanta, only to get his career string of saves cut short at 300 by that stubborn injury.

Ironically, Sutter is best remembered in Chicago for getting victimized by ex-teammate Ryne Sandberg on June 23, 1984. Ryno tied the game with a ninth-inning solo homer off Sutter, then did it again with a two-run shot in the 10th. Amid the hysteria that turned Wrigley Field into a lunatic asylum when the Cubs won, 12-11, few noticed that the Cubs reliever who gave up two runs to the Cards in the top of the 10th was Lee Smith, the new bullpen savior. Baseball is, indeed, a funny game, but Sutter kept his cool-headed approach, despite the constant pressure that knots most relief pitchers' stomachs.

"I'll never change," he told me during his first season in St. Louis. "I have a businesslike approach, because this is a business."

And much more often than not, Sutter's diving-bombing splitter gave hitters the business.

NORTH VS. SOUTH

Ron Coomer, a born and bred Chicago fan, spent most of his career in the American League. But for the 2001 season, he was part of a turnabout that had Cubs fans dreaming of a Wrigley Field October. From a dismal 65-victory showing in Don Baylor's managerial debut, they spurted to 88-74, finishing just five games behind division-winning Houston.

Pennant fever was a raging epidemic on June 8, with the cocky Cubs 15 games over .500 at 36-21, fresh from a wild weekend Wrigley Field sweep of the Cards that put them in first place—first place!—by five full games, heading to Comiskey Park for a showdown with the White Sox. If only moments like that could be bottled to get Cubs fans through all those dreary might-have-been winters, Wrigleyville's quality of life would quadruple over its normal state of perpetual optimism, even in the worst of times. And nobody was savoring that brief shining moment more than Coomer, although he confessed to being a boyhood Sox fan.

"This is really big," Coomer said, perched in the visitors' Comiskey Park dugout while the stands filled with a 50-50 blend of Cubs and Sox fans, proving that oil and water sometimes can mix. "All weekend, while we were winning three straight from the Cardinals, you could feel the electricity building up in Wrigley Field. Our fans were happy about the sweep, but we could see those 'Bring on the Sox' signs they were holding up.

"When I was a kid here, Cubs vs. Sox was the only game in town, even if it was just an exhibition. The bragging rights meant a lot more to the fans than they did for the players. Now that these games count in the standings, it just adds more excitement. This is really fun. The whole city is plugged in, taking sides and arguing baseball."

MAC'S COMEBACK

Lloyd McClendon showed some promise and some punch for the 1989 Cubs, batting .286 with a dozen homers and 40 RBI. A year later, hitting a lowly .177, the career benchwarmer got shipped to Pittsburgh for a lefty pitcher named Michael Pomeranz, who never made it to the Cubs. A Gary, Indiana native, McClendon caught the eye of big-league scouts by homering in five at-bats and walking in the other five at the 1971 Little League World Series.

But he had to struggle through almost nine years in the minors before the Reds finally called him up. The way the charismatic McClendon handled that adversity stamped him as a man with leadership potential. Besides, he had seen almost all the right and wrong ways to handle every strategic situation down there in the bushes, filing away that information for future use.

"Life is funny," McClendon reflected when the Cubs gave up on him in 1990. "It hasn't been a good year for me, but I want to go help the Pirates win some games. "

After a stint as Pittsburgh's manager, Northwest Indiana favorite McClendon switched to the American League in 2006, coaching for the Tigers. He spoiled Opening Day 2002 in Wrigley Field by steering the Pirates to a 2-1 victory, continuing the downward spiral that cost manager Don Baylor his job on July 5, just before the All-Star break. Bruce Kimm, well-liked skipper of the Iowa farm club, got summoned to shuffle the lineup the rest of the way, but couldn't stop the bleeding for the 67-95 Cubs.

AN EERIE OMEN

Little was made of it at the time, but a year later, some fans recalled what had happened to Cardinals pitcher Darryl Kile in Wrigley Field on July 27, 2001. A line drive by Robert Machado of the Cubs glanced off Kile's glove and hit him in the face. Somehow, the veteran scrambled after the ball and threw Machado out at first base, preventing a run from scoring. He collapsed on the infield grass, but insisted on coming out for the sixth inning before going to the hospital for stitches.

So manager Tony La Russa and the rest of the Cards knew something was wrong when Kile, a team leader and an intense competitor, did not show up at Wrigley Field on June 22, 2002, the day before he was scheduled to start against the Cubs. Only 33, Kile was found dead in his hotel room, the victim of congenital heart disease. That game got canceled, but the Cubs won, 8-3, the next day, although the shock of Kile's death cast a pall over fans and players alike. For once, the ferocious Cubs-Cards rivalry took a back seat to shared sadness.

"The way the Cubs fans reacted, telling our players how sorry they were about Darryl, showed me a lot of class," La Russa said.

NEW CENTER OF ATTENTION

Adding speedy spice to the Cubs-White Sox battle for Chicago supremacy in 2006 was the Juan Pierre-Scott Posednik base-stealing derby. The Cubs finally landed a thoroughbred of their own in Pierre, stealing him from the Florida Marlins for potential starter Sergio Mitre and two more minor-league pitchers. The trade was met with roars of glee from Cubs fans, snapping them out of the funk that spread over the North Side at the news that Atlanta shortstop Rafael Furcal had spurned general manager Jim Hendry's five-year contract offer, signing instead with the Dodgers.

But landing Pierre for lots less money was intended to close a glaring gap, not only in center field, but also at the leadoff spot in the batting order. Noted for his Charlie Hustle approach, Pierre brought impressive credentials as a pesky, consistent hitter, a constant threat to steal, and best of all, the potential to get on base, setting the table for sluggers Derrek Lee and Aramis Ramirez. His former managers, Buddy Bell in Colorado and Jeff Torborg in Florida, fell in love with Pierre's speed and work ethic.

"As soon as Juan gets on first base, he rattles the opposing pitcher and catcher," said Torborg, the former White Sox pilot

(1989-81), who was managing the Marlins when Pierre came over from the Rockies. "Power hitters like Lee and Ramirez will get more fast balls to swing at. Juan's a special guy."

And Pierre's specialty, swiping bases, was being counted on by manager Dusty Baker to revitalize the lumbering Cubs. In a make-or-break 2006 campaign for Baker and his team, Pierre became the central figure—not just in center field—from Day 1 in spring training.

CENTER OF CONTROVERSY

Fun was not No. 1 on the agenda for many of Patterson's center field predecessors. They've had some stormy petrels out there, like one of the best, Bill North, who got so fed up with the Cubs' contretemps, on the field and in the front office, that he fled in 1972 to Oakland, teaming with Bert Campaneris to give the A's a one-two leadoff punch that led to their third straight World Series triumph in 1974. A decade later, a new center fielder, Bob "Deer" Dernier, provided the same spark for the Cubs, even though a funny thing happened to that not-quite team of destiny on its way to the 1984 World Series.

Then there was Mel Hall, who always seemed to be seeking— and finding—trouble. He brawled with pitcher Dick Ruthven, another short-tempered Cub, during spring training in 1984, convincing general manager Dallas Green that Hall had to give way to Dernier in the lineup.

So Hall was expendable, becoming part of the fortunate June 15 trade that brought Rick Sutcliffe in from Cleveland to pitch the Cubs to the doorstep of the promised land. On the way out of town, he complained, "Who's this Sutcliffe? I wouldn't mind getting a hit off him." Hall also lamented that the only two Cubs players who didn't hang their heads over lost games were himself and Jay Johnstone, both gone long before the Cubs wrapped up their first-ever NL Eastern Division title. "Why sit around and pout about a loss?"

Jerome Walton, NL Rookie of the Year, was on the center field stage in 1989, helping drive the Cubs to the top in the East Division with a 30-game hitting streak, still the modern-era club record.

"I'll just have to start another one," the cocky freshman said.

But while Walton's ego soared, his performance dipped, and he drifted away in 1992. His wasted potential replayed the saga of Joe "Tarzan" Wallis (1975-79). He preferred to be the center of fans' attention by crashing his motorcycle into various immoveable objects rather than playing center for the Cubs. The resultant bumps and bruises caused the clubhouse whirlpool bath to be renamed the "U.S.S. Wallis," because he spent so much time soaking in it.

THE REAL FLAG WINNER

My favorite Cubs center fielder of them all was Rick Monday (1972-76). A solid hitter and a good outfielder, Monday made his most sensational defensive move in Dodger Stadium on April 25, 1976. He swooped down on an American flag, spread on the outfield grass by a couple of political dissidents, just as they lit a match to set it on fire. Monday carried the Stars and Stripes to safety while ballpark cops arrested the intruders and the normally laid-back L.A. crowd rose to give the quick-thinking Cub a standing ovation. "Rick Monday: You Made a Great Play" was the stadium's scoreboard salute, earning him another round of cheers.

"If you want to burn the flag, don't do it in front of me," Monday said. "I've seen too many veterans in hospitals who gave arms and legs for that flag."

MAC ATTACK

One of the best-hitting Cubs pitchers was Chuck McElroy (1991-93), a chunky southpaw reliever with a good bat and matching attitude.

"I won't see any more fastballs," McElroy predicted after his triple, single, and save on the mound ended a Cubs losing streak with a 9-2 Wrigley romp over the Cards on April 11, 1992. "Pitchers have long memories, so they'll throw me curves from now on. I was a pretty good hitter in high school, but I don't care where the Cubs play me as long as I get into the game."

NU, TOO, JOE

Joe Girardi dreamed about playing for the Cubs when he was a catcher at Northwestern, a few miles up the road from Wrigley Field. When manager Don Zimmer saw how the rookie handled pitchers in 1989 spring training, he turned that fantasy into reality by keeping him on the roster. Girardi got into that season's playoff with San Francisco, and he thought nothing could top it.

"I was a Cub fan growing up [in Peoria, Illinois], so this still seems unreal," he said.

But that was just a tuneup for Girardi's postseason performances—sadly, no more in Chicago. He made the scene again in Colorado and then earned three World Series rings with the all-conquering Yankees of the 1990s before returning to the Cubs in 2000. Genial Joe took that in stride, because the fans and media appreciated him, even if Sammy Sosa didn't welcome the veteran receiver's advice not to crank up the clubhouse music after the Cubs lost.

Chapter 10

HANG BUNTING, NOT CREPE

The Cubs do not have a "Mr. October" to match Reggie Jackson, who hit three home runs on three consecutive pitches in Game 6 of the 1977 World Series, leading the New York Yankees to a clinching victory over the Los Angeles Dodgers.

In fact, they lurched through the 20th century going pretty much 0 for October as a team. The Cubs did get into the World Series 10 times (1906-07-08, '10, '18, '29, '32, '35, '38 and '45) in a 39-year span, actually winning it twice with back-to-back triumphs over the Detroit Tigers in 1907 and again in 1908.

To paraphrase "The Midnight Ride of Paul Revere," hardly a man is now alive who remembers that famous day and year—October 14, 1908—when Orval Overall gave overall superiority to the Cubs by whitewashing Ty Cobb and the Tigers, 2-0. It wrapped up that World Series in five games. Much, much more significantly, it was the last postseason matchup in close to 100 years that ended with the Cubs winning the final game, at least until the magical, mystical, maybe even miraculous date of October —, 20—?

Fill in the blank yourselves, pennant-hungry Cubs fans. Supply the details from your fevered imaginations, tossing in all those leftover fantasies of an Ernie Banks (or Billy Williams or Ron Santo or Andre Dawson or Sammy Sosa) homer winning the decisive World Series game in Wrigley Field.

Ponder the wild celebrations erupting in Wrigleyville, all over Chicago, throughout Illinois—even in Little Egypt, traditional Cards country—and pretty much around the whole nation, for that matter. You know the legacy of Harry Caray created thousands of closet Cubs fans across North America, Central America and the Carribean islands—heck, just about everywhere the spoken and printed word carried the message of eternal hope that is the essence of Cub fandom.

You're aware that those millions of people are just waiting to join the Wrigley Field regulars in breaking the chain of frustration draped around the Cubs and their loyal supporters for all these years. While you're at it, dream of the final World Series strikeout, fired plateward by Kerry Wood (or, if you prefer, Fergie Jenkins, Ken Holtzman, Rick Reuschel, Rick Sutcliffe, Mark Prior—maybe even Mordecai "Three-Finger" Brown) to vanquish the White Sox and avenge last century's World Series upset by those Hitless Wonders from the South Side.

When it finally happens, Cubs fans will be able to follow Frank Sinatra's marvelous musical advice and put their dreams away for another day. Until that happy day, though, these bittersweet memories will have to tide you over. A glance back at the Cubs playoff series I wrote about years ago—1984, 1989, 1998—turned into an affectionate stroll down memory lane for me. My 1984 book, Cubs Win! was a technically, though not totally, accurate title. As we all know, the Cubs were just one game away from the World Series that snake-bitten (or perhaps goat-gored) year, with three grabs at the gold ring, only to hit a stone wall three straight times in San Diego. Summing up that playoff disaster in a single sentence, a broken-hearted Cubs philosopher said of his team's horrendous fold: "It's hard to swing the bat with one hand on your throat."

So, at the dawn of the Dusty Baker era, it might be useful therapy for Cubs fans to join me in looking back, not in anger, but with affectionate nostalgia, at those might-have-been postseason moments. I couldn't help including the summer of 1969 in these reflections, even though the Cubs didn't make the playoffs. That might have been the time when the last of our youthful illusions got swept away under the harsh glare of reality, not just in Wrigley Field, but all over America.

GARY HITS ONE FOR HARRY

In 1998, the Cubs lost both Harry Caray and Jack Brickhouse, the announcers who made them household words, spreading the legend of Wrigley Field's ivy-covered walls, fun in the sun at the Friendly Confines and finding countless ways to compensate for frustrating seasons. It looked like this one was down the drain as well, when the Cubs lost an 11-inning September 27 regular-season finale in Houston, 4-3.

They were trudging mournfully off the field, aware that the Giants were on the verge of wrapping up the NL's wild-card playoff berth by winning in Colorado.

Then, just like the last-minute stay of execution from the governor in those old movies, the reprieve arrived for the Cubs. It was delivered via a homer by the Rockies' Neifi Perez to beat the Giants, 9-8, putting San Francisco and Chicago in a flat-footed tie at 89-73. The wild card berth was up for grabs in a winner-take-all showdown, and the luck of the draw set the scene in Wrigley Field the following night.

That chilly evening, September 28, 1998, a twice-in-a-lifetime event unfolded on the North Side. Only once before—90

Mark Prior can go to the Hall—if the Cubs win it all. Photo courtesy of the Chicago Cubs.

years before, to be exact—had the Cubs been involved in a playoff to make the playoffs.

Gary Gaetti and Steve Trachsel made it a night to remember. Their 1984 and 1989 division-clinching victories took place on the road, so this would be a rare chance for the Cubs to make it happen in their own backyard.

Gaetti, an unlikely late-season pickup from the discard pile, and Trachsel, a prime target for Wrigley boo-birds through much of his up-and-down Cubs tenure, were the unlikely co-heroes in saving a Cubs season that verged perilously close to becoming another of those all-too-familiar late fadeouts. Locked in a wild, three-way struggle with the Giants and New York Mets for the wild-card berth throughout August and September, the Cubs went into a tailspin at the end, losing six of their last eight games.

Luckily for them, the Mets had nothing like the finishing kick they found in 1969 to boot the Cubs out of the postseason picture. It was the Giants, counted out with a five-game deficit and just 10 more to play, who made the closing charge that would have catapulted them past the Cubs, except for Perez's dramatic home run in Colorado.

"I want to shake that man's hand," Sammy Sosa said of his fellow Dominican Republic import. So did Cubs fans, especially the ones already clutching playoff tickets and pining to see first-round games No. 3 and 4 against Atlanta, scheduled for Wrigley Field on October 3 and 4. At least they got half of their wish, thanks mainly to Trachsel and Gaetti.

"Wrigley Field is always packed and the fans are always making noise, so I didn't feel any extra pressure," Trachsel told me on his way out of the winners' champagne-soaked clubhouse after the traditional bubble bath that follows clinching victories. "If pitchers listen to the crowd instead of concentrating on hitting the catcher's mitt, they're not doing a very good job. But this time, I noticed our fans were yelling for me instead of at me."

From Bleacher Bums to overnight converts in scalped field boxes, the frenzied 39,556 Wrigley customers witnessed mound mastery by Trachsel, who held the Giants hitless for six and one-third innings. His gem gave the Cubs a 2-0 all-time record in such one-game showdowns, with the whole season at stake.

Ironically, both wins knocked the Giants out of the postseason picture, although nine decades and 3,000 miles—the distance between New York and San Francisco—separated these gigantic Cubs-Giants collisions.

The latest one wasn't quite as dramatic—or ferocious—as the replay of a 1908 tied game between the Cubs and the New York Giants that decided the National League pennant.

If Three-Finger Brown hadn't outpitched the immortal Christy Mathewson, 4-2, before a murderously hostile mob in New York's Polo Grounds, the Cubs wouldn't even have been in the 1908 World Series, let alone won it for the last time in the 20th century. All Trachsel's Wrigley Field triumph, 90 years later, gained the Cubs was the right to get swept out of their 1998 first-round NL playoff by the Braves in three straight games.

Regardless, just getting there by beating the Giants, 5-3, to grab that wild card berth gave the Cubs and their fans a badly needed excuse to erupt.

It was Gaetti, the 40-year-old American League refugee, who lit the fuse, breaking up a tense pitching duel between Trachsel and the Giants' Mark Gardner with a two-run homer in the fifth inning to give the Cubs a lead they never lost. Most of the veteran third baseman's 360 career home runs were stroked for the Minnesota Twins, including one in the 1987 World Series, helping them to topple the St. Louis Cards in a terrific seven-game struggle. Even so, Gaetti never hit a bigger one than the two-run shot he lofted into the left-field bleachers with that 1998 playoff payoff at stake.

"I thought the wind would knock it down," Gaetti said, in between spraying Sammy Sosa and pursuing media minions to douse them with champagne during that wild postgame soak-a-rama in the Cubs' dressing room. Clubhouse mogul Yosh Kawano, who has been doing this for such few and far-between celebrations ever since the 1945 World Series, had his assistants drape lockers with plastic to protect the players' clothes, but anyone with a notebook, microphone, or TV camera was fair game.

A religious man, Gaetti credited God for bringing him to Chicago on August 19, his 40th birthday. But the Cards' decision to cut him loose didn't hurt, so the Cubs snapped him up. Nobody, including Gaetti himself, expected him to hit .320 in 37 games down the stretch in 1998, with eight homers and 27 RBI.

That unexpected punch further down in the batting order took some of the load off Sammy Sosa's back, helping the slugger to ride the whirlwind of 24-hour media demands to probe every aspect of his historic homer derby with Mark McGwire. Gaetti shared the fans' awe over Sosa's 66-homer spree.

"Every time Sammy steps up to the plate, I expect him to hit one out," he said.

Sosa's club-record total, eclipsed that season by McGwire's 70, and again when the Giants' Barry Bonds swatted 73 in 2001, had the fans in hysterics all summer. As the season wore on and the Cubs wore down, it appeared that the Sosa-McGwire circus would be the only game in both towns, with turnstiles spinning merrily at Busch Stadium in St. Louis and at Wrigley to root for this matched set of Paul Bunyan clones.

But the baseball fates wrote a different script. McGwire won the home run battle, only to watch Sosa and the Cubs win the wild-card war. And when the Cubs-Giants showdown came down in Wrigley Field, Sosa gratefully turned the hitting hero laurels over to Gaetti and seldom-seen sub Matt Mieske, whose two-run single hiked the home team's edge to 4-0. Sosa later scored on a wild pitch, and that run came in very handy when the Giants launched a desperation ninth-inning rally. Manager Jim Riggleman emptied his bullpen, even tossing starter Kevin Tapani into the fray, but couldn't prevent Bonds from stalking to the plate with the bases loaded, a run across, and nobody out. Cubs fans slumped in their seats, anticipating the game-tying grand slam, but lefty reliever Terry Mulholland kept the ball in the park, retiring the southpaw slugger on a sacrifice fly. Closer Rod Beck then touched off jubilation in Wrigleyville by slamming the door on the Giants, preserving Trachsel's 5-3 decision with his 51st save.

WAY TO GO, JOE

In yet another entry to baseball's endless list of ironic twists, the final San Francisco batter, needing a homer to tie it, instead popped out to end it. Who was that man? Why, none other than Joe Carter, providing a final dividend on the 1984 trade that sent him from the Cubs to Cleveland, bringing Red Baron Rick Sutcliffe here to pilot the Cubs toward their first-ever division title. Along the way, Carter got his own taste of glory, homering off ex-Cub Mitch Williams of the Phillies to win the 1993 World Series for the Toronto Blue Jays. Baseball is, indeed, a funny game.

"What did you expect?" asked first baseman Mark Grace, who caught Carter's game-ending popup. "A 5-0 lead in the ninth inning and we hang on by our fingernails. I guess the Cubs just have to do it that way."

They sure did, although win No. 90 was to be the last one for the 1998 Cubs. They opened the best-of-five playoff series with two losses in Atlanta and closed it by sending rookie sensation Kerry Wood out to duel with his own tender elbow and the Braves' money pitcher, ex-Cub Greg Maddux. Those stacked odds proved impossible to beat, so the Cubs' uphill battle to get into the playoffs ended with a downhill 0-3 slide out of them.

REAL FUN AT THE OLD BALLPARK

Regardless, '98 was a remarkable, ultra-entertaining rollercoaster ride. Pennant races in both leagues became sideshows, serving as window dressing for the baseball-bashing power struggle between Sosa and McGwire. Those two home run-happy superstars stopped fans from running home, bringing them back to every big-league ballpark, even in the American League, by blowing away residual bitterness from the strike/lockout that had wiped out the 1994 playoffs. That glaring gap in the chain of tradition caused many loyalists to vow they were through with the game that had been a welcome diversion for them.

The backlash hurt the White Sox, who might well have played in the '94 World Series that never was, because many of their fans accused Sox chairman Jerry Reinsdorf of being the behind-the-scenes instigator. Comiskey Park attendance shrank sharply from the all-time high of 2,934,154 in 1991 to 1,391,146 in 1998. In sharp contrast, the Cubs lured 2,623,000 cash customers to their smaller, cozier park in '98, ringing up even higher totals in subsequent seasons.

HIGH HIGHS, LOW LOWS

Wrigley thrill seekers got their money's worth throughout a zany 1998, right up to the one and only season-ending playoff game. The highest of highs, without a doubt, was Wood's 20-strikeout, one-hit museum piece on May 6. The Astros looked like cardboard cutouts holding toothpicks at the plate while the Cubs right-hander blazed his unhittable assortment past them, winning 2-0.

Perhaps the lowest of lows took place in Milwaukee on September 23. The Cubs had it won when left fielder Brant Brown circled under a fly ball by the Brewers' Geoff Jenkins that should have been the final out of a 7-5 Cub victory. Oops! Whoops! ##%*&##@%&*!!! The elusive horsehide somehow escaped Brown's glove, three runs scored, and the Cubs lost an 8-7 stunner. Ron Santo's visceral shriek of agony from the broadcast booth echoed everywhere Cubs fans huddled around their TV sets and radios.

That ninth-inning blooper could have sounded taps to Cub playoff hopes, and would have, except for Neifi Perez's ninth-inning heroics, four days later in Colorado.

"I forgot about that play before the next game," Brown insisted, forgetting that Cubs fans have memories longer than all the elephants Barnum and Bailey ever assembled under the Big Top. "But everywhere I go, people keep coming up and reminding me about it."

GAME 1: TOMAHAWKED

So the rejuvenated Cubs headed to the sunny South, intending to make the most of sneaking into the postseason picture. They wasted little time making the least of it. In the box score, this 7-1 playoff-opening loss to the Braves on September 30 looks like a rout. Yet the familiar might-have-been chorus started even earlier than usual for the Cubs, with their postseason history overburdened by such regrets. With two out and nobody on in the second inning, shortstop Jose Hernandez muffed Andruw Jones's grounder, and Michael Tucker, destined for a brief stay with the Cubs in 2001, promptly homered off loser Mark Clark. That was all John Smoltz, tough as a starter before he became Atlanta's virtually unhittable closer, needed to put his team into sweep mode.

GAME 2: TAP TRAPPED

Three words sum up this 2-1 heartbreaker—tough luck, Tap. A 19-game regular-season winner, the veteran right-hander deserved his 20th on October 1 in Turner Field, but didn't get it.

Working on a four-hit shutout and nursing a 1-0 lead with one out in the ninth inning, Tapani served up a game-tying homer to Javy Lopez. The Braves pushed over a run off reliever Terry Mulholland in the 10th, putting a stranglehold on the best-of-five series.

Eternal optimist Sammy Sosa refused to concede.

"It's not the end of the world," said Sammy, who would finish the series homerless, just two for 11. "My [congratulatory] call from the president is on hold, but if we win that first game at home, things could change."

GAME 3: STRIKE THREE

Things didn't change. Greg Maddux bested Kerry Wood, 6-2, on October 3 in Wrigley Field to go 8-1 lifetime against his former team. The Cubs batted a puny .181 in the series, wasting good starts by Clark, Tapani, and Wood. Gaetti, hero of the playoff to get into the playoffs, was a bust in the real thing, contributing a single in 11 trips.

"How about two grand slams [both by the Braves] and a wide strike zone?" Gaetti summed up the series, adding a sly jab at plate umpires' calls, which the Cubs felt favored Atlanta's pitchers throughout.

SAMMY GETS KICKS ON HOMER ROUTE 66

Wherever Sammy Sosa and Mark McGwire went in September 1998, adoring fans, TV cameras, and nosy newspaper types were sure to go. Sosa had been getting the superstar treatment ever since his phenomenal power surge in June, when he hit an unprecedented 20 home runs. On the road, the media crush grew so demanding that Sosa had to meet separately with them before the first game of every series.

As successful at public relations as he was at the plate, Sammy had been briefed about Hack Wilson's club-record 56 homers for the Cubs in 1930. When Sosa slammed No. 57 to better Hack on September 4 in Pittsburgh, he paid proper respects to the historical significance of Wilson's—and his—feats. Precisely because he made himself available while the Cards' McGwire ducked the spotlight whenever he could, Sosa found himself living in a fishbowl. The Cubs slugger seemed to thrive on it, especially the Dominican flags frenziedly waved by his backers in every ballpark.

"McGwire's the man in this country," was Sosa's stock answer about those emotional scenes. "In the Dominican Republic, I'm the man."

The next day, Sosa touched all the bases off the field, telling the media in San Diego that President Bill Clinton had called to congratulate him and wish the Cubs luck in their playoff quest. Battling a slump and concerned about hurricane damage to his Carribean homeland, Sosa broke out of it, actually grabbing a brief one-homer edge over McGwire on September 25 with No. 66, a towering blast in Houston's Astrodome. But that was it for Sosa, and McGwire roared past him again, adding five more home runs for an even 70, a standard that lasted only three seasons, until Barry Bonds's 73 rewrote baseball history.

1989: A GIANT SETBACK

This was the season of something else. The Cubs did not play their normal game, station-to-station baseball, waiting for Ernie

Banks or Dave Kingman or Leon Durham or somebody—any-body—to play longball. Their faithful fans, longing for some playoff ball, had seen their hopes implode under the weight of a collapsing team and a choking manager (Leo Durocher) on the doorstep of the 1969 playoffs.

Then, when the 1984 Cubs finally finished first, in the NL's Eastern Division, at least, they proved not to be the beasts of the East. Chicago was confident that the end of the Cubs' self-imposed 39-year postseason boycott also would end their run of 76 years (since 1908) without a World Series triumph. The emotional scars from their traumatic 1984 playoff choke-a-thon in San Diego still hung around Wrigley Field like Banquo's ghost when the 1989 Cubs got going with an old outlook, installed by a new manager.

The old approach was new to the Cubs, even if Don Zimmer wasn't. Their second-year field boss, an old-school guy, gave them a totally new blueprint in spring training: Whatever it takes to score a run, do it. The Cubs did it, to the surprise and delight of Cubs fans everywhere. They won their second NL East title in five years by duplicating the previous season's .261 team batting average and getting much more production out of those league-leading 1,438 hits. Their 702 runs, also tops in the NL, gave the main starters—Greg Maddux, Rick Sutcliffe, Mike Bielecki, Scott Sanderson—enough cushion to pile up a combined 64 wins—19 by Maddux.

Throw in 36 saves by Mitch "Wild Thing" Williams, with Les Lancaster and Paul Assenmacher combining for 14 more. Jerome Walton and Dwight Smith finished 1-2 in NL Rookie of the Year voting, and Ryne Sandberg was the power guy with 30 homers, Andre Dawson adding 21 more. It computed to a 93-69 record, six satisfying lengths ahead of those 1969 villains, the New York Mets.

S.F. WILL PREVAIL

So the NL playoff between the Cubs and San Francisco Giants, the West champs, should have been a dead-even slugfest throughout the best-of-seven series. After all, the Cubs and Giants fought to a 6-6 draw in the regular season, each team going 3-3 in windblown Wrigley Field and even windier Candlestick Park. The Cubs figured to have an edge in starting pitchers, but the Giants boasted their "Pacific Sock Exchange," left fielder Kevin Mitchell and first baseman Will Clark, a potent pair, powering up in '89 to produce 70 homers and 236 RBI. The last thing anyone expected was a decisive first-sacker sock duel between Clark and Mark Grace of the Cubs. Clark won it by a sliver, batting .650 on 13 for 20 to Grace's .647 on 11 for 17, but San Francisco took the series and the NL pennant by a margin wider than the Golden Gate Bridge, breezing home in five games.

GAME 1: CLARK'S PARK

Will Clark grabbed the Cubs by the throat immediately and never let go. Behind his booming bat, the Giants shocked a wildly confident overflow Wrigley Field throng of 39,195 to romp, 11-3, in the all-important series opener. Greg Maddux made the first of his two ineffective starts, with the Cubs' ace getting trumped—and clubbed.

GAME 2: RICK ROCKED

The Cubs pounded their longtime mound mainstay, Rick Reuschel, for a half-dozen runs in the first inning, convincing worried fans that they would be back from the upcoming three games in San Francisco with this series still on the line and the NL pennant up for grabs. The Giants refused to lie down and die, though, making it uncomfortably close before the home team won, 9-5.

GAME 3: CUBS "ROBBED"

The sight of pitcher Dave Dravecky, who broke his arm making a delivery when he returned from surgery to remove a cancerous tumor, was enough to fire up a Candlestick crowd of 62,065. The Giants got the emotional lift they needed from Robby Thompson's two-run homer in the seventh inning, just enough to nip the Cubs, 5-4. In yet another of those bizarre playoff twists that seem to bedevil the North Siders, reliever Les Lancaster lost track of the count, believing it was three and 0, so he grooved a fastball to Thompson, who whacked it over the left field wall.

"Anybody can make a mistake," Lancaster lamented. "I looked at the scoreboard, and it said 3-0. I didn't want to walk Thompson, so I threw a strike."

GAME 4: GREG'S DREGS

With everything on the line, manager Don Zimmer had no option other than starting Maddux with three days' rest. Once again, the young right-hander couldn't get the job done, so the Cubs sank into a hopeless 3-1 series deficit. This 6-4 loss got pinned on reliever Steve Wilson, but it closed out Maddux's undistinguished postseason log for the Cubs with an 0-1 record and an embarrassing 13.50 ERA.

GAME 5: RICK'S REVENGE

With Reuschel's second start standing between them and elimination, the Cubs couldn't leap the hurdle of the chubby veteran's pinpoint control. Still, they led 2-1 until—guess who?—Clark's clutch two-run single made the difference in a 3-2 squeaker, propelling the Giants into the World Series and sending the Cubs home with their sixth straight playoff road loss.

My mind flashed back more than 25 years, to when I watched the Leo Durocher era end with an orgy of Cub self-destruction. In 1972, a chubby rookie joined the team, to be joined three years later by his brother, Paul. A quiet, strapping farm boy from downstate Illinois, Rick stuck around to win 135 games for the Cubs, but had to go to both coasts for the crowning World Series experience—with the Yankees in 1981 and the '89 Giants—that eluded so many Chicago players on both sides of town.

CUBS ROAR IN '84

Blithely oblivious of the playoff fate awaiting them, the Cubs staged a hit (and pitch) show all season. They were a likeable bunch of guys, with handsome young catcher Jody Davis ("Jo-dee! Jo-dee!" bellowed the second-generation Bleacher Bums) reprising Randy "Rebel" Hundley's 1969 role as Wrigley's fan favorite. Of course, things had changed in those 15 years, so the Confederate flags that fluttered from the bleachers when Hundley came to bat were long gone by then. But Gary "Sarge" Matthews Sr., provided both charisma and punch that year, unaware that he would follow his son's footsteps back to Chicago, joining Dusty Baker's coaching staff in 2003, two years after Gary, Jr., left the Cubs to start living up to his potential in Pitts-

It's champagne-spraying time for catcher Jody Davis (left) and pitcher Rick Sutcliffe after the division-clinching triumph in Pittsburgh. Framed in the middle is longtime Cubs broadcaster Jack Brickhouse.

burgh. Bob "Deer" Dernier and Ryne "Baby Ruth" Sandberg swiped a combined 77 bases at the top of the order, while Ron "Penguin" Cey (25) and Leon "Bull" Durham (23) were the homer heroes, with Red Baron Sutcliffe (16-1 after the trade), Steve "Rainbow" Trout (13-7) and Dennis "Eck" Eckersley (10-8) as the double-digit starters.

Closer Lee Smith (9-7 record, 33 saves) should have been nicknamed "Mr. Bullpen," so Green and manager Jim Frey doubtless felt unloading Willie Hernandez would not weaken the relief corps. What happened during the '84 playoff proved them wrong, especially when the smoke cleared from that gut-wrenching Game 5 in San Diego.

GREEN LIGHT TURNS RED

On the field, everything went well—hell, went perfectly—for the 1984 Cubs. Off the field, they probably lost their first-round playoff a year before it started. Sure, general manager Dallas Green gave the green light to grabbing ace Rick Sutcliffe on June 13, 1984, in a blockbuster deal with Cleveland. The Red Baron pitched the Cubs into the postseason, but an earlier move by Green could have been the one that tossed them out of it.

On May 22, 1983, the Cubs dealt lefty reliever Willie Hernandez to the Phillies, who compounded Green's goof by letting a pitcher they deemed expendable get away to the Detroit Tigers. Both teams soon regretted that choice, though it turned out to be much more costly for the Cubs.

"I told Willie this would be his last Cub contract unless he buckled down," Green warned. "He was wasting his ability."

True, Hernandez was no Rollie Fingers or Bruce Sutter in his Chicago tenure (1977-83), and no Kenny Holtzman as a starter, either, despite his baffling screwball, hard to hit from either side of the plate.

"They tried to fool people by saying I had a bad attitude," Hernandez told me when I asked why a left-handed reliever with such explosive stuff had been sent down to the minors by the Cubs.

Manager Sparky Anderson thought Hernandez's attitude was terrific in 1984, when the Tiger closer's bullpen dominance helped the Tigers win 104 games and breeze into the World Series against the San Diego Padres. So Hernandez was sitting at home, watching the Cubs blow their NL playoff to those same, highly beatable Padres. Privately, he admitted it would have been more fun to face his old teammates.

Instead, the southpaw saved Game 3 and did it again in the clinching fifth game, while the Tigers clawed the Padres to wrap up this World Series mismatch.

"Do I feel sorry for the Cubs?" Hernandez mulled the often-answered question. "There are some good guys over there, but I don't dwell on the past."

THE IMMACULATE DEFLECTION

Cubs fans slowly began realizing their 1984 team was for real, even if Ryne Sandberg's heroics seemed unreal. For those who weren't totally convinced, what happened on August 2 swept away the last shred of doubt.

With the Cubs clinging to a 3-2 edge over Montreal in the ninth inning, one out and runners on first and third, the Wrigley crowd of 22,485 wriggled nervously, because Pete Rose, one of the all-time clutch hitters, faced Lee Smith. Sure enough, Rose rocketed a liner up the middle, ticketed for the game-tying single.

Whoops! Somehow, Smith's self-defensive glove stab deflected the ball off his shoulder, straight to shortstop Dave Owen, who turned it into the game-ending double play. Even Harry Caray's jubilant "Holy Cow!" came out as a hoarse croak after that quasi-divine stroke of luck.

"The Cubs are destined, I guess," shrugged Expos pitcher Bryn Smith.

CALIFORNIA CUBQUAKE

The 1984 Cubs were a team of destiny, all right. Sadly, it wasn't the one their fans had in mind—a rendezvous, not with destiny, but a rematch of their 1945 World Series against the Detroit Tigers, ending in satisfying revenge for that seven-game bashing by the Bengals. After the Cubs won the first two games of their National League championship series, there was no way they could go to San Diego and lose three straight times. Supremely confident Chicagoans snapped up every available ticket, enabling scalpers to demand—and get—up to $1,000 for good, not great, seats.

Pent-up hysteria on the North Side turned into absolute assurance when the Cubs blew away the overmatched Padres, 13-0 and 4-2 on October 2 and 3, for a 2-0 stranglehold on this one-sided playoff.

Or so it seemed, even to the losers, who admitted some of them huddled on the flight back to San Diego to plan hunting trips and vacations as soon as the Cubs polished them off. But not all of them quit.

"When we got off that plane, we were dead," Padres Hall of Famer Tony Gwynn told me years later. "Somehow, all that changed when we won the first game at home. Even when we fell behind Sutcliffe [in the decisive Game 5], I knew we'd get to him."

They did.

PARADISE LOST

No better way to explain it than that *Chicago Tribune* headline on October 8, 1984. It was the morning after, but the hangover wouldn't go away. Even after the last Cubs fan, player or official who suffered through that Gloomy Sunday is gone, it will hang around, like wisps of fog over Wrigley Field's scoreboard.

The Cubs led 3-0 in the sixth inning and 3-2, with six-foot-seven Sutcliffe visibly shrinking from fatigue, when the Padres came to bat in the seventh. Manager Jim Frey stuck with his valiant bearded giant too long, then brought in southpaw Steve Trout, too late. An agonizing error by first baseman Leon Durham and a bad hop on Gwynn's wicked grounder off Sandberg's shoulder at second base turned the game, the season and the Cubs' World Series fantasy into confetti, blowing away in Chicago's bitter winter winds.

Maybe, just maybe, it wouldn't have happened if Willie Hernandez had been there in the Cubs' bullpen, ready to douse that seventh-inning fire. Larry Bowa was at shortstop that day when the last echo of that season's hit song ("We'll keep 'em flyin' high for Cubbie Blue") faded away, just like the Cubs. Bowa was a Seattle Mariners coach in 2000 when we recalled the '84 Cubs' demise, just before the Mariners faced the White Sox in a Comiskey Park playoff opener.

"Chicago sure was a Cubs town that year," Bowa said. "Too bad we couldn't give their fans what they deserved."

1969: STILL ON OUR MINDS

The Cubs didn't make the playoffs in 1969. All they did was make believers out of their fans, and then break their hearts. Maybe the words of Ernie Banks, Mr. Cub then and always, can turn those memories of a sour September back toward the way it was in that fun-filled summer.

"The thing that makes 1969 stand out in my mind was our closeness, just like the neighborhood guys hanging out together," Banks said. "It was a happening in Wrigley Field."

Maybe, one of these years—or centuries—it'll happen again.

Chapter 11

THEY PUT THE WRIGGLE IN WRIGLEYVILLE

The Wrigley family gave the Cubs much more than a name for their ballpark. The Wrigley way of operating left an indelible mark on Chicago's National League franchise, on the players and managers who wore Cub uniforms, and especially on the front-office people entrusted to put a product on the field.

Judging the Wrigley era and its aftermath as an utter failure, solely by the won-lost record, the yearly standings, and the team's late-season tendency to fold up like a Murphy bed would be easy. Too easy. It is true that the Cubs took the field in 2006 with a depressing legacy—one World Series trip (1945), going all the way back to a 1938 Series setback. Ditto for their World Series forays in 1935, '32 (the year of Babe Ruth's legendary called-shot homer in Wrigley Field), '29, '18 and '10. Only the last five (1929 through 1945) came on the Wrigley watch, be-

A real slice of Cubs history comes together in 1962 when hands-on owner Phil Wrigley (center) greets players Don Elston, Billy Williams and Glen Hobbie (left), along with George Altman, Ernie Banks and Bob Will (right).

cause William Wrigley, Jr., did not buy controlling interest in the Cubs until 1919.

Regardless, a lot of easy laughs about the way their team always seemed to "gum" up the works marred the legacy of these chewing gum tycoons. It was unavoidable, since Wrigley's Spearmint met the payroll for decades. Despite that, Wrigley Field's blend of day baseball, the cozy confines that enabled fans to see their favorite player's five o'clock shadow sprout in the later innings and the el trains, buses, and trolleys (in the early decades), depositing a new crop of young fans on the doorstep every season, created generations of lifelong Cubs fans. Once they got hooked on sunshine, the outfield ivy, and the irrepressible optimism of Ernie Banks, rooting for the Cubs became a terminal disease with no known cure.

But there was a lot more to it than that. Perhaps if the Cubs had been owned by robber barons instead of the Wrigleys, a George Steinbrenner clone would have bought the team. In that case, Cubs fans feared the new owner's first priorities might be: (1) Tear down Wrigley Field; (2) Turn the Cubs into the Midwest Yankees after transplanting them into some shiny, sterile, suburban stadium, with lots of skyboxes and garish, profitable ads on the outfield walls; (3) Sign hordes of boring, overpaid mercenaries to win the pennant and World Series every year.

Maybe such draconian solutions would satisfy the win-or-else mentality that's changed sports all over America, substituting ferocity for fun at the old ballpark, Little League field, or anywhere else the outcome is more important than the game itself. It wouldn't be the way I want to go, along with what I suspect is a shrinking minority of old-time diehard Cubs fans. One man who wanted the Cubs to win, but would not bend the rules to make it happen, was Philip Knight Wrigley. He inherited the leadership—and the burden—of the Cubs when his father, William Wrigley Jr., died in 1932. What P. K. didn't know about baseball was just about everything, though he struggled manfully to carry on the family's hobby-business, with occasional success amid frequent, scatter-brained experiments.

PHIL'S HIS PHONE MAN

A gentle man and a gentleman, Wrigley was uncomfortable in the spotlight and incapable of being a hands-on owner in the daily operation of the Cubs. He much preferred to tinker with old cars in the garage of his Lake Geneva, Wisconsin, mansion and spend time with his wife, Helen, and their children.

In the meantime, P. K. answered his own telephone, taking calls on his listed number and patiently explaining to fans why the Cubs had gone straight downhill since that last pennant in 1945. He didn't snub the writers, either. I know, because I had several phone chats with Wrigley during the turbulent Leo Durocher era that turned into page one stories in the *Chicago Tribune*'s sports section.

Regardless of his ownership skills, or lack thereof, this unconventional Cubs boss—as far removed from the bombastic style of Yankees dictator George Steinbrenner as Mohandas K. Ghandi was from Blood and Guts Patton—frequently got a pass from Chicago fans and media alike. His old-fashioned decency and genuine concern for Wrigley Field and the comfort and convenience of Cubs fans overshadowed some of his bizarre brainstorms. The blue ribbon for such tomfoolery got pinned on the 1961-65 revolving College of Coaches, which quickly turned into hilarious, back-stabbing burlesque. A close second was Wrigley's hard-to-figure hiring of former U.S. Air Force Lt. Colonel Bob Whitlow as "athletic director" of the Cubs, a 1963-65 experiment that produced nothing except more front-office confusion.

ERNIE WHO?

Even what most people credited as the crowning moment of the Wrigley regime—the 1953 signing of a slender, 22-year-old shortstop from the Kansas City Monarchs—was something of a surprise to P. K.

"Why did you pay $35,000 to bring in Ernie Banks?" Wrigley asked his general manager, Wid Matthews.

"Other teams are after him," Matthews said of the youngster who became the Cubs' second black player, with second baseman Gene Baker already under contract. "Anyway, we need a roommate for Baker."

THE WRIGLEY PAPERS

Leo Durocher's 15 minutes of fame on the Chicago sporting scene actually lasted for more than seven years (1966-72). The fun times under his managerial reign zipped by quickly, but when the S.S. Durocher hit that 1969 iceberg, cleverly disguised as the New York Mets, and began to sink, Cubs fans stood by on deck for what seemed like an eternity. So did Wrigley, a very loyal man, who stuck with his embattled skipper until the waves of discontent washed away all hope of salvation. Even then, P. K. went down with guns blazing. His famous full-page newspaper ad of September 3, 1971, totally backed Durocher, unlike the traditional front-office "vote of confidence," the kiss of death that signals the manager of a struggling team to start packing his bags, send the wife and kids back to their hometown and scan the want ads.

"DUROCHER DUMPERS" DUMPED ON

Wrigley's plain-spoken case for keeping Durocher on the job caused a media sensation. Cubs fans, many still in mourning over the way the 1969 dream season ended in a nightmare, seemed evenly divided in the great stay-or-go debate. At least nobody doubted where P. K. stood. Some excerpts from his unique manifesto, which *Tribune* sports editor Cooper Rollow dubbed "The Wrigley Papers:"

THIS IS FOR CUB FANS AND ANYBODY
ELSE WHO IS INTERESTED

"The Cub organization is at sixes and sevens and somebody has to do something. The responsibility falls on me. By tradition, this would call for a press conference, following which there would be as many versions of what I had to say as there were reporters present.

"For a quarter of a century, the Cubs were perennial dwellers of the second division in spite of everything we could think of and try—experienced managers, inexperienced managers, rotating managers, no manager, but revolving coaches—we were still there in the also-rans. We settled on Leo Durocher, who had the knowledge to build a contender and win pennants, also knowing he has always been a controversial figure, because he was never cut out to be a diplomat.

"This year there has been a constant campaign to dump Durocher that has even affected the players. After careful consideration, Leo is the team manager and the 'Dump Durocher Clique' might as well give up. He is running the team, and if some of the players lie down on the job, we will see what we can do to find them happier homes."

Phil Wrigley, president, Chicago National League ball club
"P.S. If only we could find more team players like Ernie Banks."

*   *   *   *

Wrigley's unprecedented move—stating his case with paid, full-page ads in all four Chicago newspapers—produced predictably strong reactions. After all, this was no Mike Ditka, creating daily headlines by manipulating the media with his staged tantrums. When Philip K. Wrigley came out of his self-imposed isolation to tell off pouting Cubs players, grumbling Cubs fans and sharply critical media, they all had something to say about it.

FERGIE FIRES BACK

"It's a bunch of junk," Ferguson Jenkins, ace of the Cub pitching staff, said of Wrigley's blast. Milt Pappas, the Cubs' player representative, who almost exactly a year later was to hurl a Wrigley Field no-hitter that missed being a perfect game on one borderline call, was equally disturbed.

"This stuff is getting out of hand," Pappas said of the uproar swirling around the team ever since a stormy meeting on August 23 between Durocher and unhappy Cubs players. "It's a joke, and every day things get worse."

Some Cubs, fearing they were the ones Wrigley had been aiming at, fired back with anonymous barbs.

"Durocher's not the only problem," one said. "This guy [Wrigley] has done some unbelievable things. It's a sick situation."

Another player added, "Durocher gives us all kinds of hell, but he never told anybody he was laying down."

EARLY WARNING UNHEEDED

A lot of this yes-you-did, no-you-didn't kid stuff could have been avoided if the Cubs had listened to Wrigley's warning, a few days after that infamous clubhouse shouting match. I called him at his Lake Geneva home on August 26, 1971, and he didn't mince words.

"We're not playing ball," he said of the fading, quarreling Cubs. "Twenty-five years ago, I'd have gone into the clubhouse and told them myself, but I'm getting too old for that. I'll talk to Ron Santo and Ernie Banks in my [Wrigley Building] office and hope they get the message to the other players. They owe it to Cubs fans to stop piling fuel on the fire. It doesn't matter if they don't like the manager or me or anyone else."

The Cubs were six games behind East Division leader Pittsburgh when Wrigley spoke with me. By the time his full-page ad came out, a week later, the gap had grown to nine games, and the Cubs were out of the race. Soon after the season ended, Wrigley gave Durocher a one-year contract, also signing Banks as a coach at the end of his brilliant career. It simply delayed the inevitable. When the Cubs floundered early in 1972, Durocher got fired, but putting a revolving door on the manager's office in Wrigley Field didn't produce many miracles. Dusty Baker arrived in 2003, the 20th manager in the 30 years since Leo exited, with the Cubs still chasing the Wrigley World Series that had eluded them since 1945.

THE TRIBUNE TIMES

The Cubs made threatening gestures here and there throughout the 1970s, the last decade of Wrigley family ownership, never quite getting over the hump. It really was the end of an era when Phil Wrigley died at 82 on April 12, 1977. His wife inherited the estate, including the gum company and the Cubs, but she passed away soon after. That put a tremendous inheritance tax burden on the family, so selling the baseball team was a solution to easing the debt and keeping the Wrigley family business afloat.

The new owner, Bill Wrigley, found a willing buyer at a bargain basement price. The Tribune Company, owner of flagship properties in the *Chicago Tribune* and WGN, plus newspapers, radio, and TV stations, along with other enterprises throughout North America, snapped up the Cubs on June 16, 1981, for close to $21 million, plus an option on the valuable land under Wrigley Field.

GREEN LIGHT FOR DALLAS

Trib brass made a smart move by luring a savvy executive, Andy McKenna, from the White Sox to take over as Cubs president. McKenna, a behind-the-scenes power in Chicago business, sports, and social circles, had the clout to get things done. He got everybody's attention in a hurry by hiring Dallas Green on October 15, 1981, as general manager, with broad authority to remake the organization and rebuild the Cubs into contenders. And as soon as he left Philadelphia to travel to Chicago with a whip and a chair, Green began making waves.

A big, bluff, imposing man with a booming voice, Green liked the spotlight and loved baseball. Born in Delaware, he made the short move to Philadelphia for a 26-year hitch with the Phillies, doing it all, from farmhand to fringe pitcher (20-22 lifetime) to the front office to back to the dugout as manager of the 1980 world champions. His Phils won that World Series from the Kansas City Royals, managed by Jim Frey. Just four years later, Green and Frey teamed up to take the Cubs to the brink of the 1984 World Series—but no closer.

GREEN AND BEAR IT

But getting the Cubs that far created some extraordinary stretches of controversy, in-fighting, bluster and bumps in the road, including the firing in 1983 of Lee Elia, Green's personal choice as manager. One thing Green promised—and lived up to—was that he would never duck a fight. The hard-driving boss found himself in plenty of them throughout his stormy six seasons in Chicago. While I was writing Cubs Win! in 1984, with the city, the state and much of America (thanks to Harry Caray's charisma) frothing at the mouth over the prospect of this downtrodden team actually in the playoffs, I sat down with

Dallas in his office to get his state of the franchise update. As always, he was frank, open, and emotional in describing what the GM (with some justification) viewed as a personal triumph over the resistance to the sweeping changes he labeled "Building a New Tradition." Wrigley Field traditionalists didn't like some of Green's moves, even objecting when he painted that slogan on the park's outside wall at Clark and Addison. That got his dander up, so he cut loose with gusto.

"Cubs fans were used to rooting for losing teams," he said. "That's unacceptable to me. I heard people complaining that 71-91 [the record in 1983, Green's second season as Cub commander] made our New Tradition seem like the same old stuff. The Cubs were trying to rebuild with trades, but the emphasis should be on player development and scouting. That calls for patience."

OUT OF THE FREY PAN

But when the Cubs blew three straight playoff games in 1984, it was no choking matter. Green followed that with two crucial mistakes—hiring Gene Michael as manager after Jim Frey got fired in 1986 and bringing Michael back for one more losing season. Green's solution was to hire himself as manager, but he changed his mind in 1987 and went back home to Philadelphia, taking the tattered remnants of the New Tradition with him. If you're scoring at home, Green departed with one winning season, one division title, one traumatic playoff collapse (all of that in 1984) and an overall 463-504 record for his six years on the job.

Of all the million might-have-beens in Cubs history, that 0-3 postseason punishment by the Padres has been postmortemed almost as much as September, 1969, when the front-running Cubs got blind-sided by the onrushing Mets. If the Cubs had won any of those three games in San Diego, bringing a World Series to Wrigley Field for the first time in 39 years, Green could have been elected mayor of Chicago, or at least the alderman for Wrigleyville's ward. Instead, he became a footnote in Cubs history, albeit a highly entertaining one. Unhappy about what he considered uninformed interference by Tribune Company brass, Green still appreciated the irony of the situation.

"We had the Padres by the throat, and we didn't squeeze them one more time," he said. "That's why I didn't get the time I needed to start getting a steady flow of youngsters from the farm system. That's baseball. You win or you're out."

THE JIM AND ZIM SHOW

So the torch got passed to Jim Frey, another spin of the merry-go-round that assures baseball's front offices a steady supply of the same old faces, recycled into new jobs. It's the way the Good Ole Boys network works. Cubs fans weren't surprised when Frey stepped into the executive suite and tapped his boyhood chum, Don Zimmer, to complete the 1986-87 managerial switcheroo from Frey to John Vukovich to Michael to Frank Lucchesi in a bewildering who's-minding-the-store-today? sequence. Frey's four seasons as general manager also matched Green's lone division title and playoff loss, but little else to arouse Cubs fans from their lethargy.

They went into the 1990s with high hopes, inflated by an upbeat '89 showing. Overinflated, as it turned out. The Cubs displayed an inspired brand of baseball, becoming the Boys of Zimmer for that fun-filled campaign, but, like 1984, it was a one-shot deal. They were all shot in 1990. Zimmer was gone early in the next season, followed by Frey when it ended. Most of Frey's tenure was spent on the phone, in valiant efforts to trade for enough pitching to fill the void caused by Rick Sutcliff's plethora of injuries. The record shows his pleas went mainly un-heeded.

"Other teams look at the standings, and when they see you're in trouble, their price for a trade goes out of sight," Frey grumbled. "I'm trying to get a relief pitcher to shore up the bullpen, but they want a Mark Grace or a Greg Maddux in return."

CUBS LOSE GREG, THE GOLDEN EGG

The emergence of young right-hander Maddux could have given the Cubs a building block for the decade, although that dream evaporated when the 1992 NL Cy Young Award winner fled to Atlanta after a 20-11 record for the fourth-place Cubs that season. At least that defection did not happen on Frey's watch. Even though they couldn't get to the .500 mark in 1991-92, his last turns as general manager, there was plenty of talent on the Cubs' roster at the decade's outset. In his prime, Ryne Sandberg swatted 40 homers in 1991, topping the NL and becoming the only second baseman to lead the league since 1925, when Hall of Famer Rogers Hornsby hit 39.

Mark Grace was settling in for a long run at first base, pil-ing up hits at a pace that would produce more (1,754) than any other big-leaguer in the 1990s. The fancy fielder also earned his keep by scooping shortstop Shawon Dunston's throws out of the dirt. And Andre Dawson, warming up right field bleach-erites for the hero worship they soon would lavish on Sammy Sosa, paced the Cubs with a .310 average and 27 homers, closely tailed by Grace (.309) and Sandberg (.306). Cub nostalgia buffs noted approvingly that it was the first time three regulars batted over .300 since 1945 (NL batting king Phil Cavarretta, .355; Smilin' Stan Hack, .325; Don Johnson, .302). Regardless, all that potential and performance couldn't save Frey's job. With all the talent he left behind, the Cubs could be, might, be...weren't consistent contenders for the rest of the 20th century.

THE TIMES OF HIMES

What happened? In an era of skyrocketing salaries, the Cubs couldn't—or wouldn't—keep pace, at the pay window and in the standings, so the 1990s produced a familiar, i.e. sad, scenario. The movers and shakers in the *Chicago Tribune*'s ivory tower understandably wanted to turn the page, breaking away from the Wrigley era of front-office futility and inability to win consistently. They sought no more insider general managers like John Holland (1957-75), P. K. Wrigley's consigliore for a generation of Cubs ups and downs—mostly downs. Or the caretaker regime of E. R. "Salty" Saltwell (1976), the longtime manager of Wrigley Field operations, who actually filled the GM chair for that season. Bob Verdi, the quick-witted *Tribune* columnist, penned the perfect description of Saltwell's brief sojourn: "Salty has gone from counting hot dogs to signing them."

And no more revolving College of Coaches fiascos (1961-65), either. True, Andy McKenna's first foray to other, presumably greener, pastures for outsider Dallas Green did not end well; likewise for Jim Frey's twin terms as manager and GM.

HERE COMES SAMMY

So the owners went to the other end of town at the end of the 1991 season, bringing in Larry Himes from the White Sox to run the show. For some outraged Cubs fans, they might as well have gone to the ends of the earth. Himes sought to silence his critics by proving he was a man of action. Even better, decisive action, something virtually unheard of in sleepy Cubs lagoons, at least since Green fled in disgust.

"It all comes down to pitching," was the first public utterance by Himes when he took the Cubs' reins on November 14, 1991, skipping the usual glad-to-be-here pleasantries. That was typical of Himes's brusque approach. A man who knew his baseball, he was sorely in need of a charisma transplant. His lack of charm rankled the media, making it more imperative for Himes to produce a Cubs contender.

"That's a nice speculation, but it's nonsense," was his way of denying that the decision to let popular Cubs outfielder Andre Dawson go after 1992 was a payroll-slashing move. Of course it was, but Himes already had rolled the dice on a move that still has profound effects on the Cubs and their fans, not to mention baseball history, more than a decade later. On March 30, 1992, the Cubs traded veteran slugger George Bell to the White Sox for the raw potential of 23-year-old Sammy Sosa, along with pitcher Ken Patterson.

The blockbuster deal created tidal waves of pro and con on both sides of town. This early reaction from a Cubs beat writer was typical:

"I hate to say I told you so, but I told you so. Bell for Sosa was a bad trade the day it was made, and it looks worse every day. Bell instigated most of the clubhouse horseplay. Without him, Shawon Dunston has become the quietest man there. It's clear Himes wants to tear up the Cubs and rebuild. The Cubs don't need to be torn up. Himes should know there are no five-year plans with this ownership. If the GM doesn't produce fast, he's gone."

CAN'T REPEAT SOX-CESS

With a three-year contract in his pocket, Himes guaranteed results. He helped nudge the White Sox out of the doldrums by trading away South Side favorite Harold Baines in a deal that brought teenager Sosa to Chicago in midseason 1989, so he saw something in the erratic youngster that others didn't.

Ultimately, Himes was right about Sosa, wrong on his own ability to wheel and deal the Cubs into contention. At the end of Himes's three years, the Cubs had sandwiched one winning season between two losing ones, and he got kicked downstairs to a scouting post.

NO FREE LYNCH FOR CUBS

The Sosa controversy evolved into a Sosa coronation when a blend of maturity, experience, and hero worship from Cubs fans hungry for a superstar enabled this talented hombre to become The Man. Because Ed Lynch won't go down in history as the general manager who traded Sammy Sosa (although the final decision was not in his hands), he didn't go down himself until July 19, 2000. Lynch lasted five and a half years on the general manager's hot seat, longer than anyone except Dallas Green in the last quarter-century. The Cubs backed into the 1998 playoffs as the NL's wild card during his tenure, but without Sosa's gigantic presence, Lynch almost certainly would have been gone before then.

The job was too big for the former Mets and Cubs pitcher, a fact he affirmed by trying to quit even before the axe descended. Lynch was the first ex-Cub to run the front office since former first baseman Jolly Cholly Grimm, way back in the Wrigley era. He knew not to start sending out his laundry when the Cubs collapsed into the NL Central basement at 67-95 in 1999. Lynch had to run up the white flag of surrender with two months to go in that dismal season, although manager Jim Riggleman walked the plank first.

"We're looking at young people," Lynch admitted. "Mistakes will be made. All we can ask is for them to show up on time and play hard."

SAMMY HANDY FOR ANDY

Sosa's sensational socking convinced Andy MacPhail to end the stay-or-go speculation by signing the superstar to a $72 million contract in full expectation that his career would end in Chicago. Slammin' Sammy hysteria overflowed Wrigley Field as his homer output soared from 33 in 1993 to 40 in '96 to 66 in '98—the year of the great fence-busting derby with Mark McGwire—to another brace of 60-plus seasons, to the threshold of joining Ernie Banks in the 500 club when he clubbed his first 2003 round-tripper. Sosa did so, and finished his Cubs career as their all-time leader in homers at Wrigley Field (293) and on the road (252).

PUT TRUST IN DUSTY

That wasn't enough, something Cubs president MacPhail acknowledged when he stepped into Lynch's job. Lynch was out to lunch, and MacPhail's handpicked GM, Jim Hendry, found himself on the hot seat after the Cubs' 2003 playoff debacle, followed by two seasons of failing to make the postseason grade. Shelling out $18 million for Dusty Baker to shepherd the Wrigley flock led fans to expect more—lots more. Ernie Banks is sure to predict some such glad tidings this year, next year and every year, which is why his eternal optimism earned him the title of Mr. Cub. He wears it well. Some names fit snugly, like Wrigley Field's description—naturally, hung on it by Banks—the Friendly Confines.

DIZ KNOWS HOW IT IS

The great Dizzy Dean finished his career with the Cubs in 1941, unfortunately, after a liner by Earl Averill in the 1934 All-Star Game broke Diz's toe, altered his pitching motion and doused the flame in his fastball. But nothing could quench the irrepressible spirit of this homespun philosopher. His language manglings were as popular in their day as Harry Caray's "Lemme hear ya!"—for instance, "He slud into third" and "the runners are returning to their respectable bases." Dean also made a lot of sense, especially when he said, "I'd rather be lucky than good."

WHERE'S DAME FORTUNE?

The Cubs have been neither for a long time. Their fans can be excused for believing the law of averages got repealed more than 50 years ago. Luck plays a major role on the diamond every season, another reason for the game's enduring popularity. Baseball is a lot like life, because the good guys don't always win, and teams that seemed destined for the playoffs get riddled by devastating injuries. That sort of bad luck bedeviled the Cubs in 2001, when Bill Mueller came from San Francisco to solve their perennial quandary—who's the next Ron Santo? As the 16th Cub to open the season at third base since Santo departed in 1974, Mueller was answering that question swiftly and efficiently, at the plate and around the hot corner.

Then, just 36 games into his sparkling debut, Mueller broke his left kneecap in St. Louis. Just like that, the Cubs were back to their annual game of Russian roulette, rushin' hot third-base prospects into the lineup and shipping them back to the bushes when they panned out so poorly that even those ever-patient Wrigley fans panned them. The total of would-be Cub third-sackers who got the sack since Santo's 1960-73 reign is close to 100. His mark of 2,102 games at that position seems safe for the rest of the century, if not forever.

LET'S NOT MAKE A DEAL

"I've been offered a lot of trade possibilities," MacPhail said. "In my judgment, they would have been bad for the Cubs. We won't overlook any possible ways to improve the team."

For now, at least, the dream of a contending club rests with young talent in the farm system. The Cubs will go with them. The only question left for Cubs fans is obvious—in which direction?

1969—FINE VINE WIN OR SOUR GRAPES?

Finally, it all comes back to that wonderful summer of 1969. For thousands—maybe millions—of Baby Boomers in Chicago and across the country, that was a defining moment in their lives. There was joy in Wrigley Field, in stark contrast to the upheaval elsewhere in America. Then, in the last month, the prize got snatched away from the Cubs and their fans.

The unanswered questions raised then still hang over Wrigley Field, although not as severely as the hangovers at Murphy's Bleachers, the postgame hangout for True Believers in those days. Did the fold of '69 set the pattern for all the Cubs' failures since then? Or did it test the mettle of lifelong Cubs fans, making them even more determined to stick with this snake-bitten team through thin and thinner?

I honestly do not know. Of all the thousands of words written about that quixotic, crazy-quilt season, this parting reflection from Cubs owner P. K. Wrigley seems to sum it up best:

"It only takes a few minutes to go from a hero to a bum."

In the meantime, Cubs fans, just wait till next year.

EPILOGUE

In the nearly ten years since the original publication of these books, the Cubs have been to the top of the mountain, fallen off, and tried to climb back up again. They have been through three managers, three owners, two GMs, and a vast parade of players both great and not great.

The team still hasn't won a World Series since 1908. Who's at fault? The management? The players? Cubs culture itself? Certainly on- and off-field management and the players have to share the blame. But one thing is crystal clear: being a Cubs fan in over the last decade hasn't been dull.

It began with much promise. Just a few days after the Giants lost Game Seven of the 2002 World Series to the Angels, Dusty Baker left San Fran to become the new manager of the Cubs.

With Baker (who inspired signs reading "In Dusty We Trusty" all over town) in charge, an offense led by Sammy Sosa, and a pitching staff featuring young guns Kerry Wood and Mark Prior, anything seemed possible.

And indeed in 2003 everything WAS possible—in fact, everything was probable.

The everyday lineup featured fewer big-name sluggers than the fifth-place 2002 squad, but at least Wood, Prior, Carlos Zambrano, and Matt Clement provided a solid starting rotation.

After a quick start, the club struggled and found itself mired 5½ games back on July 24. But the previous day, GM Jim Hendry had swung a deal to snatch Aramis Ramirez and Kenny Lofton from Pittsburgh. Ramirez hit .259 with 15 homers the rest of the way, solving the hot corner dilemma, and Lofton took over in center field, batting .327.

By mid-August, the Cubs had climbed back into the race with the Cardinals and Astros. Chicago trailed by 2½ on September 1, but went 19-8 in the final month. Nonetheless, on September 20, the Cubs fell 8-2 at Pittsburgh and sank 1½ back of Houston.

But the Cubs reeled off three wins while the Astros lost three, and Chicago never trailed again. The Cubbies clinched their first title since 1945 on September 27, nailing down the NL Central with a 4-2 and 7-2 sweep of the Pirates at Wrigley Field.

Aside from Sosa (.279, 40 homers), the offense was good, not spectacular. But Cubs pitchers struck out 1,404 batters to set a new major league record; Wood and Prior ranked 1-2 in K's in the majors.

In the NLDS, the Cubs scored just 19 runs in the five-game set, but held Atlanta to only 15 as they won three games to two. Left fielder Moises Alou batted .500 in the series, while Wood won both his starts, including the clincher 5-1.

All of Chicago—and Cubbie Nation worldwide—was riding high. LCS opponent Florida was a definite underdog, having entered the playoffs via the wild-card route, but had beaten the Giants in their division series.

And the visitors took a wild Game One, triumphing 9-8 in 11 innings. The Cubs blew a 4-0 first-inning lead, tied the game with two in the ninth, and lost on Mike Lowell's homer. But in Game Two, Chicago whipped the Fish 12-3 with Prior working seven innings. (At the time, many wondered why he pitched so long, as the Cubs led 11-0 after five).

In Miami, Chicago won 5-4 and 8-3 to pull within just one game of the league title, but Josh Beckett kept the Marlins' hopes alive with a 4-0 shutout in Game Five.

Back at Wrigley, in front of 39,577 and countless millions on television, the Cubs jumped out in front in Game Six and held a 3-0 lead after seven innings. But Prior, perhaps exhausted, crumbled in a nightmarish eighth that included a fan interfering with a foul fly, a fumbled potential double-play grounder, a bullpen meltdown, and a three-run double by Mike Mordecai.

It seemed natural that the Cubs would then lose the deciding game, and they did. Wood couldn't hold a 5-3 lead, coughing up four runs in the fifth and sixth, and Florida went on to 9-6 triumph and, parenthetically, a World Series win over the Yankees.

Some Cubs fans have never recovered from the trauma of the 2003 series, and the club never won again with Baker at the helm.

In 2004, despite high expectations, Chicago finished third. This was an especially bitter pill as they led the wild-card race by 1½ on September 24. Despite devastating injuries to Wood, Prior, and closer Joe Borowski, the Cubs hung in before losing seven of their last nine games to finish out of the money.

The big headlines of the year—prodigal righty Greg Maddux winning his 300th game at San Francisco on August 7, Nomar Garciaparra coming over in a trade from Boston, concrete chunks falling from the upper deck, and several players complaining about perceived on-air slights from WGN-TV announcers Chip Caray and Steve Stone—merely served as sad footnotes to a frustrating campaign.

The final big headline was more significant: Sammy Sosa's time at Wrigley Field had ended. Twice down the stretch, Baker benched Sosa, who batted just .253 with 35 long balls, third-best on the club. The slugger petulantly departed Wrigley Field during the season's last game, after which a teammate—long rumored to Kerry Wood—took a baseball bat to his famous boom box. Hendry, having had enough, exiled Sosa to Baltimore during the off-season.

With Sosa gone, Derrek Lee stepped up as the Cubs' new hitting hero in 2005. The affable first sacker batted .335 to win the batting title and added 46 homers and 107 RBI. Maddux, at 39 going just 13-15, still fanned his 3,000th man. Jeromy Burnitz, one of several burnt-out veterans Hendry signed over the years to try and fill an important spot, hit .258 with 24 home runs, providing few thrills as Sosa's replacement in right field. Garciaparra, Wood, and Ramirez, among others, were sidelined for significant periods, and with no clubhouse leadership and dwindling confidence in Baker's ability to solve problems, the Cubs fell into disarray, finishing fourth at 79-83.

One of Hendry's goals in 2006 was to add speed to what everyone felt was an aging, immobile club. After acquiring lightning-fast center fielder Juan Pierre, the Cubs certainly were more agile, but didn't play any better; in fact, Chicago fell to 66-96 and finished last. Wood and Prior combined to pitch just 13 times, and Lee—who signed a five year, $65-million contract extension in April—broke his right wrist two weeks later and played only 50 games.

In July, Maddux was dealt to Los Angeles for shortstop Cesar Izturis, who contributed little. As the team lost 27 of its last 40 games, the sands swiftly ran out on Dusty Baker. He was not offered a new contract, and Hendry hired Lou Piniella to run the show in October.

A month later, in a deal partially mandated by upper management, Hendry inked star outfielder Alfonso Soriano for a now regrettable eight years.

Then, on December 6 at the winter meetings, Hendry was hospitalized with chest pains. That didn't stop the indefatigable GM from signing a passel of veteran talent, however, adding Ted Lilly and Jason Marquis to the rotation. Under Piniella, the

Cubs rose again to win the NL Central despite a weak bullpen and a thin attack, nailing down 13 of their last 20 games and clinching the division title September 28 at Cincinnati.

At age 26, Carlos Zambrano assumed the role of staff ace, posting an 18-13 mark and a 3.95 ERA in 34 starts. Lilly, Marquis, and curve-balling southpaw Rich Hill filled out the rotation admirably, although the bullpen was, at the very least, shaky.

Soriano was as good as advertised, hitting .299 with 42 doubles, 33 homers, and 19 stolen bases; during the season, Hendry acquired veterans like Jason Kendall and Craig Monroe, who provided a little bit of help.

The club could go no further than a division title, however, as Arizona swept a three-game Division Series, allowing Chicago just six runs overall.

Even bigger news came at the end of the season, when the Tribune Company—franchise owners for 25 years—sold the Cubs to its erstwhile CEO, billionaire corporate raider Sam Zell. The motorcycle-riding tough-talker kept his hands off, recognizing a cash cow when he saw one. The Chicagoans finished among the top five in NL attendance annually from 2003–07 despite what many called an obsolete park, albeit one with capacity increased by some 3,000 seats in 2006.

Hendry went international for 2008, inking Japanese right fielder Kosuke Fukudome, who batted .257 with 81 walks and played strong defense but did not contribute the power Cubs fans have historically associated with right field. Nevertheless, Kosuke was a major contributor to another NL Central champion.

The battering ballclub had five 20-homer men: Soriano, Ramirez, Lee, super-utilityman Mark DeRosa, and catcher Geovany Soto, who was voted NL Rookie of the Year. Free-agent center fielder Jim Edmonds added a fiery and still valuable piece, and young infielders Ryan Theriot and Mike Fontenot added value.

The pitching staff, featuring starters Ryan Dempster (17-6), Lilly (17-9), Zambrano (14-6), and flame throwing young closer Carlos Marmol, topped the majors in strikeouts for a record-setting eighth straight season. Wood, his arm restored, helped in the bullpen.

Zambrano threw a no-hitter on September 14, and the club clinched the division six days later. Many in the national press considered the Cubs—whose 97-64 record was the NL's best—a World Series-caliber team, but someone forgot to tell the Dodgers, who in the NLDS and blew out the Cubs 7-2 and 10-3 at Wrigley Field.

Out in Los Angeles, Chicago fell meekly 3-1 in Game Three, bringing to a distinctly sour end a season that had held much sweetness.

Despite the dispiriting playoff loss, Hendry received a four-year extension in October. For 2009, he acquired Kevin Gregg from the Florida Marlins to replace Kerry Wood—who left via free agency—and inked Milton Bradley to play right field, with Fukudome shifting to center. Neither move worked. Gregg saved 23 games but had a 4.72 ERA, while the oft-injured Bradley batted .257 before landing on the suspended list, having long before worn out his welcome with teammates and fans.

Theriot, Soto, Fontenot, and Soriano all slumped dangerously in '09, neutralizing Lee's .306-35-111 showing. Ramirez missed 50 games with a dislocated shoulder, further taxing the offense. Dempster, Lilly, and Zambrano backslid from 2008 as well, but Randy Wells emerged from the minors to lead the staff in wins at 12-10 and in ERA at 3.05.

While Chicago led the NL Central as late as August 6, they went 11-17 that month and ended up second at 83-78, 7½ games out.

Following the season, Sam Zell sold a controlling interest in the club and in Wrigley Field, as well as a 25% share of Comcast Sports Net (the Cubs' cable television partner) to the Ricketts family, whose father Joe had founded TD Ameritrade.

Tom Ricketts, club chairman and a hands-on owner, made Crane Kenney, a 16-year Cubs employee, the team's new president despite public criticism of Kenney's previous work for the organization. Tom Ricketts, his brothers Pete and Todd and sister Laura, Crane Kenney, and Tribune Broadcasting exec Nils Larsen comprised the team's new board of directors.

The club's veteran core still seemed capable of another run in 2010, but instead Lee, Ramirez, Soriano, and Fukudome suffered miserable seasons, and the Cubs were never in the race, ending up 75-87. Piniella, increasingly out of touch and annoyed with the press, the fans, and his own players, announced his intention to retire at season's end, then skipped out early on August 22. The club played well down the stretch for interim manager Mike Quade, who earned a contract for 2011.

The best news for Cubs fans in 2010 was the ascent of 20-year-old shortstop Starlin Castro, who in his first game on May 7 at Cincinnati homered, tripled, and drove in six runs. He went on to hit an even .300 in 129 games as the league's youngest player. Another rookie, Tyler Colvin, clubbed 20 homers in part-time play. Dempster was the top starter at 15-12, and Carlos Silva, a reclamation project acquired for Bradley, surprised at 10-6.

With Lee gone in trade, Hendry inked veteran first baseman Carlos Pena from the free-agent ranks. Pena infuriated some fans in 2011 with his .225 average and 161 strikeouts, but also led the club in homers and walks.

Quade and Hendry had an immediate challenge in spring training, when Silva complained about losing his job after pitching poorly in Arizona. To their credit, the Cubs simply released him and no other team called. This was just the first of several pitching disasters.

Zambrano, expected to lead the staff, instead was rocked and, frustrated, quit the team after being bombed off the mound August 12 in Atlanta. He was suspended and did not pitch again. Dempster looked lost on the mound and was regularly pounded, while Marmol, back at closer, lost some zip on his fastball and experienced several untimely meltdowns.

The 2011 Cubs' high point was a 9-8 mark on April 20. From there on the team was an almost complete shambles. Soriano and Ramirez appeared to have run out of gas, Colvin slumped and was sent to Triple-A, and Castro—the team's only All-Star and the NL's leader in hits with 207—was called out on national television for his lack of attentiveness on defense.

Quade lasted the full season, but the undermanned and motivation-less club stumbled home fifth at 71-91.

Tom Ricketts, noticing both the win-loss column and an increasing amount of empty seats at Wrigley Field, notified Hendry on July 22 his intentions to seek a new General Manager, but Hendry—to his credit—stayed on the job until August 19 to help with the amateur draft.

In October, Ricketts got his man, hiring Theo Epstein away from the Red Sox as the Cubs' new CEO. Epstein's former protégé Jed Hoyer, late of San Diego, assumed the GM role. Quade was immediately released and, after a short search, Dale Sveum, a former shortstop/third baseman and longtime major league coach, snagged his first big-league managerial assignment.

2011 marked the end of an era in Chicago, with Hendry is gone, the Tribune and Zell but mere memories, and Aramis Ramirez—one of only two players left from the 2003 club— departing at season's end free agency.

Historically understaffed in the front office, behind the curve in the use of statistical evidence, and perhaps mired a country-club atmosphere, the Cubs now have an active owner with deep pockets, a CEO who promises to create a process-oriented organization, and a manager in step with the entire chain of command.

What follows has to be better.

Or does it?

—Stuart Shea, December 2011

BIBLIOGRAPHY

Ahrens, Art, & Gold, Eddie. *The Complete Record of Chicago Cubs Baseball.* New York: Collier Books, 1986.

— *Day by Day in Chicago Cubs History.* West Point, NY: Leisure Press, 1982.

— *The Golden Era Cubs, 1876-1940.* Chicago: Bonus Books, 1985.

— *The New Era Cubs. 1941-1985.* Chicago: Bonus Books, 1985.

— *1985–1990: The Renewal Era Cubs.* Chicago: Bonus Books, 1990.

Alexander, Charles. *Rogers Hornsby: A Biography.* New York: Henry Holt & Co., 1995.

Allen, Lee. *The Hot Stove League.* New York: A.S. Barnes & Co., 1955.

— *The National League Story.* New York: Hill & Wang, 1961.

Allen, Lee, & Meany, Tom. *Kings of the Diamond.* New York: G.P. Putnam's Sons, 1965.

Anson, Adrian. *A Ball Players Career.* Chicago: Era Publishing Co., 1900.

Aylesworth, Thomas, & Minks, Benton. In John S. Bowman, ed., *The Encyclopedia of Baseball Managers.* New York: Crescent Books, 1990.

Banks, Ernie, & Enright, Jim. *Mr. Cub.* Chicago: Follett Publishing Co., 1971.

Bartell, Dick, & Macht, Norman L. *Rowdy Richard.* Berkeley, CA: North Atlantic Books, 1987.

Bartlett, Arthur. *Baseball and Mr. Spalding.* New York: Farrar, Strauss & Young, Inc., 1951.

Benson, Michael. *Ballparks of North America.* Jefferson, NC: McFarland & Co., 1989.

Bjarkman, Peter C, ed. *Encyclopedia of Major League Baseball Team Histories: National League.* Westport, CT: Meckler Publishing, 1991.

— *Baseball With a Latin Beat.* Jefferson, NC: McFarland & Co., Inc., 1994.

Bosco, Joseph. *The Boys Who Would be Cubs.* New York: William Morrow & Co., Inc., 1990.

Boudreau, Lou, & Schneider, Russell. *Lou Boudreau: Covering All the Bases.* Champaign, IL: Sagamore Publishing, 1993.

Brickhouse, Jack. *Thanks for Listening!* South Bend, IN: Diamond Communications, 1986.

Brock, Lou, & Schulze, Franz. *Stealing is my Game.* Englewood Cliff, NJ: Prentice-Hall, Inc., 1976.

Bryan, Mike. *Baseball Lives.* New York: Pantheon Books, 1989.

Caray, Harry, & Verdi, Bob. *Holy Cow!* New York: Villard Books, 1989.

Cava, Pete. *The Encyclopedia of Indiana-Born Major League Baseball* Players. Work in progress.

Charlton, James. *The Baseball Chronology.* New York: Macmillan, 1991.

Coberly, Rich. *The No-Hit Hall of Fame: No-Hitters of the 20th Century.* Newport Beach, CA: Triple Play Publications, 1985.

Crissey, Harrington E., Jr. *Teenagers, Graybeards and 4-F's. Vol. I: The National League.* Trenton, NJ: White Eagle Printing Co., 1981.

Dawson, Andre, with Bird, Tom. *Hawk.* Grand Rapids, MI: Zondervan Publishing House, 1994.

Dewan, John, ed. *The Scouting Report: 1990.* New York: Harper&Row, 1990.

Durocher, Leo, & Linn, Ed. *Nice Guys Finish Last.* New York: Simon & Schuster, 1975.

Enright, Jim. *Baseball's Great Teams: The Chicago Cubs.* New York: Macmillan Publishing Co., 1975.

Erickson, Hal. *Baseball in the Movies: A Comprehensive Reference, 1915-1991.* Jefferson, NC: McFarland, 1992.

Fulk, David, & Riley, Dan. *The Cubs Reader.* Boston: Houghton Mifflin Company, 1991.

Fusselle, Warner. *Baseball... A Laughing Matter.* St. Louis: The Spotting News, 1987.

Gilbert, Bill. *They Also Served.* New York: Crown Publishers, Inc., 1992.

Gold, Eddie. "The Player They Called 'The Mad Russian'" *Baseball Digest,* September 1982, 67-70.

Goldstein, Richard. *Spartan Seasons.* New York: Macmillan Publishing Co., 1980.

Golenbock, Peter. *Wrigleyville: A Magical History Tour of the Chicago Cubs.* New York: St. Martin's Press, 1996.

Green, Paul. *Forgotten Fields.* Waupaca, WI: Parker Publications, 1984.

Greenberg, Hank, & Berkow, Ira. *The Story of My Life.* New York: Times Books, 1989.

Greenwood, Chuck. "HOFer Williams Celebrating 29 Seasons at Wrigley Field." *Sports Collectors Digest,* October 29, 1999, 80–81.

Grimm, Charlie, & Prell, Ed. *Grimm's Baseball Tales.* Notre Dame, IN: Diamond Communications, 1983.

Herskowitz, Mickey. "When Lowrey K.O.'d Ron Reagan." *Baseball Digest,* August 1968, 58–60.

Hoffman, John C. *Hank Sauer.* New York: A.S. Barnes & Co., 1953.

Holtzman, Jerome, and George Vass. *The Chicago Cubs Encyclopedia.* Philadelphia: Temple University Press, 1997.

Honig, Donald. *Baseball When the Grass Was Real.* New York: Coward, McCann, & Geoghegan, Inc., 1975.

— *The Chicago Cubs: An Illustrated History.* New York: Prentice-Hall Press, 1991.

— *The Man in the Dugout.* Lincoln, NE: University of Nebraska Press, 1977.

Isaacson, Melissa. "Sammy Sosa: A Budding Star for White Sox." *Baseball Digest,* August 1990.

Kavanagh, Jack. *Ol'Pete: The Grover Cleveland Alexander Story.* South Bend, IN: Diamond Communications, Inc., 1996.

Kelley, Brent. *Baseball Stars of the 1950s: Interview with All-Stars* of *the Game's Golden Era.* Jefferson, NC: McFarland, 1993.

Kuenster, John. "Ryne Sandberg of the Cubs, Baseball Digest's 1984 Player of the Year." *Baseball Digest,* January 1985, 13–16.

Langford, Jim. *The Game is Never Over.* South Bend, IN: Icarus Press, 1980.

Levine, Peter. *A. G. Spalding and the Rise of Baseball.* New York: Oxford University Press, 1985.

Lieb, Frederick G. *The Story of the World Series.* New York: G.P. Putnam's Sons, 1949.

Marazzi, Rich, & Fiorito, Len. *Aaron to Zuverink: A Nostalgic Look at the Baseball Players of the Fifties.* Briarcliff Manor, NY: Stein & Day, 1982.

Marshall, William. *Baseballs Pivotal Era, 1945–1951.* Lexington, KY: University Press of Kentucky, 1999.

Mathewson, Christy. *Pitching in a Pinch.* New York: Putnam, 1912.

McGregor, Ed. "Mark Grace of the Cubs: A Non-Typical Clean-up *Hitter." Baseball Digest, June 1990.*

Mitchell, Fred. "Ryne Sandberg: He's Going to Get Even Better!" *Baseball Digest,* June 1984, 42–45.

Murdock, Eugene. *Baseball Between the Wars: Memories of the Game by the Men Who Played It.* Westport, CT: Meckler Publishing, 1992.

Nineteenth Century Baseball Stars. Kansas City, MO: The Society for American Baseball Research, 1989.

Obojski, Robert. *Baseball Bloopers & Other Curious Incidents.* New York: Sterling Publishing Co., 1989.

Pacini, Le. "Augue Galan Overcame Handicap to Star in Majors." *Baseball Digest,* February 1982, 73–76.

Peary, Danny, ed. *Cult Baseball Players.* New York: Fireside, 1990. — *We Played the Game.* New York: Hyperion, 1994.

Phalen, Rick. *Our Chicago Cubs: Inside the History and the Mystery of Baseball's Favorite Franchise.* South Bend, IN: Diamond Communications, 1992.

Reichler, Joseph L. *The Great All-Time Baseball Record Book.* New York: Macmillan, 1981.

Reidenbaugh, Lowell. *Cooperstown: Where Baseball's Legends Live Forever.* St. Louis: The Sporting News Publishing Co., 1983.

Rust, Art. *"Get That Nigger Off the Field!"* New York: Delacorte Press, 1974.

Sandberg, Ryne, & Rozner, Barry. *Second to Home: Ryne Sandberg Opens Up.* Chicago: Bonus Books, 1995.

Santo, Ron, with Minkoff, Randy. *For Love of Ivy.* Chicago: Bonus Books, 1993.

Sargent, Jim. "Arm Injuries Limited Mayer to '15 Miunutes of Fame.'" *Sports Collectors Digest,* November 5, 1999, 120-121.

"Scouting Reports on 1958 National League Rookies." *Baseball Digest,* March 1958, 73.

Shatzkin, Mike, ed. *The Ballplayers.* New York: Arbor House, William Morrow, 1990.

Smith, FredT. *Cub Tales & Trivia.* West Bloomfield, MI: Altwerger & Mandei Publishing Co., 1991.

Smith, Ira L., & Smith, H. Allen. *Low and Inside.* Garden City, NY: Doubleday, 1949.

Talley, Rick. "Bill Madlock Born to Hit." *Baseball Digest,* September 1975, 23–26.

Veeck, Bill, & Linn, Ed. *Veeck—As in Wreck.* New York: G.P. Putnam's Sons, 1962.

Voigt, David Q. *American Baseball.* 3 vols. University Park, PA: Pennsylvania State University Press, 1983.

Wasserstrom, Chuck. *1996 Chicago Cubs Information Guide.* Chicago: Chicago National League Ball Club, Inc., 1996.

Wheeler, Lonnie. *Bleachers: A Summer in Wrigley Field.* Chicago: Contemporary Books, 1988.

Wilbert, Warren, & Hageman, William. *Chicago Cubs: Seasons at the Summit.* Champaign, IL: Sagamore Publishing, 1997.

Williams, Billy, & Haag, Irv. *Billy: The Classic Hitter.* Chicago: Rand McNally & Co., 1974.

Newspapers consulted:

Baseball America
Baseball Weekly
Chicago Tribune
Indianapolis Star
New York Times
USA Today

IN MEMORY

Robert Grove Logan died in January of 2006, as the second edition of this book was going to press.

He was born October 11, 1931, in Philadelphia, two days after Lefty Grove, a pitcher for the Philadelphia Athletics, won a World Series game. Logan was named after the pitcher and became a lifetime lover of the Athletics and baseball. After serving in the military, Logan attended college and graduated from Temple with a degree in journalism. His first job was with the Philadelphia Inquirer, then with the Levittown, New Jersey Times, followed by the Illinois State Journal in Springfield. He then had a 28-year stint at the Chicago Tribune, covering professional and college basketball, football and baseball, and had his own column.

His "retirement" was followed by 13 years of sports writing at the Daily Herald. He had authored eight sports books and participated in the writing of a ninth, and he had provided an annual basketball summary for the Encyclopedia Britannica for the past 25 years.

Logan was a journalism original, an irreplaceable piece of the Chicago sports scene where characters were seen and followed on the pages of newspapers. There will never be another like him, and he will be sadly missed.